CASE STUDIES IN
CULTURAL ANTHROPOLOGY

GENERAL EDITORS

George and Louise Spindler

STANFORD UNIVERSITY

———————

SAMOAN PLANTERS

*Tradition and Economic Development
in Polynesia*

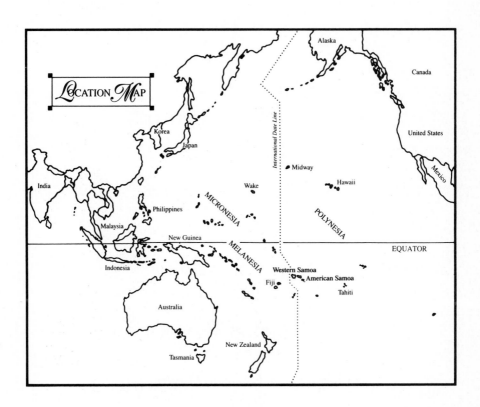

SAMOAN PLANTERS

Tradition and Economic Development in Polynesia

J. TIM O'MEARA

University of North Carolina at Wilmington

HOLT, RINEHART AND WINSTON, INC.

FORT WORTH   CHICAGO   SAN FRANCISCO   PHILADELPHIA
MONTREAL   TORONTO   LONDON   SYDNEY   TOKYO

Publisher: Ted Buchholz
Acquisitions Editor: Christopher P. Klein
Senior Project Editor: Dawn Youngblood
Production Manager: Ken Dunaway
Art & Design Supervisor: Vicki McAlindon Horton
Cover Designer: Vicki McAlindon Horton

Library of Congress Cataloging-in-Publication Data
O'Meara, Tim.
   Samoan planters : tradition and economic development in Polynesia
/ Tim O'Meara.
      p.   cm. — (Case studies in cultural anthropology)
   Includes bibliographical references.
   ISBN 0-03-022847-6
   1. Samoans—Social conditions.   2. Samoans—Economic conditions.
3. Developing countries—Economic conditions.   4. Rural development—
Samoa.   I. Title.   II. Series.
GN671.S2053   1990
306'.09961'3—dc20   89-27894

ISBN: 0-03-022847-6

Address Editorial Correspondence To: 301 Commerce Street, Suite 3700,
                                        Fort Worth, TX 76102
            Address Orders To: 6277 Sea Harbor Drive, Orlando, FL 32887
                                 1-800-782-4479, or 1-800-433-0001 (in Florida)

Printed in the United States of America

0 1 2 3 9 8 7 6 5 4 3 2 1

Holt, Rinehart and Winston, Inc.
The Dryden Press
Saunders College Publishing

Foreword

ABOUT THE SERIES

These case studies in cultural anthropology are designed to bring to students, in beginning and intermediate courses in the social sciences, insights into the richness and complexity of human life as it is lived in different ways and in different places. They are written by men and women who have lived in the societies they write about and who are professionally trained as observers and interpreters of human behavior. The authors are also teachers, and in writing their books they have kept the students who will read them foremost in their minds. It is our belief that when an understanding of ways of life very different from one's own is gained, abstractions and generalizations about social structure, cultural values, subsistence techniques, and the other universal categories of human social behavior become meaningful.

ABOUT THE AUTHOR

Tim O'Meara was born and raised in Cedar Rapids, Iowa. He went to college in California (Stanford) to study marine biology, but his fascination with other societies turned his attention to anthropology. Following graduation in 1970, he spent most of the next three years sailing around the Caribbean, hitch-hiking in Europe, and investigating Pre-Columbian ruins and remote villages in Mexico.

The Mexican experience awakened an interest in archeology, and he returned to school at the University of Hawaii in 1974 intent on unlocking the mysteries of the Polynesian migrations. He worked as an archeologist in Hawaii and Arizona, and began planning his Ph.D. research on the evolution of fishing technology in Tahiti. Overcome by doubts about the esoteric nature of the work, but already prepared for life in Tahiti, he left school in 1976 for the islands of Ra'iatea and Taha'a, northwest of the island of Tahiti. There he saw that the Tahitians, though proud of their traditions, also had a genuine desire for modernization. This desire was being manipulated by the French in order to strengthen the Tahitians' dependence on the colonial government.

Resolving to apply anthropology to the solution of problems in economic development, Tim returned to graduate school at the University of California at Santa Barbara. He began preliminary dissertation research in Western Samoa in 1979. He worked as an ethnologist for the U.S. Forest Service during 1980, and then returned to Western Samoa to complete his dissertation research from 1981 to 1983. In 1984 he continued the land tenure research on a contract with the Food and Agriculture Organization of the United Nations and the University of the South Pacific. In 1985 he returned to Western Samoa to marry Taufau Toleafoa of Fagali'i-Uta village, just outside Apia. They now have two children, Vaosa Lisa and Robert Tanielu.

After teaching briefly at the University of California at Santa Barbara, Tim took up a position in 1987 at the University of North Carolina at Wilmington where he is an Assistant Professor. In 1988 he began a new research project on traditional fishing and fisheries development in the atolls of Micronesia.

ABOUT THIS CASE STUDY

"O'Meara's *Samoan Planters* is by far the best account of what life in a Samoan polity is really like that I have ever encountered. Empirically exact, extremely well informed, insightful, and both sympathetic and honest, it provides an exemplary demonstration of modern reflective ethnography. It is delightfully written, evoking Samoan behavior and character in a style as engaging as that of Robert Louis Stevenson. At the same time, it succeeds in coming to conclusions about Samoan planters that are of great anthropological and practical significance. . . . I cannot fault O'Meara's ethnography." (From a review for the publisher by Derek Freeman.)

"*Samoan Planters* is a distinguished addition to the Case Studies in Cultural Anthroplogy as well as a major contribution to the Pacific Studies literature. It is carefully argued, beautifully written, and somehow manages to be *both* analytically sophisticated and narratively evocative. Not only is it an expert ethnography, but it is deeply saturated with the lived realities of daily Samoan life. It doesn't merely ring true; it hits dead center." (From a review for the publisher by Bradd Shore.)

Samoan Planters does much more than intrigue and captivate, it informs— not only about a way of life but about some important theoretical issues. Of great interest to economic anthropologists and development experts is O'Meara's evidence contradicting the common belief that the village economy remains undeveloped because the villagers still adhere to their economically irrational traditions. O'Meara shows that the Samoan planters' economic decisions are rational, not tradition-bound. He shows that the villagers—like other people—take into account both cultural values and the relation of gain to pain. Through detailed analysis of economic, social, and political changes, O'Meara shows that Samoans are as likely to adapt their traditions to take advantage of new opportunities as they are to mold their behavior to conform with their traditions.

Of special interest is O'Meara's argument that, in responding to economic changes, Samoan villagers have created two different land tenure systems, one traditional and communal and the other modern and individual. His analysis is supported by abundant data, gained the hard way by observing and participating in village affairs, by archival research, mapping plantations, and by interviewing scores of individuals about hundreds of plots. Though the existence of two land tenure systems will surprise some observers, the analysis is firm and his conclusions undeniably well grounded.

Another area of theoretical significance is kinship. Anthropologists have recently begun to attribute less importance to kinship terminology and prescriptive kin relations, pointing instead to deviations from the kinship "blueprint" as evidence that kin-based social systems are not as "kin-determined" as we once thought. O'Meara shows that Samoans normally use personal names when addressing or referring to others, using kin terms only when they want to emphasize appropriate behavior. Now that "appropriate" behavior is changing in response to economic and other conditions, Samoans are changing their use of kin terms as well. He also shows that while the Samoans' Hawaiian-type kinship terminology allows them to classify many relatives in a few, very broad categories when they want to recruit support, in other contexts they can use the same terms to denote the most particular genealogical relationships.

Samoan Planters raises other theoretical issues as well, but the three mentioned above should serve to indicate that this case study goes well beyond descriptive ethnography.

Students will find O'Meara's discussion of his own field experience illuminating. "When I first arrived in the village I did not know how to talk, sit, or eat properly. My hands and feet were pitifully uncalloused. I could do little or nothing useful, even if I had been allowed to try. I did not know how, when, or where to bathe or even to relieve myself properly according to Samoan standards of etiquette. People treated me as they would a fragile child. I felt as the royal hemophiliacs of Europe must have felt—honored and coddled in equal amounts. That was too much for me, and I resolved to do something about it." (Tim O'Meara, p. 36.)

What he did about it in this early moment of his relationship with the village was to prove his worth as a spear fisherman—something he had experience with elsewhere. What he did about it in the long run was to become a participant in every aspect of Samoan life. He tells us about this in the "reflective" style of contemporary ethnography so that readers can both share the experience and see the evidence and judge for themselves the strength of the resulting arguments. His experience and his vantage point as a stranger in the process of being incorporated into another human society make the telling rich, but his personal experience enhances rather than intrudes in the telling. We come to know the Samoan planters far more than we come to know Tim O'Meara—and this, we believe, is the way it should be. He had a long way to come from his ignorant state as a "fragile" newcomer to the seasoned, knowledgeable participant in village affairs. Many of us have experienced what O'Meara did in Western Samoa in some form, but here the story is better told.

Samoan Planters is indeed both a sterling contribution to the Case Studies in Cultural Anthropology, intended primarily as an instructional series, and to the literature of Pacific Studies, economic anthropology and economic development, and to anthropology and related fields at large.

George and Louise Spindler
Series Editors
Stanford University

Acknowledgments

Preliminary research in Western Samoa in 1979 was supported by the University of California at Santa Barbara. The dissertation research during 1981–83 was funded by a grant from the National Science Foundation. Research in Neiafu and Malie in 1984 was conducted under a contract with the University of the South Pacific and the Food and Agriculture Organization of the United Nations. The University of North Carolina at Wilmington and the National Endowment for the Arts, Folk Arts Program, funded brief research in 1988.

I would like to thank the government and people of Western Samoa who accepted me as a guest in their country. Tupuola Tavita, Director of Agriculture, Forests, and Fisheries, and Tapusatele Keli Tuatagaloa, Registrar of the Land and Titles Court, were especially helpful. The Chiefs and Orators of Malie and Neiafu have my deepest appreciation for their help with this research. In Apia, Fa'avaoga Tom and Olivia Yandall and their families gave their unending friendship and support.

My special thanks go to the Chiefs and Orators of Satupaitea, who treated me as a friend and honored guest during the two and one-half years I lived with them. Asiata Iakopo, Nu'u Vili, the Reverend Fogalele Fagamea, and their respective families took me into their homes and treated me as a member of the family. My friends Nu'u Vili and Faleilemilo Fa'alaga were primarily responsible for leading the very long and difficult mapping of plantation plots. Faleilemilo Faletoi shared his knowledge of fishing and many other matters, and his considerable hospitality. Sipanoa Umama'o assisted me in many research tasks, and like many other people of Satupaitea, soon became a trusted friend. Thanks also to Tapumanaia Pascal Brown, who shared his observations and insights of life in the neighboring village of Satufia with me for nearly two years.

I am indebted to many people for their comments on drafts of my dissertation, much of which has found its way into these pages. Thanks to Ron Crocombe, Robert A. Feldman, Reed Hertford, Chas Feinstein, Jon Sonstelie, and Matt O'Meara. Thanks also to the members of my dissertation committee, David Brokensha, Chuck Erasmus, and especially to Tom Harding, the chairman.

Some of the material presented in Chapter 5 of this book appeared previously in *Land Tenure in the Pacific*, R. G. Crocombe, ed., 3rd ed., Suva: University of the South Pacific, 1987. Thanks to Ron Crocombe and USP for permission to reprint it here.

Ali Pomponio edited the first draft of this book with extraordinary skill and grace. I should also thank her on behalf of the readers, who (fortunately) will never know what they have been spared. George and Louise Spindler's editorial comments were equally perceptive and helpful. Afioga Le Tagaloa Pita very kindly provided comments on the first draft of Chapters 1 through 4. Thanks also to the students in my Pacific Island Societies class here at UNCW for their editorial suggestions. Finally, Derek Freeman and Bradd Shore—both longtime students of Samoa—reviewed the manuscript for the publisher. Their helpful comments are gratefully acknowledged.

FAAFETAI
(Acknowledgments for Samoan Readers)

Faafetai i le alofa o le Atua ua faaiuina ma le manuia le suesuega sa feagai ai. Faafetai i le Malo o Samoa i Sisifo ma i latou sa lagolagoina lenei mataupu, aemaise ona sui mai le Matagaluega o Faatoaga, Vaomatua, ma Faigafaiva, lana afioga le alii pule sili Tupuola Tavita K. Leupolu, susuga ia Dick Burgess le sa avea ma sui pule o le Matagaluega ma vaaia le Vaega Fuafuaina ma Faasoasoaina le Tamaoaiga, atoa ma le mamalu o le aufaigaluega.

Faafetai foi i lana afioga Tapusatele K. Tuatagaloa le sa avea ma Resitara o le Faamasinoga o Fanua ma Suafa, faapea foi Alii Faamasino ma le aufaigaluega. Faafetai i le alii pule o le Fale Tupe o Atiinae le susuga ia Sam Leung Wai ma le alii pule o le ofisa i Savaii lana susuga Roy Slade.

Ou te momoli atu lau faafetai i alii ma faipule o alalafaga nei, Malie ma Neiafu, aemaise le afioga ia Mauala Neru mai Malie, ma lana afioga Aliimalemanu Faale ma le aiga sa ou gafa ai i Neifu.

Ao lau faafetai sili lava i le mamalu o le itumalo o Satupaitea i le motu tele i Salafai, aemaise alii ma faipule i Vaega. Faafetai i la outou lagolago mai i lau suesuega. Faamalo le fesoasoani malo le alofa. Faafetai i lau susuga le faafeagaiga o Fogalele ma le faletua sa ou gafa ai i le tausaga 1979. Faafetai i lau tofa Asiata Iakopo ma le tausi oulua valaauina au ia avea ma se tasi o outou aiga ma faaee mai ia te au se tasi o suafa matai. Faafetai i le tofa ia Nuu Vili ma le tausi mo la tatou mafutaga ma le tausiga o au. Faamalo lava le alofa.

O Nuu ma lana tofa ia Faleilemilo Faalaga sa taitai i le faiga o le faafanua o faatoaga. Malo le faamalosi. Faafetai i le taulealea matua o Sipanoa Umama-a'o sa fai ma o'u fesoasoani.

Faafetai mo ou aiga i Apia i lana afioga ia Faavaoga Tom Yandall ma le faletua ma Anne Devoe ma le aiga. Faafetai le alofa ma le agalelei.

Faafetai tele i lo outou mamalu i le aoao mai ia te au o le aganuu, masani, atoa ai ma le olaga o le aufaifaatoaga. O le faamoemoe o lau suesuega ma lenei tusi o le fesoasoani o le atiinae o nuu i tua ma le atunuu atoa. Ae peitai, e vaivai au upu, e laitiiti lou malamalama. A i ai se sese po o se pati e sala, lafo i fogavaa.

Soifua,
Mavaega Timo O'Meara

Mo Fau, Sa, ma Pati. Malo lava le tapua'i.

Table of Contents

List of Illustrations

Tala Otooto
(Summary of Text for Samoan Readers)

PE AISEA E LE ATIINAEINA AI FAATOAGA O NUU I TUA?
O SUESUEGA I FAAMALAMALAMAGA FAALEAGANUU MA MEA TAUTUPE
I SAMOA I SISIFO

O le faamoemoe o suesuega ina ia iloa ai pe aisea ua le atiinaeina ai faatoaga, pe mafua mai i le aganuu poo le maketi. Ua suesue fesuiaiga i le pulega faamatai i fanua, galuega, ma tupe o aiga, ma fesuiaiga i mea tautupe o faalavelave i Samoa i Sisifo ina ia faatusatusa ai i faamalamalamaga o loo i luga.

O iuga o lea suesuega ua tuu faatasi ma le suesuega o galuega, seleselega o faatoaga, tupe maua ma tupe faamaimau o aiga e 55 mo le tausaga atoa. Ua iloa mai nei le tupe mama ua maua i aso taitasi i galuega i maumaga ma le faiga o popo, faapea ma le afaina o nisi aganuu, galuega totogi tupe, ma tupe maua mai i fafo i le atiinaeina o faatoaga.

O lea ua maua manatu o le aufaifaatoaga e atiinae ai a latou faatoaga ma tupe maua. Ua malilie foi i fesuiaiga e masani ai ina ia faaleleia le atiinae. A fai e faatusatusa le galuega ua fai i faatoaga ma le tupe maua, e tele le galuega ae laitiiti le tupe. E faapea, e le'o se aganuu poo se masani ao le laitiiti o tupe maua ua faaletonu ai le atiinae o faatoaga.

1/Introduction

There are thousands of islands in the South Pacific, each fantastic in its own way—islands built by volcanic eruptions and by the slow, delicate growth of reef-building corals. Some of these islands supported small egalitarian societies while others supported military dynasties that ruled their subjects harshly and conquered their neighbors with brutal force. In the early centuries the islanders traded, married, and warred among themselves, sometimes across hundreds of miles of open ocean. But since the sixteenth century they have been visited by a succession of European explorers, American and British whalers, beachcombers, missionaries, traders, labor recruiters and outright slavers. Beginning in the late nineteenth century they were joined by writers, painters, and anthropologists. The mid-twentieth century brought foreign soldiers and sailors waging a savage war. Now tourists, yachties, and economic development experts flock to the South Pacific.

The islands of Samoa lie near the center of this tropical island world, just south of the equator and east of the international dateline (see frontispiece).[1] This is the heart of Polynesia, a place and a people so beautiful to Western eyes and fabled in Western myth that even professional anthropologists, like so many wide-eyed travelers, must sometimes struggle to separate fact from fantasy. When I first went to Samoa in 1979, however, I did not expect my stay to be entirely idyllic. I knew that Samoans are among the largest and most powerfully built people in the world, and I was already familiar with the rough reputation that some Samoan migrants have earned in Hawaii. Nor did I expect to find a completely traditional Polynesian society tucked away on some remote island. The Second World War rudely shook the Pacific islands out of the nineteenth century. Change has been rapid since the war. Most of the islands are now independent of their colonial masters. Western Samoa, where politics is the traditional passion, was the first island group to achieve full independence.

---

[1] Samoans pronounce *Samoa* with a long "a" (like the doctor's command to say "aah") and the accent on the first syllable: SAAH-mo-ah.

Photo 1. Cloud-covered Upolu Island, with the smaller Manono Island to the right, seen from the air over the straight between Upolu and Savaii.

A CONTEST OF POWERS

Germany and the United States divided the Samoan archipelago between themselves in 1899, thus resolving an intense rivalry that also included Great Britain. Each of these imperial powers had been intentionally fueling civil wars between rival Samoan chiefs as a way of gaining indirect control over the islands. In 1889 the colonial powers themselves nearly came to blows over Samoa. A fleet of warships—three German, three American, and one British—assembled in the harbor at Apia on the north coast of Upolu. As the naval commanders and shore-side political emissaries jockied for position, a tremendous hurricane bore down from the north, pinning the ships against the lee shore. Each commander tried to ride out the hurricane longer than the others, being reluctant to flee the harbor first and leave the island under the guns of a rival. As the winds increased during the night they became trapped, unable to set sail. One after another the anchors dragged under the force of winds and seas, and the ships were sunk or driven ashore. Of the seven warships, only the British steamship *Calliope* managed to escape at the last moment, laying on full steam and driving inch by inch out of the harbor as the crew of the sail-powered *USS Trenton* cheered them on, unable to save themselves (Gray 1960:87–90).

Today a small monument along the shore of Apia harbor recalls the tragedy and mourns the 150 sailors who died that night. There is no monu-

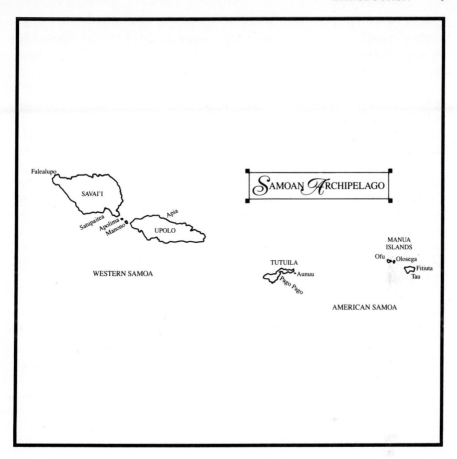

Falealupo

SAVAI'I

Satupaitea
Apolima
Manono
Apia
UPOLO

WESTERN SAMOA

SAMOAN ARCHIPELAGO

TUTUILA
Aunuu
Pago Pago

MANUA
ISLANDS
Ofu Olosega
Fitiuta
Tau

AMERICAN SAMOA

ment, however, to commemorate the heroism of the many Samoans who rushed into the violent seas to save scores of sailors who, hours before, had been their enemies.

The colonial powers soon agreed to compromise, perhaps feeling that so small and distant a prize was not worth such high stakes. Germany retained control of the two large, western islands of Upolu and Savaii, and the islets of Manono and Apolima, which lie in the narrow pass between them (see map, Figure 1.1). The United States took control of the smaller island of Tutuila, forty miles southeast of Upolu, and the tiny Manu'a group another sixty miles to the east. Great Britain gave up its claim to Samoa in favor of Germany, which then gave up its claims to Tonga, Niue, and most of the Solomon Islands in favor of Great Britain.

Germany's interests in Samoa were almost entirely commercial. Her prizes in Samoa included the large commercial plantations on Upolu, and a brisk trade in copra (dried coconut meat valued for its oil) that was developing with the local population. On the island of Tutuila, the United States gained control over Pago Pago harbor, one of the largest and finest harbors in the Pacific.[2] The U.S. had just taken the Philippines in the brief Spanish-American War of 1898, and the Navy wanted Pago Pago harbor as a coaling station on the long run from South America to the Philippines.

Germany's control over Upolu and Savaii was brief. At the outset of World War I in 1914, a small armed force from New Zealand took the territory without a fight. After the war, New Zealand's control was formalized, first under a League of Nations mandate and later under a United Nations mandate, until Western Samoa's struggle for independence was rewarded in 1962.

American Samoa, with a current population of just over 32,000 people (compared to Western Samoa's 160,000), has remained a territory of the United States. Its residents carry U.S. passports and enjoy (and perhaps sometimes endure) the full weight of American bureaucratic largesse. American Samoans are not likely to give up their American passports or share the cash bounty they receive from the U.S. with their Western Samoan neighbors. Thus, it is unlikely that the entire Samoa group will be united under a single, independent government.

THIRD WORLD TROUBLES

In many ways Western Samoa fits the image of a Polynesian paradise. Its people are proud of their traditions and of the beauty and bounty of their islands. So far, Western Samoa has managed to avoid or delay the crisis of overpopulation—and the resulting poverty and environmental destruction—that plagues much of the Third World. In the nineteenth and early twentieth centuries Samoa lost much of its population to European diseases and to increasingly lethal warfare. The worst disaster hit in 1918 when a worldwide influenza epidemic reached the islands. The New Zealand colonial government, only recently installed in the capital city of Apia, allowed a ship to disembark passengers, knowing that they carried influenza. In the ensuing weeks nearly one-quarter of the Samoans died. Older people today still recall that dreadful time when many families had no one left standing to gather food, care for the sick, or bury the dead.

The epidemic planted a seed of resentment against the New Zealand government that later grew into the Mau Rebellion. The Mau was a determined but nonviolent resistance to foreign rule that shut the would-be colonialists out of the rural villages for many years. New Zealand sometimes met the resistance with violence, sometimes by imprisoning the leaders or banishing them to distant lands. To the credit of both sides, however, the period of the Mau was largely a quiet stalemate. In the years following World War II, New Zealand gradually accepted its responsibility to prepare Samoa for independence. Today relations are remarkably friendly between Western Samoans and New Zealanders, and between their respective governments.

---

[2] In Samoan the letter "g" is pronounced like the "ng" in the English word "Sing." Thus, Pago Pago is pronounced: PAAH-ngo PAAH-ngo.

Today, the natural population growth rate in Western Samoa is well over 2 percent per year. Most of that increase is now siphoned off through emigration. The steady stream of outmigrants eases population pressure, while the return flow of cash and goods that they send back eases economic pressures at home. Nearly a third of the nation's people already live overseas, and a third of the nation's total income now arrives by airmail from overseas relatives or from friendly governments.

A QUESTION OF DEVELOPMENT

Though economically disadvantaged by its small size and its remoteness from the world's industrial and commercial centers, Western Samoa has many advantages over other developing nations. No foreign enemies press against its borders. Foreign aid is plentiful. The modest size of the country itself makes problems more manageable. Western Samoa still has some breathing room to develop its resources without the urgent threats of overcrowding and malnutrition that send many other developing countries reeling from one crisis to the next. Most villages on Upolu, and especially on Savaii, still have extensive land for farming. Towering forests still cover many of the rainy mountain slopes. There are still fish in the shallow lagoons and deep offshore waters. Above all, the Samoan people are highly literate, healthy, and as yet lightly burdened by the struggle for survival.

In spite of these advantages, development does not come easily. The local economy stumbles along, selling cheap agricultural commodities abroad and importing expensive processed foods and manufactured goods. The value of imports is now six times that of exports. There is little industry to create new jobs, and the pay scale is so low that the departure of well-trained people has increased from a "brain drain" to a dangerous torrent. Western Samoans, for example, now hold half of the skilled government jobs in American Samoa, where they are drawn by salaries that are five to ten times higher than at home.

One of the most intractable economic problems in Western Samoa (and many other developing countries) is the low production of semi-subsistence village farmers, locally called "planters." These village planters grow or catch most of their own food, selling a small surplus locally or through middlemen to international markets. Individually their outputs are low, but together they dominate the country's economy. Their harvests must be increased to raise export incomes and reduce food imports for the rapidly growing urban population. Farm incomes must be raised to reduce the growing economic inequality between urban and rural areas, and to slow the rush of rural people to the city.

Recognizing the growing seriousness of the problem, both international aid organizations and the local government have begun to emphasize village agriculture development. In Western Samoa this means not only increasing the size of harvests, but also the proportion of the crop that villagers sell in the marketplace, particularly for export. Villagers could greatly increase production with the land, labor, and capital that are currently available. They have also been involved in the cash economy for decades, but cash cropping remains poorly developed. Villagers even seem to ignore or resist government attempts to intensify agriculture. In the face of numerous development programs, export production has stagnated or even declined. The threat to the nation's financial stability is clear, but unfortunately the causes of the problem have remained obscure.

THE DEAD WEIGHT OF TRADITION?

Most local and expatriate development experts in Western Samoa believe that great economic rewards are possible for diligent planters who would limit their involvement in village social life. Roads and other infrastructure in Western Samoa are adequate for marketing produce (Leung Wai 1978). The Development Bank, the Rural Development Programme, and other branches of the government encourage and sometimes even subsidize the production of various cash crops. The government-owned Agriculture Store provides heavily subsidized fertilizers, pesticides, and capital equipment.

Numerous Department of Agriculture reports and farmer education brochures herald the money to be made from village agriculture. Several reports estimate that profits from agriculture are high (see Lockwood 1971, GWS 1977, and Burgess 1981). In the early 1980s the Department of Agriculture estimated that the potential return from the staple root crop, taro, was an astounding WS $57 (US $48) per day of labor.[3] They also estimated that planters could earn a still attractive WS $6.95 (US $5.90) per day producing coconuts and copra.[4] These estimates compare very favorably to the usual wage of about WS $4 per day for unskilled labor. Nevertheless, villagers neglect their plantations and flock to the wage jobs.

Assuming that economic incentives are already adequate to inspire greater output, many observers conclude that village agriculture stagnates because Samoans prefer to pursue traditional social goals rather than modern economic goals. Many observers also believe that villagers are too conservative to change or abandon those traditions which inhibit their economic development. Samoans do have a reputation for extreme cultural conservatism. For example, Farrell and Ward state:

[3] Western Samoa's currency is called the *tālā* (from the English, "dollar"). In Samoan, vowels are pronounced in three lengths, with different meanings. The longest of the three occur in accented syllables and may be indicated by a macron, as in *tālā*, pronounced with equal accents: taah-laah. Samoans rarely use such diacritical marks, however, and omit them entirely in proper names. During the time of my research, one Western Samoan *tālā* (WS $1) was worth about 85 cents in U.S. dollars (US $0.85).

[4] Department of Agriculture paper, n.d.; see ADB 1985(2):49 for a similar account including additional crops.

Tradition dies hard in Samoa. The many aspects of the Samoan way of life are vigorously and steadfastly protected. Nowhere else in the Pacific is innovation so resolutely resisted, and in few other territories is the cult of custom so deeply revered (1962:232–33; see also Homes 1980).

People have blamed those customs for the country's underdevelopment since the early colonial days. George Turner, an early Protestant missionary, believed that Samoa's "communistic system is a sad hindrance to the industrious, and eats like a canker worm at the roots of individual or national progress" (1884:160). Nearly a century later, Ward states that:

> In Samoa, the traditional communal pattern of life inhibits private saving and investment, and . . . privilege, status and respect require the dissipation of capital on churches, weddings, and other ceremonial purposes (1962:322).

Farrell and Ward add that "The present state of Samoan agriculture is far from encouraging, and this is to be attributed largely to the *matai* [family chiefs] system of land control" (1962:234). Western Samoa's *Third Five Year Development Plan* charges that Samoa has a "cultural system which many observers, Samoan and foreign alike, believe discourages economic achievement beyond a certain level" (1975:57–58). Similar views are often stated in the nation's English-language newspapers. Fairbairn (1985) presents the consensus list of cultural impediments to Samoan development:

1. communal land tenure causes insecurity of tenure for the producer and a consequent reluctance to develop the land;
2. nonproducers [i.e., chiefs] control agricultural incomes, so that producers do not gain the full benefit of their labor;
3. sharing and ceremonial gift-giving levels incomes between households, thus reducing the incentive to produce for those who give and for those who receive, and limiting the farmer's ability to save and invest;
4. villagers are satisfied with their traditional standard of living—that is, they have fixed or limited wants or aspirations;
5. villagers have a high leisure preference; and
6. they are resistant to change.

Pirie and Barrett state that the traditional social system is largely to blame for the Samoans' "pathetic" response to economic stimuli (1962:76). Nayacakalou graphically summarizes the position when he concludes that production is inhibited by "the dead weight of tradition" (1960:117).

If this explanation is true, development would depend not so much on creating better economic opportunities for Samoan planters as on changing their attitudes and social institutions. In fact, this is an important goal of many development programs. Radio talk shows, agriculture fairs, the declaration of a national "export year," harvesting competitions, and a host of other government programs seek to persuade and educate planters into increasing production. Villagers are constantly told to plant and harvest more crops, both for their own good and for the good of the country. Government officials, newspaper editors, and other city dwellers often chastise villagers publicly for not planting enough crops, and for not tending or harvesting the crops that they do plant.

Are villagers reluctant to develop because they are at a "temporary plateau of satisfaction," as Ward and Proctor (1979:373) and Fairbairn (1985:320) believe? What are the villagers' desires and strategies for increasing their own well-being? What are the real economic benefits of development for the planter? How do village social organization, politics, land tenure, religion, and personal values affect economic development? Do villagers even *want* development? Examining the relationship between tradition and economic development will help answer these questions and bring us closer to the solution of practical development problems.

THE DEVELOPMENT IMPERATIVE

When Western Samoa finally gained its independence in 1962, the country immediately began a rush towards modernization. Funded almost entirely by foreign aid, they rapidly built new roads, schools, hospitals, a satellite telecommunications system, hydroelectric dams and power stations, and an international airport. Today the word on the lips of government officials, city merchants, and village planters alike is *atiinaa'e*, "development." But while the material signs of modernization have increased rapidly since independence, Western Samoa has found it difficult to sustain its own, internally generated development. The country struggles along, poor cousin to its relatively affluent neighbor, American Samoa. The cost and volume of imports rise inexorably higher while erratic commodity prices repeatedly set Western Samoa's agricultural export-based economy on the verge of collapse. The national government relies heavily on foreign aid, while parents send their children overseas to work, hoping that they will remit money back home.

Villagers increasingly measure their economic well-being by the new yardsticks of local and overseas wage and business incomes. By those yardsticks, Samoan planters consider themselves *mativa*, "poor." Their poverty is not entirely illusory. Once the romantic beauty of the seashore and the thatched roofs is left behind, much of Samoa looks like other Third World countries. I was shocked the first time I came upon a scene that reminded me of the dead-end rural poverty I had seen in Mexico, Guatemala, and the West Indies.

I was talking with a middle-aged chief named A'asa in his house one day shortly after my arrival in Western Samoa.[5] My legs hurt terribly from sitting cross-legged all morning, so I persuaded A'asa to take me on a tour of his coconut plantations. We limped slowly up the gravel road, A'asa because his rubber sandals had been stolen and the gravel hurt his bare feet, and I from what felt like distended hip joints. Even moving slowly, A'asa began breathing

---

[5] The apostrophe in "A'asa" is pronounced as a glottal stop, as at the beginning of each syllable in the English exclamation, "Uh-oh!" or the Cockney pronunciation of "t," as in "le'er."

heavily. Like most aging Samoan men, he has been a heavy smoker for several decades.

At A'asa's urging we detoured to rest at the house of his sister at the back of the village. It was a small board house with corrugated iron roof of the kind Samoans refer to as *fale pālagi,* or "European houses." Once painted an unnatural green, the walls were now splotched with dark mildew stains. Around the gaping front entry the yellow-painted trim was almost totally obscured by the accumulated grime of passing hands. Inside, the one-room house was completely bare. Not a single mat graced the concrete floor. The walls were disfigured with layers of greasy hand prints, as if the house had once been used as a mechanic's shop, and was now left vacant.

Three filthy children, only partially dressed in rags, peered out from a dark kitchen partition in the back of the house. A'asa called out repeatedly. Finally an equally filthy teenage girl appeared in the rear doorway. A'asa asked her several brief questions that I could not understand. Though the girl replied to each question, she kept her head bowed slightly and avoided looking directly at her high-ranking uncle. The girl departed, and A'asa motioned for us to sit down on the bare floor to rest. Immediately the children approached for a more intimate inspection of the stranger. Seated now at their own level, I noticed the open sores on their legs and the ill-kept state of their noses. As I inspected them, they grinned back at me with the starry expressions of wonder that Samoan children reserve for visiting foreigners. In a few minutes the girl returned with a gigantic ripe banana. Apparently there was no cocoa, no tea, and no other food to serve the guests. A'asa handed the banana to me as I rose and coaxed him out of the house.

Many Samoans now harbor unrealistic hopes for material plenty, their aspirations buoyed by a flood of unearned wealth and video values from overseas. Most people cannot realize their dreams even now—at least not at home. Should the flow of foreign aid and private remittances ever dry up, or the gates close on future migrants (all probable results of a worldwide depression), both national and family goals will quickly turn from fulfilling dreams to escaping the desperation and meanness that grips so much of the Third World. If local development fails, the loss or reduction of overseas support would quickly reduce Western Samoa to the common push and shove of modern life.

PRIVATE MOTIVES

Like other anthropologists, I have many reasons for doing field research in a strange and distant country. One important reason for doing the research described in this book was my desire to contribute to the solution of the practical problems discussed above. Another reason is a private fascination with other worlds—a desire to live a life radically different from my own. Perhaps I also needed to rationalize the fantasy of a beachcomber's sojourn in Polynesia with a desire for success in American life.

With fascination comes the desire to understand. Why do people in other societies act so differently from us? Are their capabilities, emotions, or desires fundamentally different from our own? Are other societies less wealthy than ours because they lack some character trait—perhaps the boundless desire for material gain that seems so central to Western culture and psychology? Or are differences of custom, belief, and action the result of living in different social, economic, political, and environmental conditions, and possessing different knowledge about the world? Are these differences—however dramatic—merely surface manifestations of a universal human nature, differently elaborated or expressed?

A PLAN OF ACTION

I set out to find my own answers to these questions in Western Samoa in 1979. Funded by a small grant from the University of California at Santa Barbara, I first spent a month in the capital city of Apia getting my bearings, studying the Samoan language, and talking to government officials. With their permission and the advice of some new Samoan friends, Tom and Olivia Yandall, I then began visiting rural villages looking for a research site.

After three practice runs in other areas, I headed for Palauli Bay on the southeast corner of Savaii. I was looking for a relatively traditional, agricultural village that grew all of the major crops. The village could not be so remote, however, that transportation to markets was an obvious impediment to cash cropping. I also wanted a village where planters had alternate sources of income from fishing and from local wage labor, but without either of those dominating the village economy. From reading the literature and studying the maps, I expected the villages at the head of Palauli Bay would be ideal for my work. When I arrived there on the bus from the wharf, however, the gravel road running through the center of the villages was torn up for construction of the new round-island road (a foreign aid project). The formerly placid villages were engulfed in dust and noise.

Dismayed by the destruction, I stayed on the bus and improvised a new plan. After passing through a large coconut plantation where a European-style house commanded a view of a clear, rocky stream, we reached a quiet junction in the road. I got off and began walking seaward along a dusty, one-lane road. I hoped it would lead me to the villages of Satupaitea district, which line the western shore of the bay.

Soon I was in the midst of houses. Some were oval, thatched, and open in the traditional style. Others were rectangular with corrugated iron roofs and painted board walls. It was midday and the tropical sun was blazing hot. No one was about the village. Out on the bay the tide was dead low, and a faint breeze wafted the pungent odor of decay in from the mud flats that began only a few yards from the road.

Finally, I saw a woman and a little girl sitting in one of the open houses.

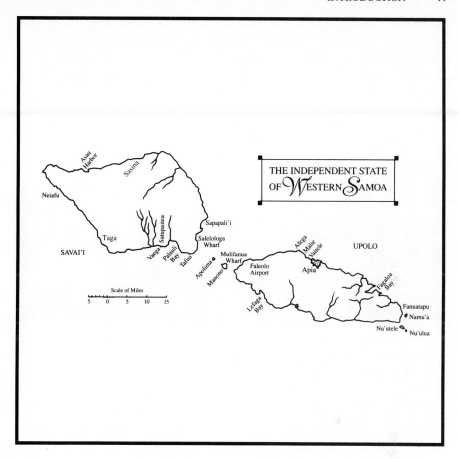

I approached the house, trying to look as if I often walked unannounced into strange villages in foreign lands. Just as I reached the steps of the house the little girl began to scream hysterically, terror in her eyes as I approached. I greeted the woman and then tried a simple Samoan sentence, the rough product of four weeks of study with a dictionary and a Peace Corps language book. My new friends in Apia had told me that if I went to a village where I did not know anyone (which, of course, included every village in Samoa), I could go to the local pastor's house and he would receive me as a guest of the village. That did not sound like a reasonable request to me, but lacking any other plan I forged ahead. I asked the woman where the pastor's house was. The moment I spoke the little girl redoubled her screams of terror.

"What?" the woman replied, trying to shout above her child's cries. I repeated my question louder, then louder again.

"Which one?" she shouted.

"L.M.S." I shouted back, guessing that the dominant "London Missionary Society" would have a church in the village.

Photo 2. Air view of Palauli Bay facing south. The villages of Palauli District lie in the foreground at the head of the bay, while the villages of Satupaitea line the southwestern side of the bay in the upper right of the photo.

I understood only one word of her reply—*Metodisi*, "Methodist."

"Where?" I yelled, hoping that I had not confused the Samoan words for where, what, and when. Her reply was unintelligible to me, but she pointed on up the road. I thanked her and departed quickly in the same direction.[6] I figured that I could spot a church easily enough, but I had no idea what a pastor's house might look like.

I missed the first pastor's house in the village of Pitonu'u, but landed successfully at the second one in Vaega, a couple of hundred yards further down the road. There the houses sit upon a rocky shore and look out across the broadest expanse of the bay. A young man came out to meet me. I tried to explain the reason for my visit in three or four rehearsed sentences of simple Samoan. With a puzzled expression on his face, the young man led me into the large whitewashed house. Some time later his father, the pastor, came in. I repeated the brief explanation of my presence and my request that I be allowed to stay with them. I did not understand much of the pastor's response, and from his own puzzled expression I guessed that either I was not making sense, or I had overstepped the bounds of propriety—or both. He granted my request, however, and I stayed with the kind pastor, Fogalele, and his wife, Fale, for three weeks. They and the other villagers were friendly,

[6] Much later I discovered that Samoans often try to control small children by telling them that they will be devoured or beaten by a *pālagi*, or "European," if they misbehave. This child's reaction was a common one.

courteous, and tolerant of my ignorance of things Samoan. During my brief stay I learned a bit about village life and something more of the Samoan language. The village leaders also consented to allow me to return the next year to begin my dissertation research. It was not until February of 1981, however, that I returned with a grant from the National Science Foundation to study the "Social and Economic Causes of Underproduction in Samoan Village Agriculture."

After my return, I spent the next twenty-nine months in Western Samoa. I lived for most of that time in Vaega village, though I also worked in and around Apia and in several other villages on both Savaii and Upolu. I returned to Western Samoa again in 1984 for three and a half months to continue my study of the effects of land tenure on agricultural development. During that time I worked mainly in Neiafu, on the southwest corner of Savaii, and in Malie, on the northwest coast of Upolu. That research was supported by a contract with the Food and Agriculture Organization of the United Nations and the Institute of Pacific Studies at the University of the South Pacific in Suva, Fiji. I also returned for month-long visits in 1985 and 1988.

The only person in Vaega who spoke English was a young teacher at the village's primary school. He spoke English well, though reluctantly. The master and one of the teachers at the neighboring Wesleyan High School also spoke English, but since they were not members of the village, they did not participate in most village affairs. A few other villagers have some acquaintance with the language, though they are careful not to display it in public for fear that they will be embarrassed by a mistake. During my residence in Vaega and in several other villages, and in all of my research work, I spoke English only with a few officials in Apia and with some part-European plantation owners. Otherwise I spoke Samoan.

A MATTER OF TENSE

Most of the material I present in this book comes from the period from 1981 to 1984. Some aspects of Samoan culture, and of Samoan village life in general, have changed very little over the years. Other aspects are changing more or less rapidly. In writing this book I have tried to pay close attention to my use of verb tenses. I avoid completely the so-called "ethnographic present" tense that anthropologists commonly use to describe customs that once were, but are no longer. Instead, I use the present tense to indicate only those things that existed during the time of my field work and will most likely continue to exist in the near future. Thus, when I say that Samoan parents "teach" their children to obey them without objection, I mean that they did so during the time of my field work, they do so now as I write, and they will probably continue to do so into the foreseeable future. That statement alone implies nothing about their actions in the past. Some conditions have changed significantly between the time of the field work and the writing of this book, or I expect them to have changed by the time the reader sees this book. In those cases, I use the past tense.

A NOTE ABOUT FRIENDS

It is a sobering experience to write a book about a people and a place that one loves, knowing that many of those people, or their children or grandchildren, will read the book, judging me and perhaps even themselves on what I have said. It is a humbling experience because I also recognize that those Samoan readers know far more about their lives than I could hope to learn or to express in these pages. My research purpose, however, was not to capture the full intensity and complexity of Samoan life and culture, but to answer a few practical questions about the motivations and desires of Samoan planters. I wanted to know how people strive to achieve those desires in the circumstances that surround them. I do claim some expertise in the answer to those questions.

My answer is that the aspirations of Samoan planters are not fundamentally different from those of Americans or other Westerners. Given the circumstances in which they live, villagers' strategies for satisfying those aspirations are explainable in the same terms as our own, more familiar strategies. My goal in this book is to communicate to you that simple conclusion and the evidence upon which it is based. My hope is that by understanding Samoans better, you will accept them and other people like them as worthy of your respect. More pragmatic is my hope that by seeing village planters as real people, economic development experts will reject paternalism and redouble their efforts to put people first.

In order to communicate to you something of the lives of Samoan planters as real people, my message must range beyond the factors that directly influence their economic behavior. I must also touch the lives of friends. Since an account half told is unbelievable and therefore of no use at all, I will lay out the good with the bad, as honestly as I can. As a group, Samoans are intensely sensitive to public criticism or embarrassment, yet they are equally proud of public recognition. How can I protect people's privacy *and* recognize their personal contributions while telling the tale honestly? My solution to this quandary is to publicly recognize individual people, families, and villages by giving their real names whenever it might be a matter of pride to them or whenever the reference is neutral. I will give fictitious names whenever identification might cause embarrassment or lead to other difficulties. Sometimes I will also alter the description of people, places, and events to hide their identities. I will not, however, alter significant attributes.

2/Western Samoa: Profile of a Modern Polynesian Nation

Samoa has changed considerably since the first European explorers came ashore two hundred years ago. Samoa was then a society of shifting alliances and family chieftainships that frequently warred among themselves. Today Western Samoa has a parliamentary government. It is also a member of such international organizations as the United Nations, the British Commonwealth, and the South Pacific Forum. Traditionally, Samoans prayed to a pantheon of Polynesian gods, including Tagaloa, Founder of the Universe, and to their own families' gods. Today Samoans pride themselves on being among the most devout Christians in the world. Before contact with Europeans, every family and every village was nearly self-sufficient, with little local or inter-island trade. Today even the most remote village is dependent on the outside world.

In spite of the many profound changes, however, Samoans have maintained their reputation for cultural conservatism and their pride in the *fa'a-Samoa*, or "Samoan way of life." Samoan families are still ruled by their elected chiefs, or *matai*, and all of the more than 300 rural villages are still governed by their *fono*, or council of chiefs. Samoans have also managed to retain their identity. Though two hundred years of contact has allowed the genes of foreigners to mix widely, the population remains almost entirely Polynesian. Western Samoa boasts the largest population of Polynesians in the world, with over 150,000 in the home islands and half again as many living overseas. Most of the early migrants went to New Zealand, but now many also go to nearby American Samoa, and to Australia, Hawaii, and the U.S. mainland.

Western Samoa's two main islands, Savaii and Upolu, are tropical and mountainous. All of the islands are of recent volcanic origin, and beneath the lush vegetation lies more lava rock than soil. On the northeast side of the largest island, Savaii, a series of eruptions wiped out entire districts only two generations ago. Undulating lava still blankets the island for miles where it flowed down from the mountain top and spilled into the sea. Only an occasional tuft of grass or a stunted sapling shows green against the expanse of black rock.

THE BIG ISLAND OF SAVAII

Savaii resembles its namesake, the big island of Hawaii some 2,200 miles to the northeast, in both its outline and its geologic history. Savaii is much smaller though. Encompassing only 1,600 square kilometers (about 620 square miles), it is roughly the size of Oahu. But there is no city like Honolulu here. Savaii is Samoa's "outback." Only 43,000 people live on Savaii (compared to over 700,000 on Oahu), primarily in villages of from 300 to 600 people scattered around the coast.

Savaii does not have a single city. The closest approximation is the growing trade center of Salelologa, strung along the asphalt road leading from the inter-island ferry wharf on the southeastern side of the island. Inland from the wharf is Taylor's bar with two pool tables (always occupied), the government's dilapidated public works yard, and a large new produce market. The sides of the market are open to the breeze, and the roof covers a wide expanse of concrete floor, broken only by a few vendors who sit patiently behind their small piles of taro, cucumbers, or cocoa beans. Near the market is the new, gleaming white public library that was built recently by the Japanese. Further inland, at the intersection with the newly surfaced round-island road, stands a loose collection of perhaps a dozen shops. A compound of new government buildings lies a short way along the round-island road. Within the compound are the postal and telephone offices, branch offices of the Development Bank and the Agriculture Store, and the offices and warehouses of the Copra and Cocoa Boards.

The new asphalt, round-island road was nearly complete in 1983, and electric poles were beginning to appear as the government slowly extended power to the villages. People are also building new houses along the inland portions of the road to take advantage of the improved transportation. They also move inland to be closer to their plantations, and because the preferred house sites along the shore are becoming overcrowded. Along with its intended benefits, the new road provides plenty of crushed rock which villagers now use instead of stream pebbles or coral rubble to surface the floors of their houses. The road is also a handy source of tar for patching cracks in canoe hulls.

The new road, the new government buildings, the power line, and most other capital improvements in the nation are the product of gifts or low-interest loans from foreign donors. Aid has poured into this tiny nation since independence. Individual donor nations include New Zealand, Australia, Germany, and the United States, all of whom feel a post-colonial responsibility in the area (and also want to deflect unwanted migrants). Japan, who has fishing, economic, and political interests in the islands (not the least of which is its troublesome desire to dump radioactive waste in the Pacific Ocean), is also an important donor. Even the People's Republic of China gives substantial aid, though its own per capita income is perhaps one-fourth that of Western Samoa. Aid also comes from many international agencies. These include the World Bank, the Asian Development Bank, the International Monetary Fund, the European Economic Community, numerous branches of the United Nations, the British Commonwealth, and OPEC.

In fact, there are so many aid proposals to handle, so many technical experts and dignitaries to welcome, and so many overseas training programs and official meetings to attend, it sometimes seems there are not enough people left in government to do the work. Everyone is either in Rome, Manila, Bangkok, or Auckland, or they are showing someone from one of these places around the islands.

Neither the foreign aid nor the cash remittances from migrants has produced much self-sustaining development in the local economy, but the flow of money from overseas has greatly modernized Samoa. Even in rural Savaii many European-style houses line the road—rectangular and wood-framed houses with low-peaked, corrugated iron roofs, and louvered glass windows. Some of the houses are brightly painted, but on most the paint has weathered and soiled to a sad blend of pastel colors and dark mildew stains. A few families even own pickup trucks, new or in various stages of tropical decay, always parked conspicuously in front of the house.

With only rare exceptions, people pay for both the houses and the pickup trucks with cash gifts from relatives who have gone overseas to work. For most residents, income from selling crops or working for wages is barely enough to support their daily needs and perhaps the yearly school fees of their many children. Like the nation as a whole, money for improvements and sometimes even for daily support comes from overseas.

Standing between the European-style houses, and behind them in the less desirable inland sites, are many Samoan-style houses. Their rectangular foundations are built of black volcanic boulders, and their floors are rounded stream pebbles or road gravel. Their roofs are either high-peaked and thatched or low-peaked and covered with sheets of corrugated iron. These Samoan-style houses are left completely open, their roofs supported only by posts made of local tree trunks, in order to let the sea breeze blow unimpeded through the house. During the frequent rain squalls, people lower horizontal shutters of plaited coconut leaves to keep the interior of the house dry. Otherwise these blinds remain tied up under the eaves, lest the neighbors suspect that something illicit is going on inside.

Behind many of these substantial houses are smaller thatched houses without stone foundations. In these small houses only roughly laid platforms of boards or split logs raise the human occupants above the marauding pigs, chickens, and dogs. Most of these small houses are occupied by a married son or daughter of the couple that lives in the bigger house. A few, however, are occupied by mature but poor families who join the households of wealthier relatives.

Behind each cluster of residential houses are one or two low, thatched cook houses with sticks nailed across their supporting posts in a generally futile effort to fence the animals out. Often the cook house closest to the main house is reserved for the common chores of boiling and frying (which are almost always done by women), while a more distant cook house is used for making the stone oven, or *umu* (a chore usually performed by young men).

Clumps of banana trees, with their tubular trunks and high arching leaves, shade the houses. Large, spreading breadfruit trees stand a little distance from the houses, where their large, starchy fruits will not drop on the rooftops. There are several varieties of breadfruit, each with distinctively shaped, many-fingered leaves that identify which variety is best for making *taofolo*, baking in the stone oven, or roasting on an open fire. The banana and breadfruit trees not only provide shade and food, the family also uses their leaves as cooking and serving materials. People rarely use the breadfruit leaves anymore to make kites for fishing or for fine-grained sandpaper as they once did.

Surrounding every house is a pavement of loose cobbles or gravel of black lava. This pavement protects the family from the mud that develops from the eighty to one hundred twenty inches of rain that fall each year. The clatter of the loose rock also acts as a simple warning device whenever someone approaches the house. A close search of the cobbles around almost any house will turn up several polished stone adzes, chipped stone adze blanks, or fragments of shattered adzes—a startling reminder of how recent the traditional past is in Samoa.

Between the houses and the road are neat, grassy yards. Many have small gardens of tropical flowers bordered by bushes with glossy, variegated leaves of green, yellow, and red, or hibiscus bushes with their deep red, pink, or yellow flowers. In the yards of many houses are simple, stone-marked graves, and the painted cement tombs of more recently departed parents. The ornateness of these graves and their prominent placement in front of the family residence expresses the tremendous respect and devotion most Samoans feel for their parents. The placement of the graves also documents the surviving family members' claim to the land—an important point since most boundaries and ownership claims are recorded only in people's memories.

Outsiders are often surprised to see crouching children "mowing" the grassy lawns with rhythmic sweeps of their machetes. In the early mornings children also pick the yards clean of fallen leaves, and then sweep the smaller refuse into the lagoon with long-handled brooms made of coconut leaf midribs. If the young men are down from the plantations, a scrawny horse may be staked in the yard as well, cropping the short grass. Small, wiry chickens zigzag around the borders of the yard, scratching the dirt while trailing a brood of little chicks that often catch the hungry eye of the fat black pigs that root insolently here and there.

AN UNANNOUNCED VISIT

Foreign visitors are rare in a rural village, and so they are welcomed with some excitement. I have stopped many times in distant villages at the homes of both friends and strangers. One of the first times was in a village on the south coast of Savaii. I arrived unannounced at an open, corrugated iron-roofed house that sat high on a stone foundation beside a lagoon. I climbed the stone steps at the front and sat cross-legged on a pandanus mat just inside and to one side of the entrance. A middle-aged man looked up as I entered. He sat facing me with his back to the bright light of the lagoon. Following local custom, neither of us spoke until I was seated. Then the man put aside the coconut-fiber rope he was braiding, adjusted the simple cotton skirt, or *lāvalava*, around his bare waist, straightened his back, and greeted me formally: *Susū maia lau susuga* . . . "Welcome, sir . . ."

When our formal greetings were completed, he called impatiently to the children who watched from the corners. With a curt order he sent them scurrying this way and that, bringing more mats to cover the floor in front of me and a coconut leaf fan to ease the heat and keep the flies at bay. Finally they carried in a heavy Samoan meal: a thick, black, cocoa drink of overpowering sweetness, heaps of cold, purple-grey taro dripping with white coconut cream, and a chicken they had hastily stoned and roasted. As the children went about their chores, they gave me wide-eyed glances and shy smiles. Their father tapped his fingers impatiently on the floor mat, doing a very good job of looking important in his modest surroundings.

I watched a group of men out in the shallow lagoon. They were setting a nylon net in a deep "V" shape, leaving their outrigger canoes with shark-nosed bows and upturned sterns tethered nearby to the scattered coralheads. I made small talk with my host. I would wait until after the meal to ask him about the new cocoa variety he had recently planted—which was the real purpose of my visit. In the background I could hear the sudden shouts of the fishermen, distorted by the light wind blowing in from the sea. A white flurry of splashing rose from the water as they drove the reef fish into the net. The fish were small, but the fishermen untangled each one in turn, cautiously biting their heads behind the eyes to kill them, and then tossing them into the nearest canoe.

The fishermen stood chest-deep in the warm sea, facing back toward the mountain slopes that rise slowly from behind the metal roofs of the houses. For two miles inland the slopes are covered with coconut palms. Then the palms give way to lighter patches of fallow land. Still farther up, the grasses meet the deep green of the taro plots, only recently cleared from the forest. Above the taro plots the dark forest stretches upward in a smooth arc, shaped by the lava that once flowed from the peaks of the interior.

THE LIFE IS GOOD, BUT . . .

This is the rural Samoa that Samoans can afford on their own. It is a world of thatch and corrugated iron, machetes and firewood, of pebble floors, muddy foot paths, and dugout canoes. It is a delightful world in many ways, but far from Eden. Contrary to popular Western belief, it is not a world of ease and leisure, except for those who are old and important. Nor is it a world that can presently pay for the things its people want—the pickup trucks, better houses, books for the schools, better medical services, a better and more varied diet, electricity and the household fixtures that go with it, and clothes they do not have to stitch themselves or buy second-hand from Australia.

Villagers often speak proudly of the good life in Samoa where they can *'ai fua*, "eat for free"—as opposed to life in New Zealand or America where they believe that people will starve if they have no money to buy food. But Samoans also speak often of their *mativa*, "poverty." Some of them chafe at the lack of opportunity or the slowness and conformity of village life, hoping to leave for Apia or New Zealand. Many others enjoy village life, wishing only that they had more money. As my friend, Nu'u, once remarked: *E lelei Samoa* . . . "Samoa is good. Food is easy to get." Then he added with a sorrowful laugh, "But Samoa is also bad. The search for money is very hard!"

To a casual visitor these quiet villages of Savaii may appear isolated, lost in their own palm-frond world. Nothing could be further from the truth. Many former residents of rural villages live permanently in Apia or overseas, yet remain closely attached to their families and villages. Many current village residents travel overseas, often for periods of up to six months, and they are constantly traveling to and from Apia. Many villagers are also knowledgeable about current international affairs, especially those concerning the Holy Land and the rest of the Near East, and those concerning superpower rivalries. One of the first questions a Savaii villager asked me during my residence there was whether the Russian navy is really larger now than the U.S. navy, as he had heard on the radio. Rural villages are greatly affected by events in the wider national and international arenas. In turn, rural villages play important roles in the social, political, and especially the economic life of their nation.

THE NATIONAL ECONOMY

Western Samoa's economy subsists on three sources of income. First is the export of a few agricultural products. The main exports are coconut products, including: (1) copra, the dried meat of the coconut; (2) coconut oil pressed from copra, which is used in a variety of soap and food products; and (3) canned coconut cream, or *pe'epe'e*. Cocoa beans, which are made into chocolate, are also an important export, along with the starchy root crop, taro (*Colocasia esculenta*, or "elephant ear"), and some bananas. The second source of national income is foreign aid. The final source of income is private aid in the form of cash and purchased goods remitted by relatives working overseas. These sources supply the country with roughly equal amounts of income.[1] The nation's Gross Domestic Product (GDP) was roughly WS $140

---

[1] In 1983 exports were worth over WS $25 million (US $18.5 million). Foreign aid was slightly higher—over WS $26 million (US $19 million), or about US $120 per person. Private remittances from overseas were officially estimated at over WS $31 million (US $23 million), or US $144 per person (GWS 1984:173). This estimate of remittances includes only cash transfers, however. My research in Vaega indicates that remittance totals would be one-third higher if the value of goods received from overseas was also included.

million in 1983 (ADB 1985[2]:198), including a substantial contribution from the "subsistence sector" (i.e., food and other goods that were consumed directly by their producers). Thus, private gifts and foreign aid together made up at least 30 percent of the nation's total income, which averaged WS $1,230 (US $911) per person in 1983.[2] Since a large part of the GDP itself comes from recirculation of the remittance and aid money, probably one-half of the nation's total income comes directly or indirectly from overseas gifts.

Semi-subsistence village planters control 80 percent of the nation's land, and they produce most of the export crops. The remainder of the export crop comes from private and government-owned commercial plantations. When export prices are high, the country is relatively solvent. Even in good times, however, the nation imports three times more goods than it exports. When export prices drop, the country quickly falls into financial trouble.

Over the years nearly a third of foreign aid and the government's own development expenditures have gone to support agricultural development. Most of those funds, however, have gone to the government-owned Western Samoa Trust Estates Corporation (WSTEC) or to larger-scale commercial farmers, rather than to village planters.

THE PASSION FRUIT SCHEME

The brief history of passion fruit production in Western Samoa is a good example of how development often bypasses village farmers. The passion fruit is very sweet and delicious, and though little-known in the U.S. (outside of Hawaii, where it is known as "lilikoi"), its popularity is growing worldwide. The plum-sized yellow fruit grows on a dense and heavy vine, which has to be supported off the ground like a grape arbor. The passion fruit program was first started by the Department of Agriculture in the late 1970s in quarter-acre village plots. The purpose of the program was to diversify village agriculture and utilize surplus labor in the villages. The new program was soon overcome by problems, however. One notable problem was that in order for the vines to bear fruit, the planters had to hand pollinate each flower. Another problem was the rapid deterioration of trellis posts, which caused the mature vines to collapse.

After a couple of years of experimentation with village plots, a productive system was worked out. The post problem was solved by using chemically treated coconut logs to support the trellises. Commercial beehives eliminated the need to hand pollinate the flowers. At the same time, the program was moved out of the Department of Agriculture and placed under the direction of a full-time manager, who was hired from overseas. The new expatriate manager eliminated most of the project's input subsidies, but doubled the purchase price of the fruit. He then signed contracts with selected commercial

[2] The Western Samoan currency went through a series of devaluations in 1983. During that year the exchange rate averaged about WS $1.35 = US $1.00.

growers, guaranteeing to buy all of their harvests at the attractive new price. He also personally supervised extension services and the supply of planting stock and trellis materials.

The result was a near frenzy of planting, almost entirely among middle- and upper-class Samoans who own freehold land near Apia.[3] I talked with many of these passion fruit growers, and all were excited about their newfound source of wealth. These freehold landowners are mostly of part-European or part-Chinese descent. Some were actively involved in the work, but many others were absentee owners employing hired managers and labor, virtually all of whom were full-Samoan.

Many observers contrasted the dismal failure of the passion fruit scheme when it was directed toward village planters with its tremendous success since it began catering to more Westernized, commercial farmers. Many people took this as another indication that village planters are "uneconomic" and that they could never be induced to develop their plantations. What these critics ignored, of course, was that the new passion fruit scheme was entirely different from the scheme as it had first been tried with village planters.

Although the later passion fruit scheme did not actively discriminate against Samoan village planters, several factors combined to almost totally exclude them. The manager would not accept any growers who did not contract for the entire, expensive package. Village planters had neither funds nor mortgagable land to secure loans to finance the heavy initial costs of production. In order to simplify extension services and other logistics, the expatriate director wanted only "a few good, efficient growers" with concentrated holdings of at least ten acres of passion fruit. The commercial beekeepers, whose services are critical to production, also required a concentration of large landholdings. Neither group wanted to dilute its efforts by providing the extra services that small-scale, village farmers would have required. Finally, though the director's expertise and personal supervision were of great benefit to the commercial farmers (and were undoubtedly responsible for the program's initial success), his personal supervision also served to exclude all but a very few (well-placed) village planters. Planters are reluctant to approach any government official other than a relative, and they find it virtually impossible to approach a European officer who does not speak Samoan.

After three years of spectacular increases in both harvests and farm profits, the passion fruit scheme collapsed. Inattention to marketing combined with an unexpectedly large crop resulted in huge, unsold surpluses just as a few village planters were beginning to participate. The project did not have the funds to purchase even the contracted fruit, and countless other uncontracted producers suddenly appeared with truckloads of fruit to sell. Tons of unsold

---

[3] "Freehold land" can be bought and sold, as opposed to "customary land" which, by Western Samoa law, cannot. Customary land is held "according to the custom and usages of the Samoan people."

passion fruit juice sat frozen in lockers, and many more tons of fruit were simply dumped.

Like the passion fruit scheme, most agricultural development projects are geared toward large-scale, commercial farmers or government-owned plantations rather than toward common village planters. Most projects that have made it to the villages—such as commercial poultry, pig, and cattle schemes—have been failures. One important reason is that in Western Samoa, as in other countries, it is sometimes difficult to get benefits past the more-savvy, urban people and into the hands of the less-savvy, rural people. Another reason is that many of the people who design, fund, and implement projects do not have detailed knowledge of village social and economic conditions. They believe that village planters are fundamentally uneconomic and will never develop their plantations voluntarily. As a result, they design projects that bypass village planters in favor of commercial farmers, or they advocate legislative changes that would force village planters to produce more. A good example is the following proposal by an anonomous development expert:

A LAND TAX

The author of Western Samoa's latest three-year development plan strongly advocates that the government institute a tax on agricultural land. The purpose of the tax would be to force local planters to produce and market more cash crops (GWS 1987:28, 34, 66). The tax would be levied on all agricultural land according to its size and productive potential. Agricultural land taxes are common in Western countries where such taxes encourage farmers either to use their lands productively or dispose of them to someone who will. The proposal to institute such a tax in Western Samoa, however, is based on ignorance of local conditions.

First, in order to impose such a tax, the government would have to survey all village agricultural plots accurately to determine their areas, and then permanently mark the plot boundaries. Surveyors would also have to assess each plot's productive potential. Finally, all claims to ownership would have to be settled, including the many new disputes that would erupt during the surveying. I spent six months, full-time, surveying the 195 agricultural plots in Vaega and then recording ownership claims, without marking boundaries or trying to settle conflicting claims (see Chapter 5). Very few of the nation's 60,000 or so other agricultural plots have been recorded even to that degree. A nationwide survey is clearly impossible with any reasonable commitment of resources. In addition to these logistical problems, such a survey would raise incendiary legal and social problems of its own.

Second, the proposal to institute an agricultural land tax assumes that all land could and should be valued according to its potential for producing cash crops. This may be a reasonable assumption in an industrialized country like the United States or New Zealand, but it is absurd in Western Samoa where villagers must reserve at least half of their land for producing food and other subsistence crops. The imposition of a land tax would have the effect of forcing village planters to produce cash crops for sale when it is not to their economic advantage to do so. Thus, the tax would result in no conceivable benefit to the planters (even if some of the tax was returned to them, perhaps to improve rural education). The tax would benefit urban dwellers, however, who purchase food in the local market and who also depend heavily on foreign imports. Storekeepers can import these goods only if village planters export enough cash crops to maintain the nation's foreign exchange reserves. In short, an agricultural land tax would be just another technique for transferring wealth from rural people to urban people.

Third, the imposition of a land tax assumes that there is some mechanism for transferring agricultural land from owners who cannot or do not want to produce enough cash crops to pay the tax to those who do. In Western Samoa, very little agricultural land is freehold land. Eighty percent of all land is held by "customary" tenure. The nation's constitution prohibits people from selling this land, even to other Samoan residents in the same village.[4] Villagers can lease their customary land, but they almost never do. Short-term leases are unattractive to those who want more land because they need time to make the development pay. Conversely, long-term leases are unattractive to those holding surplus land because their families are growing rapidly and the future economy is uncertain. Another problem is that long-term use traditionally implies ownership and people lack faith in the Court's ability to enforce a paper contract that contradicts that tradition.

The imposition of a land tax might force villagers to lease some of their land. The short-term effect, however, would probably only be to increase pressure on overseas relatives for remittances. Villagers commonly employ this method now for collecting school fees and other large expenses that they find difficult to raise from local sources. A land tax would probably not increase agricultural production in the long term either. Instead, the long-term effect would be to increase the already considerable pressure on villagers to scatter their children overseas where they could earn the money to pay the new land tax.

AN URBAN VIEW OF VILLAGE PLANTERS

Western Samoa is a tiny and homogeneous country by world standards. There is comparatively little distance, either geographic or social, between rural villages and the center of government in Apia. A common language, culture, and religion unite the people, and they speak their collective will in an independent, democratic government. Most of the Samoan officials and

[4] On rare occasions villagers may transfer land nevertheless. I recorded three examples in Vaega where land was transferred permanently from one family to another, once as a kind of dowry, once in exchange for fine mats, and once in exchange for forgiving a monetary debt.

bureaucrats who plan and direct rural development projects were themselves born and raised in nearby rural villages, though most left early in their childhoods to attend school in Apia or overseas. Virtually all urban officials visit their village relatives occasionally to attend important family ceremonies, and when villagers travel to Apia they visit and usually reside with their urban relatives. Expatriate development officers who make the effort find village planters to be accessible, cooperative, relatively free of suspicion, and even aggressively friendly.

Yet with all these avenues for communication, urban-dwelling officials are often perplexed by the planters' actions (or inaction). Several high-ranking Samoan agricultural officers complained to me privately that they were often baffled and exasperated by the behavior of village planters. Expatriate officers (some with several years of experience in Western Samoa and other Pacific countries) sometimes admitted that they had little or no understanding of village life. From their urban environment, these development officers often conclude that the planters' economic behavior is strange or even irrational. One highly placed expatriate officer had been trying for years to implement his pet development plan, yet he admitted that he had no idea whether villagers would even tolerate it, much less participate in it. He asked me if I thought they would.

"I don't know," I replied, "why don't you ask them?"

"But I can't," he moaned. "I can't talk to them." Then he added candidly, "I've been living here for five years, and I don't have any idea what is going on out in those villages."

When his boss arrived on a junket from Europe, the local officer asked me to take them both on a day-long tour of Savaii. In order to avoid being received with the pomp and ceremony due their rank, the local officer refused to stop and talk with anyone in the villages we passed through. He was visibly uncomfortable during the entire trip, and he did not relax again until we returned to the more familiar surroundings of the city.

UPOLU AND THE CAPITAL CITY OF APIA

Thirteen miles east of Savaii is the smaller but more populous island of Upolu. Here the villages are more prosperous and modern, largely because of their greater access to government and other wage work in Apia. Along the heavily populated northwest coast and in the villages just east of Apia, many people are able to combine the best of both urban and rural life: the access to jobs, shopping, and entertainment of the city and the peace, security, intimacy, and cheap living of a rural village. In each of these coastal villages at least one large concrete church (and often several smaller ones as well) stands prominently above the houses, deliberate evidence of both the residents' devotion and their wealth.

Apia is the capital of Western Samoa and the nation's only city. Nearly 45,000 people live in the city and in the many suburban villages that crowd around it. Most of the amenities of modern life can be found in Apia, though not everyone can afford them. By Continental standards Apia is a small, almost lethargic port town. To those coming in from Savaii, however, it seems a busy, bustling place. It is a world of shop clerks, civil servants, and occasional tourists—an almost pure service economy of government offices, retail stores, small hotels, movie theaters, pool halls, dance halls, and bars. Except for the government brewery and copra mill just outside town, little is produced here.

I remember Apia best from my last visit. I arrived by bus at the central market next to the harbor. The market was jammed with people and island produce—neat piles of taro, coconuts, and vegetables watched over by villagers sitting cross-legged on newspapers, fragments of cardboard, or tattered mats spread out on the concrete floor. Brightly painted buses, the Samoan version of converted longbed trucks that are a familiar sight in many tropical countries, rumbled up to the market to unload more people and produce, and then fanned out again through the dusty town and across the island.

Down the sidewalks near the market, villagers spread cocoa beans for sale on little squares of newspaper or pages torn from old school notebooks. Passersby dodged from one patch of shade to another. Schoolchildren, in their white shirts and brightly colored wraparound skirts called *lāvalava*, straggled home in groups, laughing and talking gaily. A few village youths loitered around a corner shop. They wore secondhand T-shirts and flowered *lāvalava* knotted loosely in front. Crude tattoos marked their upper arms, and their black hair curled just long enough in back to provoke comment from their elders. Errands completed, they stood idly, smoking hand-rolled cigarettes and shifting their weight from one calloused foot to the other.

The older women were dressed in colorful *puletasi*, matching long blouses and skirts. The women's dresses were uniformly tight fitting, not from immodesty, but from immodest girths. The village *matai*, or family chiefs, were easy to identify. They wore sport shirts and somber-colored *lāvalava*, held decorously in place with leather belts. Barefoot or in rubber sandals, they each carried a briefcase—either a rectangular attache case from relatives in America, or a satchel-shaped portfolio from relatives in New Zealand. Inside the briefcases were probably nothing more than a comb, a small jar of scented hair oil, a battered notepad, and a baked taro.

A pair of burly *matai* passed in front of me carrying their briefcases and long, black, bamboo-handled umbrellas from China. Small hand towels were wrapped around their necks and tucked under their collars to absorb sweat, making them look like small-time prizefighters, which they once may have been.

There were also part-European men in from their nearby plantations. They were driving one- or two-ton Toyota or Isuzu trucks, big enough to carry laborers to the plantations and produce to town. There were Samoan civil servants, clerks, and shopkeepers, the men wearing dark pants or formal *lāvalava* and white shirts, the women in ankle-length dress uniforms. A group of expatriate consultants passed by on the sidewalk looking very colonial in their thigh-length shorts, shoes, and knee-high white socks, their faces pinkish

Photo 3. Apia harbor, looking southeast from the Reclaimed Area.

against the darker crowd. A young Peace Corps volunteer came out of a shop with a small knapsack slung over one shoulder. A helmeted Japanese volunteer sped by on a motorcycle. There were even a few tourists from Europe and Australia peering idly into the shop windows and looking thoroughly out of place in their sensible wash-and-wear clothes.

Across the harbor a huge container ship dwarfed the rest of the city. It slowly unloaded manufactured goods, machinery, building materials, and tons of food onto the wharf, and loaded in turn only a couple of containers full of island produce. In the center of the harbor a lovely blue ketch rode at anchor, the sea breeze pointing its stern in toward the bar at Aggie Grey's Hotel.

Most of the buildings in town look boxy and plain against the backdrop of rugged mountains. Only the new, six-story John Williams and National Provident Fund office buildings rise above the one- and two-story profile of older buildings. A few white, wooden buildings with red, iron roofs and delicate fretwork embellishing their façades still remain from the early colonial days. Built by the Germans shortly after the turn of the century, these buildings defy the termites, dry rot, and rust that quickly mar later construction.

Behind the row of waterfront offices and stores are the Chinese shops, as well as the pool halls, movie theaters, and bars where unemployed men spend the money they have begged from working relatives. Women shop or wander only briefly in town. They spend most of their time either tending the counters in nearby shops or at home minding children and doing household chores. There is always work to be done around the house. People also think it unseemly, as well as unsafe, for young women to wander about the town.

Behind the last row of shops are rows of tiny wooden houses jammed together between open ditches that drain what used to be a large swamp. On the higher ground leading up to Mount Vaea are more substantial homes. Still higher, along the cross-island road where the air is cooler, are the luxurious homes of the island's elite. Among them sits the late-nineteenth century mansion of the famous writer, Robert Louis Stevenson. Today the large wooden structure is the official residence of the Head of State, Afioga Malietoa Tanumafili II.

Like other villagers from *i tuā*, "out back," visitors from my research village of Vaega come to Apia often for entertainment, business, social and political affairs, education, and for work. Some even settle permanently with relatives in one of the many urban villages that surround the town center. But it takes money to live in town. Most people from Vaega say that when their money runs out on their brief sojourns to Apia, they are glad to return to the security and familiarity of their families and village.

3/Vaega: A Village on Palauli Bay

It is a tiresome journey from the city of Apia, midway along the north coast of Upolu, to the village of Vaega on the southeast corner of Savaii.[1] After a long wait at the downtown market, the bus takes an hour and a half to traverse the twenty miles to the ferry landing at Mulifanua. Watching the Samoan social hierarchy being acted out at every stop offered me some diversion. A child waits by the side of the road and waves the bus to a halt. An elderly man steps out of the meager shade of an electric pole and rises with labored dignity up the bus steps. A polite young man in the front row quickly leaves his wooden seat, stepping over the boxes and baskets in the aisle. Halfway to the rear he slides into a seat just vacated by a schoolgirl who has been hoisted onto the lap of a matron at the window seat. The bus pulls away toward the next stop a hundred yards down the road—where the passengers reshuffle once again. By the time the bus reaches the ferry landing, the young men are jammed into the rear seats, and the school children are all sitting on adults' laps. The women and middle-aged men are scattered among the center seats. The older chiefs and a pastor and his wife sit in dignified twosomes in the forward seats.

There is often a long wait for the ferry to depart. The open vehicle ferry is a rusting, battered, and grease-covered hulk of welded iron plates that spent its better years plying the monsoon seas of some Asian nation. Many passengers push and shove rudely for the few seats on the wheelhouse afterdeck. The less fortunate squeeze in between, under, and on top of the half-dozen trucks, pickups, and cars for the nearly two-hour crossing.

The tan and green Satupaitea bus waits at the ferry landing at Salelologa, ready to embark on its half-hour run across the Tafua peninsula and then around the shore of Palauli Bay. Vaega lies just inside the reef along the western shore of the bay, facing the trade winds and the sun as it rises over the volcanic cinder cone of Tafua. Vaega was my home for more than two of the three years I have spent in Western Samoa, though I also stayed for shorter periods in eight other rural and urban villages.

The district of Satupaitea is composed of three villages with a total pop-

---

[1] In Samoan most vowels are pronounced separately. Thus, Vaega is pronounced in three syllables: "Vah-e-NGAAH." Following this rule blindly will cause problems for the student of Samoan language, however, for there are many exceptions, including the assimilation of phonemes, the production of glides, and the existence of true dipthongs (e.g., the "ai" in *tautalaiti*).

Photo 4. The central malae, *or village green, in Vaega. The boys in the foreground are returning from the Wesleyan school wearing their school uniforms while a group of young men play cricket behind them.*

ulation of about 1,500 people. Pitonu'u village (with its suburb of Mosula) begins at the junction of the tarred, round-island road and the gravel Satupaitea road. Vaega lies in the center of the district between Pitonu'u and Satufia village, which lies to seaward. Vaega is also the political and religious center of the district, though it has recently been eclipsed in size by Pitonu'u.

Vaega is the oldest coastal settlement in the district. During the wars of the nineteenth century (and many times before), the entire population lived two miles inland to protect themselves from surprise attack. There villagers also sought temporary refuge inside a circular stone fort surrounded by a ditch. When peace was restored at the end of the nineteenth century, the people began to settle back along the lagoon shore. Today, as the growing population clears the forest higher and higher up the slopes for their taro plots, they slowly uncover an elaborate maze of stone walls, mounds, and platforms. These mark the former residences and the tiny, intensively cultivated plots of the inland village of Uliamoa.

The modern village road follows the shoreline. In the center of Vaega is a large grassy area called a *malae*, or village green. Open-sided Samoan houses sitting atop basalt foundations surround the *malae*. Important village or district ceremonies are held on the village green, but today it is more often the scene of Samoan-style cricket games. Like all other Samoan villages, there is now a narrow cement cricket pitch laid down the center of Vaega's village green. Samoan cricket games tend to be raucous affairs, with the teams shout-

Photo 5. View from the shore of Satufia looking northeast into Palauli Bay. Children jump from the lava rocks and swim in the protected waters just inside the reef.

ing and dancing in unison to celebrate every "out." Villagers have modified the rules to allow thirty or forty people to a side, and they swing a long bat that is shaped more like a war club than a British cricket bat.

Beyond Vaega is a stone-walled compound that encloses the European-style buildings of the Wesleyan intermediate school, a district institution now for three generations. Beyond the school, an aging medical clinic sits on a slight rise above the lagoon. The clinic appears deserted, but it usually houses one or two patients and their families, along with four or five resident nurses. Below the rise stand the houses of Satufia, spread around the inland side of an enormous, grassy *malae*. Beyond Satufia lies nothing but a few coconut groves overgrown with brush, and then miles of forest.

Vaega is primarily an agricultural village. A few wage jobs are available in the village and in the shops and government offices at Salelologa. Of the 524 people living in the village in 1981 (see census diagram in Figure 3.1), there were only fourteen generally full-time wage laborers: two teachers, a nurse, five bus drivers and their helpers (called "supercargoes"), two Agriculture Department employees, one Member of Parliament, one plantation worker, one family shopkeeper/part-time postal employee, and a pastor. Two families run small stores and copra trading stations in the village. One family runs a home bakery business. Another runs a very prosperous transportation business with four buses, two heavy trucks, and a pickup.

In addition to these residents, at least 143 former residents have left the village within recent memory, migrating either to the Apia urban area or

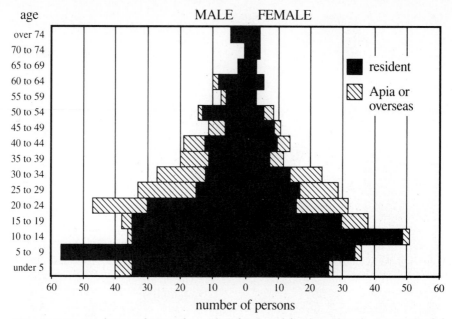

Figure 3.1 Census of Vaega showing the number of male and female residents by age group (solid areas), and the number of recent migrants (out of the village) (hatched areas).

overseas.[2] Thus, over 20 percent of the village population has departed for urban areas. Half of these migrants left the country entirely—a level of overseas migration that is only about half the national average (Government of Western Samoa 1976). As one village chief noted, the villages in Satupaitea district are noticeably poorer than their neighbors on the main road in Palauli because fewer Satupaitea people have migrated overseas. Hence, the remaining residents of Satupaitea now have less remittance income than the other villages.

Vaega presented an ideal location for my research into the effects of tradition on agricultural development. Vaega is a strongly traditional, agricultural village, yet it is not isolated. Some wage labor is available, but the village is not dependent on it, as villages near Apia are. Land is still adequate for the expansion of cash cropping. Though many people have left, much labor remains idle in the village. Vaega also had the advantage of being a compact, closely knit village with effective leadership. Though not completely harmonious, it was without major factional disputes. Such disputes might have disrupted both my research and the village's development efforts. Because all of these obvious and mundane obstacles to development were lacking in Vaega, the interplay between traditional social forces and modern economic forces was more readily apparent.

---

[2] This number does not include those people who relocated to other rural villages.

THE ASIATA TITLE AND VILLAGE POLITICAL ORGANIZATION

The residents of Vaega are divided into thirty-two extended families. At the head of each family is a *matai*, or chief. Different families own different *matai* titles, each with its own name. A family elects one (or more) of its members to hold its particular title, whereupon that individual takes the title name as his first name, with his given name following.[3] The *matai* titles themselves are ranked in a traditional hierarchy of importance and power. Thus, the families who own the titles and the individuals who currently hold them are also ranked.

Matai titles are divided into two kinds. The most important are *ali'i*, or "high chief," titles. Subservient to particular *ali'i* titles are one or more *tulāfale* titles. *Tulāfale* often act as lieutenants and spokesmen for their high chiefs, so *tulāfale* are referred to in English as "talking chiefs" or "orators."

The chiefly title of Asiata is the highest *matai* title in the district. It was formerly a *tulāfale*, or orator's, title. Many generations ago, however, an early holder of the Asiata title usurped the highest position in the district from the *ali'i*, or high chiefs. Today, holders of the Asiata title have the prerogatives of both high chiefs and talking chiefs. As a high chief, holders of the Asiata title have the power to create new *matai* titles. They are also supported by a retinue of orators. Yet holders of the Asiata title retain the symbols of orator status—the ceremonial speaking staff and fly whisk. They may also give speeches in the manner of orators, while other *ali'i* sit in dignified silence.

Like all major titles in Samoa, the Asiata title has been hotly contested. In 1920 a decision of the Land and Titles Court split the title among several branches of one family. Not all of the branch titles are currently filled, while some are shared by more than one person. Nine men currently hold the title, but only four live in the district, all in Vaega.

Every extended family in the village is related in some way to one of the branches of the Asiata Family, or *Sā Asiatā*. Most are related by direct descent from a previous holder of the title. Others are related indirectly by descent from another chiefly title that is subservient to the Asiata title. The Asiata Family itself is made up of all those individual descendants of the original Asiata who actively maintain membership in the group. This includes virtually every person born in the village. When the villagers say *E tasi le 'āiga*—"We are one family"—they are very nearly correct. Most blood relationships are not so close, however, that intra-village marriage is entirely prevented.

Each family runs its own internal affairs, led by its chief (or chiefs). Inter-family or villagewide affairs require group action. The four resident holders of the Asiata title decide many village matters among themselves in private meetings. This is possible since together these men represent the entire village. Larger or more serious matters (along with much mundane business) require the joint decision of all the village *matai*. To decide these matters, the chiefs meet periodically as a village council.

[3] Less than 0.02% of all *matai* are women, and there were none at all in Vaega.

Photo 6. Asiata Iakopo and Muta in their receiving house. The kapoc mattress behind Muta is where the author spent most of his first weeks in the village, alternately sleeping and eating.

At the head of this political structure today sits one man, Asiata Iakopo. He is the traditional leader, or *sa'o*, of the village. He holds this position by village consensus, in recognition of his personal abilities and his commitment to the welfare of the village, and because the great majority of Vaega residents belong to his branch of the Asiata family. The district has also elected Asiata Iakopo twice to be its Member of Parliament. During his second tenure he served briefly as Minister of Lands.

Asiata Iakopo is the epitome of a Samoan high chief. He is a large, handsome man of 65 years with powerful arms and shoulders, a bull neck, and a square jaw. Like other men his age, he keeps his white hair cut short in the fashion of the 1940s, when U.S. Marines occupied the country. Asiata's manner and bearing are dignified. His look is sometimes thoughtful, sometimes disdainful, occasionally fierce. He gives the impression of a man who possesses greater power than he uses openly. Dressed in a dark, ankle-length *lāvalava* and a fancy New Zealand sport shirt, his feet bare and calloused, he continually ministers to the affairs of his family, the village, the national government, and the Methodist Church.

I have watched Asiata many times as he sat cross-legged in quiet dignity at the far end of a meeting house, just to one side of the center post (leaving the position of highest honor vacant as a sign of respect to the greater authority of God). His eyes squinting and his brow furrowed in thought, he draws continually on an imported Benson & Hedges cigarette, while most of his fellow *matai* roll their own. He speaks with the authority of one who knows he will have the last word. He begins softly. The other chiefs stop their murmured gossip to hear the measured words of a master orator as he weaves together the details of Samoan legend, Biblical verse, village affairs, and his personal wisdom in the esoteric language of the chiefs.

Yet neither Asiata Iakopo nor any other person has decisive power in Vaega. All decisions are made by consensus at the appropriate level of authority, the highest level being the village council. Each family, led by its *matai*, jealously defends its prerogatives against the slightest encroachment, from whatever level. A challenge to a person's or a family's honor or authority, however limited, will immediately cause a confrontation.

Samoans are known for their elaborate social and political etiquette. Because of this politeness, they are sometimes thought to be a serene and easygoing people. The elaborate etiquette is designed, however, primarily to prevent slights or political confrontations, for wounded pride can quickly explode into anger or violence. I was sitting with a chief named Auala one afternoon when his wife burst into the house, crying and swearing at the same time. Her dress was torn and she waved her arms around in fury. When she finally settled down, we learned that another woman had tried to take her seating position at the Women's Committee council meeting and she had fought with the woman. At formal meetings each *matai* sits in the position appropriate to his rank in the political hierarchy. At women's council meetings, the wives of chiefs sit according to their husbands' ranks. Thus, when the other woman tried to take her seat, she interpreted it as an attempt to usurp the political position of herself, her husband, and their family.

In his own home, Asiata Iakopo is treated with deference by visitors and by his own family. His wife, Muta, who is equally imposing in the women's councils, sits by his side. When other families in the village cook a pig, they often send Asiata the upper part of the back—the piece reserved for high chiefs and pastors. Also like the pastor, Asiata often receives gifts of fish after an especially bountiful catch. These offerings are wrapped in a coconut leaf and delivered quietly to the back of his house by a child.

Any time a fisherman catches a turtle—the "sacred fish" of Polynesia— he must take it directly from the reef to Asiata's house. Shortly after I returned to Vaega in 1981, I was sitting with Asiata in his meeting house, which projects out into the shallow bay on a foundation of lava boulders. A fisherman from Pitonu'u paddled up to the rear of the house and silently unloaded a large hawksbill turtle from his canoe. He had caught it barehanded while it slept in a crevice of the reef—a rare occurrence. Without rising, Asiata pulled $2 from his briefcase and handed it to one of his granddaughters who had approached unbidden to carry out his errand. She carried the money to the fisherman and deposited it in his hand. The fisherman then turned and, still dripping wet from his exploits, climbed back into his canoe and paddled off toward his own house.

Asiata and the pastor both reciprocate the more frequent gifts of food that they receive, but rarely is the reciprocation so direct as with the turtle. Other chiefs or their wives come visiting at meal time as often as they send food. Sometimes Asiata summons them for a discussion of village or family affairs. Other times they come on their own to seek a favor or ask advice. Frequently they come simply because there is no good food at their own homes and they know that Asiata and Muta will be eating better than they. Some afternoons Asiata also hosts a group of village chiefs for afternoon "tea" and a friendly game of dominoes.

TURTLES AND THE STATUS OF A YOUNG ANTHROPOLOGIST

A few weeks later, I used the high status of the turtle to help raise my own status in the village. A common problem of anthropologists is that they begin their field work being largely ignorant of the skills by which their hosts measure personal competence. In my case, although I was accorded all the politeness and respect of an honored guest, my attempts at "participant observation" in the daily tasks of the household caused some bemusement among my hosts. Their idea of an honored guest is one who reclines all day on a kapoc mattress, alternately eating and sleeping in full view of all curious passersby—of which there are many.

When I first arrived in the village I did not know how to talk, sit, or eat properly. My hands and feet were pitifully uncalloused. I could do little or nothing useful, even if I had been allowed to try. I did not know how, when, or where to bathe or even relieve myself properly according to Samoan standards of etiquette. People treated me as they would treat a fragile child. I felt as the royal hemophiliacs of Europe must have felt—honored and coddled in equal amounts. That was too much for me, and I resolved to do something about it.

I had been surprised at the meager catches of Samoan fishermen. Most of their catch comes from spearfishing along the reef shallows. Their simple gear consists of a pair of goggles, a five-foot long spear made of one-quarter inch reinforcing bar, and a slingshot made from a forked stick and a piece of surgical rubber tubing. Since virtually all Samoan men are addicted to cigarettes and virtually none know how to equalize the pressure in their ears as they dive, their spearfishing is confined to the shallow, overfished waters just above and inside the reefs. Their normal catch includes several palm-sized or smaller fish and sometimes an octopus pried from its coral cave. Since I considered myself a pretty good spearfisherman, I saw a chance to prove my worth.

I set about making a proper speargun modelled after the homemade spearguns I had used while living in Tahiti several years earlier. My first efforts were conspicuous failures, however, which only exacerbated my problem. I had not yet learned to deal with the verbal thrust and parry of the common Samoan conversational style called *ula*—a form of good-natured but often biting ridicule that expresses the ambivalence of friendliness and aggression which seems to mark many Samoan relationships, including those with Europeans. Every failed fishing trip brought more snickering.

Finally one afternoon everything worked properly. I paddled back to Asiata's house with the fully laden canoe riding dangerously low in the water, trying to force the half-smile of triumph from my face. Luckily, several other *matai* were playing dominoes with their host. Both family and guests craned their necks to see over the low back wall of the house as I unloaded two large turtles, while leaving the fish in the bottom of the canoe. It took several giggling grandchildren to haul the flapping and gasping turtles up the rocks to the open area behind the house. Asiata sat in the background, grinning and shaking his head. His wife, Muta, went to the locked storeroom and brought out a new flowered *lāvalava* which one of the young girls carried out to me. I thanked Muta in the Samoan fashion by bowing slightly and raising the gift over my head. Then I departed in the canoe—my status elevated and the snickering finally halted.

THE ANTHROPOLOGIST AS VILLAGE MASCOT

During my first, three-week scouting trip to the village in 1979, I had stayed with the village pastor and his wife. On my return in 1981, they were away in Apia, and Asiata Iakopo invited me to stay with his family. A few weeks later, I was sitting in Asiata's meeting house when he abruptly rose and headed over to the nearby Women's Committee building where the other *matai* were gathering for a council meeting. One of his lieutenants, Tauatama, bid me to follow him to the meeting. As Tauatama and I approached the meeting house, he told me that Asiata was going to give me a *matai* title. I quickly protested, fearing that perhaps I was being set up somehow, for I certainly did not qualify for *matai* status. I said that I did not know enough of the Samoan language or culture to accept a title, but Tauatama stopped me.

E pule Asiata, he said, "Asiata has the authority." Then he guided me into the meeting house to sit at Asiata's side.

The title bestowal began with a kava ceremony, which consists of an elaborate round of speeches followed by the formal presentation to each *matai* of kava drink made from the pounded root of a pepper bush (*Piper methysticum*).[4] Asiata then presented a cooked pig and a finely woven pandanus mat, or *'ie toga*, to the village council. By these acts Asiata Iakopo and Asiata Fatu (the aged leader of the other major branch of the title) bestowed on me the newly created orator's title of *Mavaega*. Already respected as a foreign visitor, the new *matai* title further enhanced my status. The title also legitimized my participation in village councils and in the social affairs of my Samoan families.

I was surprised and perplexed at first over the bestowal of the title. I did not know then that bestowing a title is a common method for both honoring

---

[4] As prepared in Samoa, this drink has virtually no "narcotic" affect, except that it numbs the mouth slightly for a few moments.

a foreign visitor (or a Samoan visiting from overseas) and attempting to bind the visitor in mutual obligation to the village or family that bestows the title. Those whom I dared ask declared that the title was a great honor. Still wary, however, I sought the advice of the English-speaking master of the nearby high school. He was highly critical of the title bestowal, declaring that the title was a sham since it gave me control of neither lands nor a family to work them, as Samoan tradition required. He warned me that the title bestowal could only be an attempt to seduce me into giving over cash and goods to the villagers. My hosts seemed sincere, though, and no one had asked me to contribute anything for the bestowal ceremony.

I was not sure what to conclude at the time, but I gradually learned that both the title and the motives were genuine. While it was once true that bestowing a *matai* title simultaneously granted the titleholder authority over an extended family and its lands, that is no longer the rule today. Many men (and a few women) now receive the titles and the social and political prerogatives of *matai*, but without authority over the lands and labor of an extended family (see Chapter 5). Thus I joined the junior chiefs of Vaega, many of whom (as I learned later) held newly created titles like my own.

I also learned that I had been presented with an important lesson early in my fieldwork. The Samoan schoolmaster had been quite wrong in his analysis of the situation. I realized that in order to understand the operation of Samoan society and the behavior of its members, I could not depend on second-hand reports from English-speaking informants.

I finally became convinced of the genuineness of my title when the village chiefs began encouraging me to register it at the Land and Titles Court.[5] Later on when I became more adept at ceremonial affairs, Asiata Iakopo often urged me to use my title by acting as his official representative when I travelled to another village where an important ceremony was being held. In this way, he said, I could receive more gifts than if I represented only myself. At other times when I was tagging along in the company of people from Vaega, they would sometimes push me to the fore, urging me to speak or play some minor ceremonial role, as if they wanted to show off their village mascot.

I was fortunate that the people of Vaega not only encouraged me to participate in their affairs, they also allowed me to shift back into my role as an outside observer whenever necessary. For example, people encouraged me to participate fully in the gift exchanges at a village funeral. During a lull in the formalities I asked and readily received permission to leave the meeting house to talk with the younger men and women who were preparing food in the rear houses, or to record the quantities of gifts that had been amassed. Villagers would have frowned on such behavior by one of their own *matai*.

---

[5] Most villagers were not aware that national law requires a person to be a citizen of Western Samoa in order to register as a *matai*.

A HOUSE WITH BAMBOO WALLS

Two months after my return to the village in 1981, Asiata Iakopo graciously organized a work party to build a small Samoan house for me. I needed some personal privacy, but more importantly, I needed a neutral place where I could talk with people away from both their own crowded houses and away from Asiata's imposing presence. Asiata himself had no unoccupied land in the village, so he arranged to build my house on the land of a nearby relative, Nu'u Vili. I did not know Nu'u then, so I went to speak with him in his house.

I found Nu'u to be a bright and very pleasant man of about 40, short and stocky, with his hair beginning to bald in the middle. He has one front tooth missing in his warm smile (knocked out by a cricket ball in his youth). In the years that followed, I came to know Nu'u well. Like everyone I met in Samoa, he is a perfectly understandable person. I was somewhat surprised (and perhaps a bit disappointed) that there was nothing bizarre about Samoans, nothing that was impenetrable to the Western mind. I found no unbridgeable gap between cultures or people. That did not mean, however, that there were no surprises.

Building the house was an education in itself. Not knowing how to compensate the workmen, I asked Asiata for his advice. Since I was now a chief, he said, I might conduct the affair in traditional style. That meant an elaborate round of kava ceremonies, gift giving, feeding the workers, and finally a ceremonial payment to the *tufuga*, or "master" carpenter. On the other hand, he suggested, I might just give him WS $100 (US $85) and leave the rest to him. I thought that the first method was too full of pitfalls for a novice on a short linguistic and cultural tether, and perhaps too elaborate for the small, thatched house of a bachelor. I feared that the second method, however, was inherently uncontrollable. I therefore opted for an approach that I thought would be more familiar to me. I offered to pay the workers the going wage (WS $3 at that time) plus tobacco and a midday meal until the house was finished. The only housing material I needed to supply was two pounds of nails. Asiata soon assembled a small group of orators and a few untitled men from among his closest adherents, and we started to work.

I had chosen to conduct the housebuilding through a worker/employer relationship because I thought it would be more controllable. The way that relationship actually works in a Samoan village, however, is quite different from what I expected. I immediately began to fret about the slow pace of the work. There were lengthy interruptions for this or that village affair. On the days we did work, most of the men did not arrive at the house site until ten o'clock, and they frequently drifted away during the day or sat in the shade for long periods, smoking and talking. I had worked on construction crews in the United States where we also spent a lot of time doing nothing, but at least we tried to *appear* busy.

One evening I described my frustration to Seupule Ropati, a burly man of about 45 years who had been particularly kind to me. I suggested that

Photo 7. Nu'u Vili returning from church.

instead of paying everyone $3 a day, I should cut the wages back to reflect the time actually worked, hoping that this would inspire the men to greater activity. Seupule shook his head. He explained to me that in Samoa, respect for *matai* status requires that all workers receive full pay, even those who appear uninvited near the end of the day. That seemed to be a highly improbable story. I thought he must be joking, or simply trying to hoodwink me into continuing the full payments.

"If it is a matter of respect," I asked, "why don't the workers show respect for me by working?"

"Yes, they should," Seupule replied, "and it is wrong that they do not, but you must show respect to the *matai*, nevertheless, for they honor you by coming to help."

When I left Seupule's house that night, I was not sure whether I had found an honest friend or a sincere liar. Over the next two years, however, I kept his words in mind, and I saw that he was right. Honor and respect are the twin pillars of Samoan culture. But while mutual respect implies reciprocity, it need not imply balanced reciprocity in a material sense. The person who first requests assistance carries the burden of showing respect. Otherwise, the one who heeds the call is placed in an inferior position, giving assistance as if it were the other person's due. Some helpers shirk their duties, but they must receive a gift of thanks nevertheless. Such people trade their own respect for a material gift, and they humble themselves to their hosts in the process.

The work dragged out for nearly three weeks. First we repaired the stone platform and set the posts, then we built and raised the roof and covered the floor with coral pebbles. Finally we thatched the roof with plaited coconut leaves. The builders left the house open in traditional Samoan fashion, with neither interior nor exterior walls between the support posts. I decided to add low, exterior walls of plaited bamboo between the upright posts, however, in order to shield myself somewhat from the young gawkers who gathered on the road. I was still an object of wonder to the village children at that point, and I had not yet adjusted to the almost complete lack of privacy in a Samoan village. The pastor's son, Sala'i, and Nu'u's nephew, Selesele Ma-laki, stopped to see what I was doing. When I explained, they immediately chided me for the design change.

"What is wrong with having walls?" I asked.

"It is not according to Samoan custom," Selesele declared.

"Why is it not according to Samoan custom?" I countered, showing my irritation.

'Ua sā, Sala'i replied earnestly. "It is prohibited."

I looked up and down the road at the other village houses. There were no Samoan-style houses with low walls like the ones I planned to make, but there were several European-style houses completely enclosed by walls. That led me to suspect that the men's comments were largely rhetorical. Several times before I had felt that villagers wanted me to follow their customs more closely than they did themselves, as if they wanted visible reassurance that I respected them and their ways. I was usually careful to comply, but privacy was too important to me then to abandon my plans so easily.

"Why are walls prohibited by Samoan custom?"

"When people see that your house has walls," Selesele explained, "they will think you are doing something bad that you must hide."

"But staring into other people's houses is also prohibited by Samoan custom, and the kids stare at me just the same."

They had to agree, for at that moment a group of children stared intently at us from the road. I suggested that Samoans do not need walls on their houses because no one stares at them. But since I was still a curiosity in the village, I needed walls around my house. Selesele and Sala'i understood my unusual situation immediately, and they accepted my unorthodox plan just as easily. And I understood why, in a country where only the sea breeze alleviates the midday heat, people might suspect deviance of someone who shields his house with walls.

I did not know what to expect from my neighbors when I moved into my

Photo 8. The author's house with bamboo walls on the shore of Palauli Bay. The fence in the foreground was a futile attempt to keep the village pigs out of a vegetable garden. In the background a fisherman returns from the reef early Sunday morning as the smoke from scores of stone ovens wafts out over the water.

new house. Nu'u and his wife, Meaalofa, immediately welcomed me as a member of their family, and we soon became very close friends. I thus became Nu'u's younger "brother," while Asiata Iakopo continued to act as my Samoan "father." Nu'u was then the village *pulenu'u*, a government/village liaison officer elected by the village council. These early relationships—first with the village pastor, then the village leader, and finally with the village liaison officer—gave me quick access to the major arenas of village affairs. The other village chiefs and their wives also warmly welcomed me into their company. I was still young and single, however, and that un-chiefly state of affairs led me to many close friendships with the younger men and women of the village. And when my strangeness in the eyes of the village children gave finally way to familiarity, they also befriended me.

THE VILLAGE CHURCH

In the middle of Vaega, on a slight rise just above the road, stands the Methodist church. The villagers constructed the immense concrete building twenty years ago, replacing an earlier structure that has now crumbled. In keeping with its Protestant heritage and with the villagers' own relative disinterest in visual arts, the church is rather plain. The walls are whitewashed,

Photo 9. The Methodist church in the center of Vaega. The crowd of people on the steps has arrived late for the service, and must wait for the doors to be unlocked after the pastor's long opening prayer.

the rectangular windows are trimmed in blue-green, and the low-peaked roof is painted a flat red. The only concession to style is a modest portico with squat Roman columns that adorns the entrance.

The two adjacent families donated the land for the church, and the building now straddles the old boundary between their plots. As a result of giving up much of their land, these families have had to squeeze their own houses in beside the church, or even behind it where the sea breeze never stirs. The entire village contributed to the construction of the church. Every family donated money to purchase building materials, and virtually every adult helped in some way during the lengthy construction. The village hired specialists to direct the work, but the people of Vaega themselves supplied the unskilled and semi-skilled labor. At stages during the construction, and especially when the building was finished, the villagers presented gifts of fine mats, pigs, and money to these specialists as payment for their services.

Many Samoan villages are divided between two, three, or even more religious denominations, each supporting its own church and its own pastor or priest. In Vaega, there is only the Methodist Church. Vaega's leaders strongly discourage straying from the Methodist Church, not only because of their spiritual conviction, but also because they fear that religious divisions would disrupt village harmony.

The people of Vaega feel a strong local pride in their tradition of Methodism. They claim that the first Christian church in Samoa was founded in

Vaega. The first missionaries landed in Savaii in 1828, just inside the reef on the small beach near my house. Surprisingly, the first Christian missionaries were not Europeans, but Tongans. They voyaged to Samoa in a double-hulled sailing canoe, just as their warrior ancestors had come some 600 years earlier. But this time the Tongans came to proselytize, not to conquer.

Two years after the arrival of the Tongan missionaries, John Williams arrived with the gospel according to the London Missionary Society. The L.M.S. was already locked in competition with the Methodists in other parts of the Pacific. Upon his arrival in Samoa, Williams was startled to find that much of the south coast of Savaii was already firmly Methodist. Today, the nation as a whole prefers to honor the later arrival of the European missionary, Williams, rather than the earlier ones from Tonga. Nevertheless, local orators proudly claim their district's priority.

Religious hegemony has not gone uncontested in Satupaitea district. In recent years both the Mormons and the Congregationalists (formerly the L.M.S.) have built churches there. The Methodist faithful forced the converts and their churches out of the villages proper, however, to live inland along the round-island road. Recently, a Samoan Seventh Day Adventist pastor established a modest church further down the road, and a few people in Satufia have converted to the Baha'i faith.

Each congregation has slightly different rules for private behavior and for participation in village ceremonies. Each congregation also maintains a different schedule for public worship. These differences express the personal faiths of the members and satisfy the religious requirements of their respective denominations. The differences also allow the members to demonstrate publicly their respective loyalties and their group's autonomy.

Some church rules have a significant effect on village life. The Methodists are rather puritanical compared to most other denominations in Samoa. They allow precious little in the way of entertainment. The Church does not permit dancing at night (and discourages it during the day). It bans card playing of any kind, day or night, and strictly forbids the drinking of alcohol. Sundays are reserved for church services, for eating and sleeping, and for reading the Bible. Neither work nor play is allowed on the Sabbath, at the very least not until the afternoon service is completed.[6] During the Christmas and New Year's holidays in Vaega, several entrepreneurial families ran bingo games (WS 5¢ per card) by the light of gas lanterns in their homes or on the cricket pitch. The pastor banned the popular games after only two nights. And when another villager rented his house to an urban entrepreneur as a movie theater, the village leaders closed down the theater after only a couple of shows.

All of these prohibitions apply to villagers wherever they are, but slackness sometimes creeps in when people travel to Salelologa, Apia, or overseas. Young men sometimes even hold clandestine poker games or drinking parties

---

[6] To the dismay of most Westerners, who chafe at these unfamiliar restrictions, the period between Sunday church services is nevertheless a favorite time for women to wash the family laundry and for boys to wash the family horse.

behind the village, though *matai* almost never attend these affairs. Villagers are generally willing to overlook breaches of proper conduct as long as violators remain discreet. If misconduct leads to a public outburst or to fighting, however, the village council imposes heavy fines on offenders. Merely to be seen drunk in public is a terrible shame for a *matai* and will bring censure and a stiff fine from the council.

Vaega's historical role as the local citadel of Methodism seems to have encouraged its residents to adhere more strictly to church doctrines than its neighbors. Village life is noticeably gayer in Satufia, only a few hundred yards away. For example, though there is no Church prohibition on singing, no one in Vaega owns a guitar, and only children sing popular Samoan songs along the road on a moonlit night. In Satufia, on the other hand, small groups of young people (usually segregated according to sex) often meet on the village green at night before curfew to play a guitar and sing softly. Other times they listen to Samoan music played on giant cassette players, gifts from relatives in New Zealand.[7]

A FRIEND IN SATUFIA

A few Satufians are more brash. My close friend and spearfishing partner, Milo Faletoi, sometimes held "private" drinking parties in full view of the village. Milo is a handsome and powerful man with a square-cut jaw. He is also intelligent and able, with a wry sense of humor (he once named his dog "Idi Amin") and a ready smile that, nevertheless, often reveals the clenched teeth of competition.

At just over forty years, Milo is in a difficult period of life for an ambitious Samoan man. No longer young, he is charged with the duties and responsibilities of a *matai* and is the leader of a large family. He is old enough, however, that his eldest sons are nearly fully grown. Like most other men his age, he is therefore able to leave the more common and arduous forms of labor to his sons while still engaging in fishing, cutting coconut meat from the shells, and the occasional skilled tasks, such as house and canoe construction, which are the proper employ of *matai*. This leaves him with a good deal of idle time. Milo stands out as among the most capable men in the district. Yet he is still relatively young and inexperienced in the esoteric practices of village politics. He knows that many years will pass before he achieves the political prominence to which he aspires.

On rare occasions Milo or one of his friends brought a quart of vodka back to the village, usually purchased at the duty-free shop at the airport in American Samoa. Then we would meet at night in Milo's open-sided house, high up on its stone foundation on the ocean side of the village green. Illu-

---

[7] In the rural villages where few people speak English, almost everyone dislikes Western pop music unless it has been translated into Samoan and played with a Samoan air. In Apia, however, and especially in American Samoa, American pop music is all the rage.

Photo 10. Milo Faletoi posing with a turtle that he shot through the eyes with one of the author's homemade spearguns.

minated by the blazing light of a Coleman lantern, Milo played the guitar and sang the popular ballads of his youth while we encouraged the littlest children to dance the Samoan *siva*. Milo's wife, Valelia, and the older children watched from the background, or covered themselves with a sheet to sleep along the shadowy perimeter of the house. Milo's younger brother sometimes came to the house with a friend for the party, but since they were not chiefs and owed respect to Milo as their elder, they did not join us directly. They sat quietly by themselves, sipping from their glasses and rising frequently to pour the ghastly mixture of vodka, tap water, and orange flavoring syrup for us from a glass pitcher.

CHURCH AND POLITICS IN VAEGA

People sometimes try to manipulate inter-church rivalries to their advantage. One of my more distant neighbors was Fiamamafa, a short, unkept man whose appearance reminded me of a small-time Mafioso from an old gangster movie. He is a *matai* of little account in the village, but he continually challenges people whenever he sees an opportunity to increase his importance or authority at their expense. If done with skill, wisdom, and a measure of forbearance, this could be one mark of an important and influential man. But Fiamamafa has little of these qualities, and he generally succeeds only in alienating people. At one point Fiamamafa challenged the village council over a trivial matter. The resulting dispute quickly escalated in gravity as the council levied greater and greater fines against Fiamamafa each time he refused to accede to its authority. Finally the council banished him, a move that traditionally would have meant the complete removal of Fiamamafa and his entire family from the village. National law now prevents village councils from playing this trump card, however, so the sentence effectively meant only that Fiamamafa's *matai* title was no longer recognized in the village and neither he nor his family could participate in formal village affairs.

The combatants remained locked in a standoff for several months until Fiamamafa suddenly announced that he and his family would convert to Mormonism. He reinforced his threat by marching his large family, dressed in their Sunday whites, single file past Vaega's own Methodist church during the Sunday service while on their way to attend the rival Mormon service in Mosula.

Fiamamafa's desertion from the church forced the hand of the council. It also precipitated a long and earnest discussion about the role of the church in the unity of the village and the village's duty to support the Methodist Church. Finally they reached a compromise. Fiamamafa and his family would return to the Methodist Church and he would pay a reduced fine of one roast pig and several boxes of ship's biscuits. In return, the council would rescind its banishment order. When the time came, Fiamamafa presented the pig and ship's biscuits to the council in a triumphal manner, as if he were feasting them rather than paying a fine.

The village's desire to prevent defection from the Methodist Church does not spring primarily from religious prejudice or antipathy toward members of other Christian denominations. Most people of Vaega agree that if a person believes in Christ and worships God, it is less important how they go about it. Villagers extend their tolerance with more difficulty to people who follow non-Christian religions, to agnostics, and to atheists. They describe their own, pre-Christian past as the time before they "saw the light." They rarely speak of that time, and then only with some embarrassment.

THE VILLAGE PASTOR

Over the years the people of Vaega have supported many pastors—first Tongan and then European missionaries, and now local Samoans. The pastor and his congregation are bound in a special relationship, each serving the other. The pastor, of course, serves the religious needs of his village. In return, the village provides the pastor and his family with as fine a house as they can afford, with agricultural lands, generous monetary support, and with many personal services. Villagers respect and honor their pastor because of his religious position and his religious knowledge. They also honor him because, after six years of postsecondary training at the seminary on Upolu, he is the best educated person in the village.

The formal relationship between the pastor and the village sets the pastor apart from other village leaders. While the pastor has authority over church affairs, he has no formal say in the secular affairs of the village. By the covenant between church and village, pastors cannot hold *matai* titles or participate in village council meetings. Methodist ministers are always assigned outside of their natal villages, and neither Vaega's pastor, Fogalele, nor his wife had relatives in the village. As a result, they did not participate as individuals in local family affairs or in village ceremonies. Fogalele was often involved in his role as pastor, but church and village etiquette required him to leave the ceremonies immediately after giving the opening prayer.[8]

While a pastor has no formal say in secular village affairs, some pastors exert powerful influence informally. Vaega's pastor did not, primarily because Asiata Iakopo and the other village leaders are such capable and powerful individuals. Many Samoan pastors are also capable and powerful individuals, however, and if village leadership is weak, an aggressive pastor may influence secular village affairs. I heard two different pastors from villages on Upolu boast that they exerted decisive influence over parliamentary elections in their villages. I assume that they were exaggerating their powers, but not without some basis. Villagers hold their pastors in very high esteem and also reward them very handsomely, so it is not surprising that the ministry attracts ambitious men seeking just those rewards.

The people of Vaega gave a large amount of cash and goods to support their pastor and his family (the exact amount must remain confidential). Their main contribution comes during the church service once a month, when every chief gives to the pastor's *peleti* ("plate"). In 1982 donations ranged from WS $3 to WS $65 per *matai*, and totalled well over WS $400 per month. During the service one of the chiefs (the church "Treasurer") announces each gift by name and amount, along with the total amount of all gifts. This adds a strong element of pride and competition to the contributions, which helps to maintain a high level of giving. Samoans announce all contributions publicly,

---

[8] Etiquette also required that he always receive gifts at these ceremonies, but not give them. The only exception to this rule of which I am aware is that upon taking up a post in a new village, a pastor presents gifts to the assembled *matai*. He has, however, just received an equal or larger gift from the village that he has just left.

Photo 11. The Reverend Fogalele Fagamea and his wife, Fale, on their way to church.

however, not just church contributions. They do this partly to encourage and to recognize generosity, and partly to prevent embezzlement by providing a public accounting of all donations.

These monthly donations to the pastor are technically gifts, rather than a salary. Villagers say that their gifts to the pastor are really gifts to God, physical expressions of their love and devotion. They say that the gifts reach God through His earthly conduit, the pastor, though they have no mystical conception of how that is accomplished. As such, the villagers' personal relationships with a particular pastor have little to do with the size of their gifts. Villagers remember some pastors as being humble, kind, and charitable. Other pastors were less so. But villagers give generously regardless of the individual pastor's character. They say that the pastor will be judged in heaven, like all people. It is not their position to judge him here on earth. I would be remiss as an ethnographer, however, if I did not report that while pronouncing these words of equanimity, some villagers show a noticeable strain in their faces. In private, unguarded moments, even some of the leading deacons expressed doubts about the earthly ways of the Church. No one, however, expressed any doubt about their Christian God.

SELESELE TANIELU, A VILLAGE ENTREPRENEUR

The most generous contributions to church and village affairs come from Selesele Tanielu, a 39-year-old *matai* who owns the local transport business, and his widowed mother. Selesele Tanielu is a very capable businessman, and he is both kind and generous to his fellow villagers. He is thus highly regarded. He devotes nearly all of his time and resources to building up his business. He inherited the business from his father, Asiata Lagolago, when it consisted of a single bus. Asiata Lagolago was one of the first generation of modern village entrepreneurs in Samoa.[9] Asiata Lagolago became Satupaitea's representative to Parliament, and he was a respected member of the Prime Minister's Cabinet during the years following independence.

With the money he earned from his bus and from his government salary, Asiata Lagolago hired other villagers to develop large coconut and cocoa plantations for him behind Vaega. During the early 1980s, prices were too low to warrant harvesting the crops, so Selesele Tanielu allowed the plantations to stand virtually idle. Twice a month the "supercargoes" on his buses harvested 200 coconuts to feed Selesele's pigs. The other nuts and all of the cocoa were left to rot (or be pilfered by other villagers). Only a part-time laborer tended the barbed-wire fences that surround and divide the plantation. The fences control a small herd of cattle that grazes under the coconut trees and on a small area of open pasture.

Selesele's buses run from dawn to dusk six days a week, and half-days on Sunday. Selesele often drives one bus himself. There are also constant repairs to supervise, often continuing late into the night so a bus will be ready for the next day's run. Inside the back entrance of his two-story, European-style house, adjacent to the bus parking area, the dark hallway is piled with engine parts and boxes of oversized tools. A wooden table in what might otherwise be a dining area is completely covered with pistons, a crankshaft, greasy rags, and cans full of bolts soaking in oil.

The grounds around the main house are cluttered with rusting truck bodies and bus chassis. In the middle of the compound, now almost obscured by junk, is a wooden store with iron bars across its dusty windows. Selesele abandoned the store a few years ago to focus all of his attention on the more lucrative transport business. The building is now locked, its shaded porch a convenient snoozing platform for a half dozen enormous black pigs.

Selesele says that in another ten years or so, when the business is firmly established, he will turn his attention to politics. When he does, I have no doubt that he will become the district's Member of Parliament. In the meantime, his attention to business precludes his direct participation in village social and political affairs. Except for attending the Sunday morning church service, Selesele is rarely seen about the village. *Matai* should attend all village affairs, but Samoan villagers are pragmatists, and if people have more pressing affairs, they are readily excused. Selesele makes up for his physical absence by contributing the most money, pigs, and other resources to most village affairs. In this way he is able to conduct his business without neglecting his social responsibilities.

---

[9] Local entrepreneurs appeared at the first onset of trading with the Europeans, but as soon as the colonialists became well established, they crushed their island competitors (see Pitt 1970).

In addition to his feeling of social responsibility and his natural generosity, Selesele has two other reasons to be what villagers call *lima foa'i*, or "giving handed." Though he is still a political youngster and he holds only a relatively minor title, there is no question that he is the heir to his father's high title, Asiata.[10] Thus, since Selesele has the financial means, he can contribute more than other chiefs of his present rank, and even more than those who far outrank him. He gives partly in memory of his father's high status and partly in anticipation of his own future status.

The second reason for Selesele's generosity is that while his business success is admirable in the eyes of other villagers, it puts him in a delicate social position. He runs the only bus lines on the entire southeast coast of Savaii. He thus provides an essential service. But while providing the service at a moderate price (both the routes and the fares being regulated by the government), he has become very wealthy, and that wealth has come directly from the passengers—his neighbors. Operators of successful village stores face the same problem. Demonstrating their generosity frequently and publicly helps to deflect criticism. It is a measure of Selesele's success that I never heard another villager speak ill of him or show any jealousy toward him.

Though the scale of entrepreneurism and philanthropy is small in Vaega, the pattern has obvious parallels in the United States and other Western countries. One important similarity is that philanthropy has little or no effect on the distribution of wealth in the community. In Samoa (as in the U.S.) wealthier households give larger sums to charity and to other civic causes than poorer households give. As a percentage of total income, however, poorer households in both countries are more generous than wealthier households.[11] Thus, philanthropy does not help to level either current incomes or accumulated wealth between households in a Samoan village.

BEAUTIFYING THE VILLAGE CHURCH

Samoan villages engage in a nearly continuous series of civic projects. In Vaega, construction of the new church in the late 1960s was soon followed by construction of a new pastor's residence and community hall, then new residences for teachers at the Wesleyan secondary school, then an entire new elementary school. During my brief visit to Vaega in 1979, I joined a gang of more than fifty men building a new dormitory at the Wesleyan school. In 1982, when Satupaitea district had paid off its government loan for the new elementary school, the chiefs of Vaega built another student dormitory at the Wesleyan school. Soon after that, they refurbished the nurses' residence at the local medical clinic. Early in 1983 the people of Vaega turned their attention to beautifying their church.

---

[10] The Selesele title is the highest orator title in the village, but since it has been split among thirty-five people, holding it is no longer a matter of great prestige.

[11] My evidence for Samoa comes from the economic survey and from other field records.

When the shell trumpet sounded Monday morning, I joined Nu'u and his nephew, Selesele Malaki, and we strolled together up the gravel road to the church. By the time we arrived, most of the other chiefs were already there, standing around waiting for something to happen. It was a motley group. We were all wearing our work clothes—an assortment of secondhand sport shirts, holey T-shirts, and faded *lāvalava*—all clean, but greyed nevertheless by mildew and plantation dirt. A few of the men were smooth-shaven with their hair neatly combed. Most were still disheveled and sported a stubble of beard, fringed along the bottom by a few wispy neck hairs, left as a kind of scraggly fashion statement.

Samoan villagers live their entire lives in view of their neighbors. There are few secrets among them and even fewer attempts to disguise their everyday appearances. They love to look good and to dress well, and they are as impressed as anyone by a handsome face or figure or a fine suit of clothes. But since they are visible to their neighbors from the moment they are born, and from the moment they awake each morning, most villagers realize the futility of trying to maintain a public image that differs much from private reality. Like campers on an extended outing, they go about their affairs with little of the self-consciousness that characterizes more private societies.

I was not sure what was going to happen at the church, and Nu'u answered my questions only with *Se'i iloa*, "We'll see." Mid- and lower-ranking chiefs are frequently uninformed about decisions of the high chiefs, and we had assembled that morning at the direction of the *Sa Asiata* (literally "the Family of Asiata," but referring figuratively to the four men then resident in the village who held the paramount title of Asiata).

Soon the pastor and his wife arrived. Though the high chiefs had called the work party, Fogalele and his wife, Fale, had instigated the project, and they were on hand to oversee the work. Following them from the pastor's residence across the road came several men carrying gallon cans of paint. They brought over a dozen cans of white latex paint—a rare sight in a village since each can costs nearly WS $40.

I wondered where the money had come from. Village projects are usually funded by collecting WS $5 or so from each *matai*. For an especially big project, the collection might be extended to include untitled men, or collections might alternate between the two groups. Those decisions are only made by consensus at village council meetings, however, and there had been no meeting for several weeks. I soon learned that the paint had been donated by Selesele Tanielu.

With the arrival of the paint that Selesele had contributed, our task became clear. There were only a few paintbrushes, however, and about three dozen painters. Only two of the brushes were new. Most of the others were caked with old paint or worn down to pitiful nubs. Surprisingly, the shortage of brushes presented no difficulty. Several of the men went off to nearby houses and returned with sections of coconut husk, which they quickly worked into serviceable brushes. Others returned with empty cans that a few days before had contained headless mackerel or pressed corned beef. After a perfunctory wiping, these served as paint cans. Other men appeared with homemade pole ladders.

Instead of going right to work, everyone just stood around. I was about to ask what we were waiting for when two men returned with buckets of water. To my astonishment, they walked straight up to the cans of paint, and as everyone watched they began diluting the paint with vast quantities of water! I tapped Lautafi Esau on the shoulder and asked him what was going on. He replied nonchalantly that they did not have enough paint. They did not want to waste it by applying it in a thick coat, so they were diluting the paint into a thin whitewash that would cover the whole church.

In political affairs, villagers observe a strict hierarchy of honor, status, privilege, and (to a lesser extent) power. In both men's and women's communal work groups, however, people work almost entirely on their own initiative without anyone directing the work. This is partly because the high chiefs and their wives (who are all elderly anyway) do not participate, so the members of a work group are all of relatively equal rank. In addition, most people are usually familiar with the task at hand. As a consequence of relying on individual initiative, work groups like the one painting the church sometimes suffer from egalitarian chaos. The work proceeds slowly but with everyone in good humor, and if the result is imperfect in some respects, no one seems to mind.

Individuals work at their own pace. Since there were more of us painting the church than the job required, it was of no concern if someone dropped out for a long smoke break, or even to attend to some matter at home. Before the morning was half over, several men were sitting in the shade rolling cigarettes or just lounging while the others painted. Some men worked very little, others worked almost non-stop, but no one ever commented on another's performance. The only reward was a reputation for industry, the only penalty a reputation for indolence. We continued in the same pattern of work and periodic rest throughout the week, though the number of workers decreased every day (and the number of domino players in a nearby house increased proportionally).

Near the end of the week, when we had begun painting the interior doors and window trim, we heard a rumor that the pastor and his wife wanted to cover the rough concrete floor of the church with linoleum. Other churches, they said, had linoleum-covered floors, and ours suffered by comparison. For the first time I saw a look of concern on the faces of the workers. The church floor covers several thousand square feet, and linoleum is very expensive. No one voiced disapproval of the plan, but the villagers' sudden lack of enthusiasm was obvious. "Perhaps we could just cover the raised area around the pulpit," one of the men suggested.

The following day several rolls of linoleum arrived as cargo on the bus from Salelologa. Someone had purchased the linoleum on credit at the direction of the four Asiatas, leaving the village a debt of WS $800 to repay. We set to work immediately removing the pandanus floor mats from the isles and the more finely woven sleeping mats from the area around the pulpit. In

Photo 12. The elders of Vaega and Satufia taking communion in the church at Vaega.

their place we unrolled the linoleum. There was no glue to affix the linoleum to the concrete, so we simply laid it out, cutting it to a rough fit around the pillars. When one roll was finished, we overlapped it with another, though each roll was of a different pattern and color. The pastor, Fogalele, directed the work personally. His son took over the difficult task of fitting the linoleum around the base of the pulpit. In a couple of hours the center aisle and the front one-third of the church floor were covered with linoleum and the renovation was complete.

A SENSE OF COMMUNITY

Vaega is a community in a sense that is now rarely found in Western countries. The families of Vaega have lived among their neighbors for many generations. Neighbors have known each other all their lives, and their families have known each other for centuries. Village traditions bind them to their ancestors even farther into the dim past. Neighbors live close together in houses without walls, intimately but discreetly aware of each other's affairs. They attend each other's births. They play together as children, and later they go to school together. As adults they fish together, weave together, build their houses together. They work their plantations side by side. Sometimes they marry each other. They worship together, celebrate together, and finally they mourn together.

To an outsider, the most pervasive qualities of Samoan village life might be cohesiveness and intimacy. The entire village moves as one in most of its affairs. As an American used to city ways, Vaega often seemed to me to be the ultimate expression of good neighborliness and small town democracy. At a village council meeting every *matai* has a chance to speak and decisions are reached by consensus. When church or government officials visit, members of all the village families receive them, serving a formal banquet to the visitors and to their own leading *matai*. When a member of the village dies, the entire church choir, dressed in long white robes, sings gentle hymns through the night. The next morning the village *matai* gather in a nearby house, bringing gifts of fine mats and money. The village women, dressed entirely in black, sit throughout the day in another open house, while scores of relatives arrive from around the country and even from overseas to offer their support.

Everyone has a place in their family and village. No one is alone, no one is a stranger, no one is without support. Samoans who visit the United States are shocked to see bedraggled people wandering along our country's highways or huddled together on back city streets. "Where are their families?" they ask, uncomprehending. "Why don't their families take care of them?"

At other times the closeness of village life seemed oppressively conformist and authoritarian. Virtually every event is planned and directed by either the leading *matai* or the pastor. The pastor announces the numerous church obligations along with the gospel during the Sunday morning service. When attendance declines, the village council appoints an orator to patrol the village during church services, fining anyone who does not attend.

Every evening people gather in their homes for a short family service. An orator at the inland entrance to the village signals the beginning of the prayer session by blowing a long, foghorn note on a trident-shell trumpet. This first call is quickly answered by another trumpet of slightly different size and tone, then another and another as the call passes down the road to the seaward end of the village. This signal temporarily seals the village from all intrusion. People who are walking along the road must step off to one side and wait patiently for the *sā*, or "prohibition," to end. If a person's home is nearby, the orators guarding the road hustle them off to join their families in prayer. Those who do not live nearby, but are especially devout, may join the nearest family in their service.

Soon after the trumpets sound, the robust singing of both adults and children fills the air. The children sit cross-legged along one side of the open house, shifting and squirming until it is time for them to read a short passage from the Bible. They pass the Bible from hand to hand as each child reads, their noses pressed almost to the page in the failing light of evening. Sitting a few feet away are the young men and women of the family. They have learned to be shy and reluctant in public in a way that still escapes the more exuberant children. Once the Bible is set aside, the family members shift to their hands and knees, some with their heads bowed onto the mat, as the head of the household delivers a prayer. No matter who delivers the prayer—

aged *matai*, middle-aged mother, or young father—the prayer is long, flowing, and earnest, and often punctuated by soft declarations of "Thank you, Jesus" from other family members.

When families finish their prayers, the trumpet shells sound again along the road, freeing the villagers to go about their affairs. Young men quickly light hurricane lamps, or the occasional gas pressure lamp, in the now-darkened houses as the younger children serve the evening meal. For some families the meal is delayed while the *matai* delivers a stern lecture to the assembled family, recounting their past failings or those of a particular member. At other times a simple statement suffices concerning the chores that the junior members of the household will carry out the next day.

Later in the evening, the orators' trumpets sound again, signaling the nine o'clock curfew after which only *matai* are allowed out of their houses. The purposes of the curfew are to assure that schoolchildren get to bed early; to prevent theft, clandestine meetings of unmarried people, and other illicit behaviors that might go undetected in the darkness; and to generally maintain the peace and quiet of the village. Following the announcement of the curfew, orators again stand watch on the village road, and they may fine offenders. These nightly patrols are not a hardship to the orators, however. Most of them are middle-aged men with large families, and they welcome the excuse to gather by themselves in small groups, talking quietly and smoking in the night air.

Once or twice a month a mid-level orator acts as town crier, announcing village social, political, and economic affairs along the road. I sometimes walked along the dark village road with my friend and host, Nu'u Vili, when he acted as crier. He paused before each group of houses, their interiors illuminated by the soft firelight of kerosene lanterns. Facing the houses, he gave a long, low blast on his shell trumpet and then shouted the village orders for the week:

> Tomorrow will begin the planting of taro tops. Each *matai* must plant five hundred for the inspection on Thursday, three weeks from now. Beginning tomorrow morning at the sound of the trumpet, the untitled men will cut the bush alongside the inland work road. It is prohibited that you not attend. It is also prohibited that young men continue to wear their hair long. Those who do will be fined fifty cents at the next council meeting. It is prohibited to again play bingo on the cricket pitch after dark.

VILLAGE AGRICULTURE

Vaega's lands theoretically stretch from the lagoon shore all the way to the mountain tops behind the village. Villagers have cleared only 1,290 acres of land, however, extending in a ragged strip four miles inland (see Figure 5.1). Each of the village's large extended families (and almost all of their constituent households) have their own scattered plots within that area. Local

Photo 13. Young man preparing to harvest taro in a plot that he has newly cleared from the virgin forest.

English-speaking people refer to these plots by the rather dignified title of "plantations," corresponding to the local term, "planter," for those who work the land.

The main food crop in Vaega and throughout Samoa is taro (*Colocasia esculenta*). Taro is a starchy root crop, familiar to some Westerners as the ornamental plant called "elephant ear." Samoans also grow several other staples, including breadfruit, bananas, yams, and another root crop called *ta'amū* (*Alocasia sp.*). Breadfruit has the great advantage of requiring very little production effort, but Samoans do not like it as much as taro or yams. The breadfruit harvest is also limited to one major and one minor season during the year. Breadfruit trees grow within the village proper and in the coconut plantations. The villagers also planted breadfruit trees along a stretch of the upland plantation road several years ago. This was in response to a government development project—soon abandoned—to produce livestock feed from the starchy fruit.

Bananas grow in fallowed lands between the coconut and taro lands, and around village house sites. The clumps of banana trees adjoining every house are safe from theft, and they regenerate themselves without tending. The yards are already well kept, so additional weeding is not necessary. Natural fertilizer from the animals that roam the yards seems to be enough to keep the bananas propagating themselves indefinitely. Bananas growing around the houses thus require no more cultivation effort than a swipe with a machete to bring down a bunch of fruit. People almost always harvest bananas when they are still green and immediately bake or boil them as a starchy staple food.

Bananas and breadfruit add variety to the taro diet with very little extra effort. This gives the cultivators an occasional respite and reduces the total labor requirements for food production. When a family is temporarily short-handed—because of illness, travel, or social obligations—these tree crops also act as a valuable food reserve for people who have no other form of larder. One stormy October when I was living with Nu'u, our entire family was sick with the flu. No one went to the taro plantations or out fishing on the reef for almost three weeks. The most anyone could do was stagger out of the house a few yards to the nearest breadfruit or banana tree and pull down some fruit.

Ta'amū is a larger cousin of the taro. It produces a huge, starchy corm up to six or seven feet long and as big around as a person's thigh. It grows much like the smaller taro, except that it does not mature within a single year as the taro does. Taro matures within six to twelve months, depending on soil, weed, and weather conditions, as well as on the size of the planting stock. Taro roots, or corms, will rot if left in the ground longer. *Ta'amū* has the advantage of continuing to grow for several years without rotting. While it is not as palatable as the taro, it provides another reserve of food, as well as being desirable simply for variety.

Yams contribute only a minor part to the diet, though most people consider them to be even tastier than taro. The yam plant is a climbing vine that produces one or more large tuberous roots. Villagers usually plant several yams in a circle around a small, dead tree. They lean bamboo or *fu'afu'a* poles against the tree for the vine to climb until it reaches the branches of the tree. Yams require fertile, rock-free soil, of which there is very little in Vaega (or elsewhere in Samoa). Planters must loosen the soil thoroughly if the tuber is to grow well. They must also weed the area around the roots repeatedly since the yam, unlike the broad-leafed taro and *ta'amū*, never shades its own ground. Thus, while the yam is a favored food, it requires more work than other crops.

Village planters grow taro and the other root crops in a shifting, bush-fallow system. The most common practice is for planters to clear virgin forest and immediately plant the first taro crop. Their planting material is the stems of other taro plants that have been harvested recently. They harvest taro by pulling it out of the ground, cutting the corm from the bottom of the stem, and then cutting the leaves from the top of the stem. This leaves a thick stem about eighteen inches long, from the base of which new roots will soon sprout. Once the land is cleared, men begin planting the stems one at a time. First, the planter punches a hole in the soil and loose rock with a stout planting stick. Then he pries up on the stick, loosening the rocky soil enough to insert a stem. Finally, he packs the soil or rock down around the stem with his foot.

After harvesting the taro from a new plot, the planter (perhaps aided by his wife and older children) immediately weeds it thoroughly to encourage a second crop to grow. This second crop develops from suckers that have sprouted from the main taro corms. After harvesting the small sucker crop two or three months later, the planter allows the plot to rest long enough for fast-growing vines and creepers to cover it again. These vines suppress the growth of more noxious weeds.

My neighbor, Vila, showed me how to clear these vines for the next planting. He hitched his *lāvalava* up around his thighs to keep it out of the way of his machete and then stooped to pull a mass of tangled vines and creepers a foot or two off the ground. As he tugged on the vines with his left hand, he swung the razor-sharp machete with his right hand, hacking off a mass of vines and then flipping them over to bake in the sun. There the vines continue to suppress the growth of grass and forest seedlings, while helping to retain moisture in the soil and providing compost for the new taro crop. It was arduous work, and it was not long before I was covered with dirt and bugs, and dripping with sweat. I was a little nervous too about swinging the machete so close to my bare legs and feet, as the blade frequently glanced off rocks that were hidden beneath the vines.

Machete accidents are common in the plantations, and most men have scars on their legs from cuts. One evening about a month later I was sitting in Nu'u's house when I saw Vila riding his horse slowly through the village. I immediately knew that something was wrong because village law prohibits riding a horse inside the village proper. Vila was sitting tall, but as he neared I saw that his face was deathly pale and he swayed slightly on his makeshift saddle of creepers. His right knee was bandaged with a piece of soiled *lāvalava*, and clotted blood caked his lower leg.

"Vila, do you need help?" I called, afraid that he would fall from the horse before he reached the clinic 200 yards farther down the road.

"No, it's nothing much," he replied, smiling somewhat dreamily. "I was just weeding taro when my machete glanced off a rock and cut my leg."

In older plots the planters have to weed the taro two or three times, first by hand and then by machete, before the taro grows large enough to shade out the weeds. Weeding may be completely unnecessary, however, in areas they have just cleared of trees. Few weeds grow naturally under the forest cover, and the debris from clearing covers the ground and helps to suppress weeds. The soil in these freshly cleared plots is also richer than in older plots. The combination of richer soil and fewer weeds can produce a crop of very large taro (weighing several pounds apiece) within only six months. Older plots only produce one-pound corms in ten or even twelve months, and require several weedings in the process. After many years, the lengthening fallow periods can no longer suppress the growth of hardy grasses and weeding becomes very strenuous. At this point the planters either abandon the plot until secondary forest grows up again, or they replant the ground with co-conuts (or less often with cocoa). They carefully weed around the new saplings until they are well established. The planters then cut the weeds back only sporadically for the next five or six years, until the trees begin to bear nuts.

Sometimes the planter judges the soil and weed conditions incorrectly and the newly-planted taro does not grow rapidly enough to stay ahead of the weeds. In that case, he usually abandons that section of the plot without wasting further effort on it. In older plots where the soil is nearing exhaustion and grasses are displacing other weeds, this produces taro plots with an exaggeratedly haphazard, ill-tended appearance. Rather than indicating indifference to his crop, however, this pattern reflects the planter's judicious expenditure of his time and energy. Clearing the land, planting it, and weeding the crop is very demanding work, and no one wants to waste his efforts on a poor crop. Once the tree cover has been partially removed, the tropical sun can be painfully hot, and planters are careful to guard against heat exhaustion and dehydration. If there is no urgency to their work, the men may rest in the shade and smoke for as much as fifteen minutes out of every hour.

Taro planting and harvesting go on all year, except during the drier months of July and August, and during the main breadfruit season in April and May. The rest of the year planters visit their taro plots almost daily, both to get fresh taro and to guard against theft. One quarter of their trips to the taro plantations are only to harvest food for the evening meal, replant a few taro stems, and to guard the plot against theft. Planters are able to improve their efficiency considerably when they grow and harvest large lots for sale. Their highest development priorities are to increase their share of the limited taro export market, and to extend the work road up to the taro plantations so they can haul large loads out by truck, rather than on their backs and the backs of their horses.

Young to middle-aged men do most work in the taro plantations, though younger boys also do some hand weeding and often help with the harvesting. The only work that women or girls commonly (though not exclusively) perform in the upland taro plantations is the hand weeding of short grass and herbaceous weeds. Women almost always have more than enough chores to do around the house, and parents do not want their daughters to venture far from home unless a parent or older brother is along to protect and supervise them.

Unmarried brothers may work together on the same taro plot. A few young men occasionally form temporary clubs, working each other's plots in turn or hiring out to work on other families' plots. Sometimes the few families who are short on labor but have money to spare also hire a few neighbor youths for a single day of labor. Otherwise, each nuclear family or each unmarried man usually works his own taro plots independently.

The *taulele'a* (more formally called the *'aumāga*) are the untitled men of a village. In former times they might plant a communal taro garden for a special purpose. Today the only occasion for communal plantation labor is when either the untitled men, the *aualuma* (the group of unmarried women of the village), or the full *komiti* (from the English "committee") of all village women tend the taro and coconut lands of the village pastor.

Economic development projects that originate outside the village are often designed to require a communal production effort, as well as requiring communal ownership of land and other productive resources. There are two good

Photo 14. Young men and a woman of Vaega rest during their walk up to the taro plantations. Two other young women are outside the picture to the right, giving an indication of the usual ratio of young women to young men working in the taro plantations. The stones that they sit on are part of the large stone fort that once provided refuge for the inhabitants of the inland village of Uliamoa.

reasons for this communal emphasis. First, both the local government and international development agencies want to spread the benefits of limited funds as widely as possible. Second, they want to prevent their development efforts from widening the already cavernous gap between rich and poor villagers. These goals are laudable, and the villagers support the goals. Unfortunately, the projects themselves are founded on the mistaken belief that village production is essentially communal. While villagers do organize temporarily for communal production on special occasions, they greatly prefer individual or household production in their everyday, long-term efforts. As a result, the vast majority of these communally organized development projects are temporary successes and long-term failures. The effect of these failures on development planning has been even worse. Since many development agents believe (incorrectly) that the communal projects they design conform to village cultural requirements, the failure of these projects unfortunately and unjustifiably reinforces the experts' already low regard for the Samoan planter.

In my experience in Vaega, both the most industrious and the least industrious planters seemed to drop out of communal production efforts early. The more energetic knew that their rewards will match their efforts better on their own plantations. The less energetic feared that as their own contri-

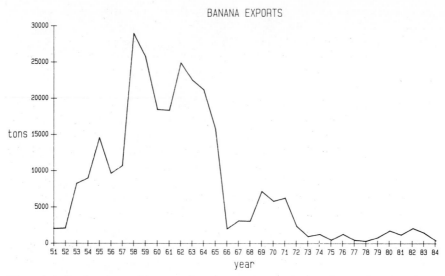

Figure 3.2 Yearly exports of bananas from Western Samoa showing the rapid boom and bust of the banana market.

butions dropped off, their more conscientious neighbors would seize control of the project (and the ultimate rewards). Lautafi Pemita is a young and talented *matai* whose interests do not center on plantation work. When I asked him why he dropped out of a communal project, he replied: *E lē tutusa tagata.* "People are not the same." Seupule Ropati and Milo Fa'alaga, both middle-aged orators who dropped out of the same project, gave identical replies. Everyone realizes that individual efforts will differ greatly, and except in times of hardship, no villager enjoys supporting the members of other families with his own labor.

A few decades ago, villagers seldom needed to clear virgin forest lands. They rotated their garden plots among fallow lands where they had to clear only secondary growth. The only cash crop at that time, coconuts, occupied permanent plots nearer the village. In the 1950s Western Samoa (and Vaega village) became a major producer of bananas for the New Zealand market. Since villagers generally planted the bananas on lands that had been cleared for taro, this interrupted the cycle of forest regeneration. The banana boom soon collapsed, however, due to problems with bunchytop disease (a viral infection of the leaves), recurrent shipping problems, and competition from production giants in Ecuador (see Figure 3.2 above). The collapse of the banana market left Vaega planters without an alternate cash crop, so for the past two decades they have planted coconuts in most fallow taro plantations.

With greater population pressure and more demand for cash today, people extend their land holdings by clearing most new taro plots from virgin forest. Seeing this primary expansion, planters now rush to clear the forest farther and farther from the village in order to claim as much new land as possible and thus avert land shortages for their families in the future. Some wealthy village planters even hire gangs of workers with chainsaws to clear land for them. The unfortunate result of this secondary expansion is that people often replant only part of their old taro plots in coconuts—just enough to seal their long-term claim to the land. Then they push on higher up the slopes to clear more virgin forest. Even when they fully replant the fallow land in coconuts, their choice is dictated by the lack of a good alternate crop, rather than because of any economic opportunity they see in coconuts.

As a result of this expansionary strategy, many families have far more coconut lands than they can currently work efficiently. Many plots are only half-planted, rarely weeded, and seldom harvested. The return to their labor on these poorer lands is simply too low to be worth more than nominal effort, unless special social or economic circumstances temporarily increase a family's need for cash. People carefully maintain and thoroughly harvest their better coconut lands, however.

Samoan adults rarely eat the thick, white meat of the mature coconut unless they are in the plantations without other food. Children sometimes do, but a nearby adult is likely to deride them by asking, "Are you a Tokelauan?" The reference is to the atoll dwellers of Tokelau, north of Samoa. As in other atolls in the Pacific, root crops are sometimes in short supply on Tokelau, so people traditionally ate coconut meat as a staple food (imported food is now common on Tokelau). For a Samoan, eating coconut meat indicates poverty and lack of food—like an atoll dweller—and hence is a source of embarrassment.

Samoans do grate the coconut meat from the shell and squeeze the thick cream from it to use as a condiment, as other Pacific islanders do. Coconut cream, or *pe'epe'e*, seasoned with salt accompanies virtually every meal. People usually pour the coconut cream over boiled taro or the other starchy staples and then heat it briefly over the fire just before serving. The resulting slippery mass is called *fa'alifu*. It is the main (and often the only) course of the two daily meals served Monday through Saturday. On Sunday mornings villagers bake their food in the traditional stone oven.

Men, women, and children share the work in the coconut plantations more evenly than in the taro plantations. During the early 1980s, no villager hired laborers to work his coconut plantations because, as we shall see shortly, the income was too meager to pay anyone to do the work. Children harvest a few coconuts for their families' food several times a week after school. Because of village law, they can gather these nuts only from the plots immediately behind the village proper. Most of these plots lie on lava bedrock and are subject to flooding in heavy rains. These plots are also heavily intercropped or overgrown by weeds, and the coconut trees themselves may be sixty or eighty years old, well beyond their years of peak bearing. These plots thus produce too few coconuts to be gathered efficiently, so they are useless for copra production.

In Vaega (and many other villages), collecting nuts from the better plots further inland is *sā*, or prohibited, except during times specified by the village leaders. There are two reasons for this restriction. First, it prevents the wholesale theft of nuts from unattended plantations. Second, it ensures that every family will be able to meet its financial obligations to the village. The village leaders schedule coconut harvesting periods to coincide with those obligations so that people cannot avoid paying their share by claiming to be *gau*, or "broke."

For example, early in my stay the district was repaying a Development Bank loan that they had used to build a large new elementary school behind Vaega. Every *matai* was taxed WS $5 (about US $4 at that time) each month. For three or four days at the end of each month village leaders lifted the *sā* and every household collected coconuts on their inland plots. The following week members of the School Committee collected the loan payments and then paid the monthly installment on the district's debt.

German, British, and American plantation owners introduced the cocoa, or cacao, tree into Samoa in the late nineteenth century. It is now so ubiquitous and so important that most Samoans believe that it is a traditional crop like taro or coconuts. The best cocoa-producing areas are on the north and north-west coasts of both Savaii and Upolu, where rainfall is moderate. In Vaega, where rainfall averages from about 80 inches along the coast to probably 120 inches in the highest plantations, cocoa does not grow or bear as well. Both the trees and their pods are prone to disease. All Vaega families grow cocoa for home consumption, however, and some for occasional sale. Villagers usually interplant cocoa trees rather casually among the coconut trees, which grow much taller and provide the cocoa trees with the partial shade they need.

The cocoa crop is highly seasonal, unlike coconuts, which bear fruit all year. The cocoa pods mature during the dryer months beginning in mid-May and lasting to late September or early October. In Vaega the peak harvest usually occurs in late July and early August. Another very minor harvest occurs in December, and a few stray pods mature at other times of the year. People usually cut the pods from the tree with a knife and carry them home in baskets for processing. They cut the pods open with a knife and extract the beans, which are coated with a sweet, white gelatinous substance that is delicious to eat.

If they have only a few pods, villagers roast the fresh beans over a fire. Women or young girls almost always perform this unpleasant task, which requires sitting on the ground next to the fire and stirring the beans constantly as they roast, and then picking the hot beans off one by one and removing the papery husk. Then they pound the beans with mortar and pestle. Finally they mix the resulting paste with boiling water and brown Fijian sugar to make a rich, hot cocoa drink. Proper processing, however, requires a basket full of wet beans. They cover the basket with banana leaves and allow the beans to ferment for two or three days, which brings out the best flavor. Once fermented, they dry and roast the beans, and prepare them as before. People call the drink *koko Samoa*, and it is delicious. Villagers consider that no meal, however grand, is complete without cocoa, and the addition of a pot of cocoa to plain boiled taro or breadfruit makes a respectable meal.

Photo 15. Lafai Faleupolu showing cocoa pods from his plantation in Neiafu. In his right hand he holds a passion fruit.

Whether for home consumption or market sale, villagers produce and prepare all of their crops using only simple technology. A bushknife is the only essential tool. Many families use a horse for transport, while they almost always hire a local pickup truck to haul large harvests of coconuts to the village. Villagers apply no chemical fertilizer or herbicide to their coconut plantations, but the few cattle enclosed in some of those plots help to restrict the growth of weeds and add some natural fertilizer to the soil. People in Vaega never apply artificial fertilizers to their taro plots.

Most families have sprayed a herbicide on their taro at least once, but only a half dozen families use a backpack sprayer regularly. One reason for the unpopularity of herbicides is that, lacking adequate markets, a single family's taro sales are rarely large enough to support expensive technology. Moreover, most families have ample labor to do the same job without expense. Villagers are also concerned about the long-term effect of herbicides on the soil. Some farmers believe that their use eventually encourages the hardier grasses to dominate, rather than forest plants which are easier to weed and which make better compost. Perhaps most importantly, many families are reluctant to store weed killer around the house for safety reasons. Suicide has been epidemic recently in Western Samoa, especially among young people, and drinking the herbicide, paraquat, is the method of choice (see Chapter 4).

THE GOLDEN YEARS OF VILLAGE LIFE

Times were not always so difficult. In the minds of many older Vaega residents, the banana boom years of the 1950s and 1960s were the "golden years" of village life. People made relatively good incomes from the sale of bananas and from copra, and the village prospered. The Women's Committee had its own banana plantation from which the women earned enough money to purchase materials for construction of a large, partially open, wooden building with cement floor and tin roof. The women purchased the materials, and the men constructed the building on the shore in the center of the village, facing the village green. The women still hold their council meetings in the building, and they gather there to weave their mats in each other's company. One small room at the back of the building sometimes serves as a birthing center, though most women prefer to give birth at home. The village *matai* also hold their council meetings in the Women's Committee building.

The use of the Women's Committee building is a good indication of the difference in power and status between men and women. Women have their own sphere of authority, and they are able to initiate and carry out important projects on their own, as evidenced by the construction of the building itself. The women have daily use of the building and are responsible for it. Everyone refers to the building as the *Fale Komiti*, the "Committee Building." When the Women's Committee holds one of its irregular meetings at the same time as the council of *matai*, however, the women give way. The Committee meets at a smaller private residence nearby, while the chiefs occupy the Committee Building.

During the prosperous years of the banana boom, the entire district had electricity. The district pooled its new banana wealth and purchased a large generator secondhand in Apia. With the help of the former owner, they installed the generator at a central point in Vaega. After several years of operation, someone forgot to check the oil in the generator and the engine froze. By then the banana market had collapsed and the district lacked the funds to replace it. For the next twenty years the district had no electricity, except for two small private generators that recently lit the homes of prosperous families and the nearby pastor's residence.

A few years ago the district purchased a new generator. This time the funding came not from local sources, but from a 65 percent subsidy (and technical assistance) from the government's Rural Development Programme.

District residents collected the remaining funds from their New Zealand relatives and from the New Zealand Rotary Club. This project immediately fell victim to inter-village rivalry, however. The generator sits in Pitonu'u, and the electricity never reached Vaega and Satufia.

I think there is a simple lesson here for understanding the lack of success of many aid-supported development programs in Western Samoa and in other parts of the world. A generation ago the people of Satupaitea were much less sophisticated in the ways of the industrial world than they are today. They had none of the financial resources or technical expertise that are now available to them through aid programs and from their overseas relatives, but they did have a viable export crop. The villagers worked hard growing bananas, saved their money, and together they purchased, installed, and maintained their own electric generator. Today, lacking a viable internal source of income, they rely on external gifts. In many ways their village is more backward now than it was a generation ago.[12]

The boom in banana exports occurred when Samoan traditions were much stronger than they are today. This contradicts the common assumption that those traditions are inhibiting the villagers' production of cash crops. The early, village-sponsored electrification project similarly contradicts the argument that villagers are content with their lives and do not want the material advantages of modernization. The sequence of events shows instead that villagers want to modernize. It also shows that they are willing to work and save to acquire certain benefits of modernization, and that they are capable of initiating and directing much of their own development effort. Outside aid projects—while often of great help—are no substitute for policies that contribute to an economic environment where villagers can increase their own incomes, create their own projects, and improve their own well-being in a manner that they choose. Nor are the banana boom and the village-sponsored electrification project isolated incidents. There was a similar boom in cocoa exports in the 1950s (see Figure 3.3). As the number of Samoan migrants to New Zealand increased after independence, their desire for Samoan foods set off a boom in taro exports in the late 1970s (see Figure 3.4).

During these periods when cash cropping temporarily expanded, the people of Satupaitea district built or improved much of their agricultural road system. They also donated land and built a substantial medical clinic and nurses' residence. More recently they donated land for an elementary school and built several large, European-style school buildings and smaller residences at both the elementary and intermediate schools. They made all of these improvements on their own initiative. They contributed their own land, labor, and money, and they completed each of these projects with little or no outside assistance.

One reason that life was easier during these "golden years" is that there

---

[12] In 1988 a new development project brought electricity to Vaega from a generator on the other side of the island. With heavy subsidies, all but a few households can now afford at least one bare lightbulb in their homes. Three families now have VCRs, and a few are considering freezers.

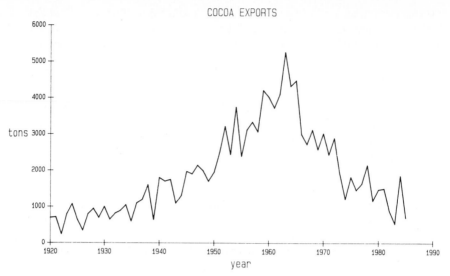

Figure 3.3 Annual cocoa exports from Western Samoa.

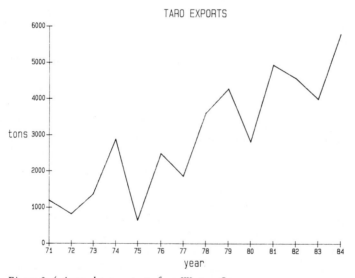

Figure 3.4 Annual taro exports from Western Samoa.

were fewer people to support. In the early 1960s there were just over 400 people in Vaega, 100 less than today. With fewer fishermen, the fish were more plentiful along the reef. With less forest clearing, the stream at the head of the bay carried less silt into the lagoon. There was once a small shipbuilding industry in Palauli, and steamboats passed Vaega on their way to the head of the bay. Today the head of the bay is a shallow mud flat. Asiata Iakopo told me that when he was a boy, the lagoon water in front of his house was over his head. Today the high tide barely covers the mud.

A generation ago the taro plantations were only about two miles inland, where the more fertile slopes rise above the lava plain that bounds the coast. Now the men clear their new gardens nearly four miles inland, higher on the slopes where the taro does not grow so well for lack of sun. The move to higher plantations also adds greatly to the daily walk to the plantations, and to the backbreaking labor of transporting the taro back to the village. Returning from the plantation, each planter carries his daily produce in two coconut-leaf baskets lined with taro leaves. The baskets hang from either end of a stout pole that he shifts from one shoulder to the other to ease the pain of the heavy load, the muddy blade of his machete jutting rakishly from one basket as he hurries down the path.

A generation ago when the population was smaller and there were fewer children, the village's elementary school was housed in a single, open-sided building near the shore. Today the district has a large, three-wing, wooden schoolhouse behind Vaega. Because of the constant traffic to and from the new school, the stone fence that once protected the village from roving pigs can no longer be maintained. Today neither pigs nor horses are banned from the village proper, as they once were. Now when the men come down from the plantations they stake their scrawny horses in the yards in front of their houses. Pigs roam freely, fouling the ground and spreading flies and parasites.

A generation ago the village was more isolated than it is today. Temporary visits and permanent migration to Apia were both uncommon, and travel overseas was very rare. By 1981 when I conducted a village census, villagers travelled frequently between their village and Apia. Just over two-thirds of all adults then living in the village had visited American Samoa. Thirteen percent had visited New Zealand, and several had visited Hawaii and the mainland U.S.

In those golden years a generation or more ago, people did not have the benefit of cash remittances from urban and overseas relatives as many do now, yet in many respects life was easier then. According to villagers who are now middle-aged, their childhoods were spent largely in play and in rather casual schooling. They performed few chores around the house, and while they often accompanied their parents to the plantations, they did little work. Even church attendance was largely a matter of preference.

The population has grown considerably since then, and neither the plantations nor the sea yield so easily as they once did. In gaining greater exposure and greater access to manufactured goods, villagers have acquired new needs and new desires. This combination of increasing material desires and decreasing resources has led to a perception of scarcity. Villagers have recruited more child labor to help fill the gap. Children still have time to play and they do so with great exuberance, but only when their many household chores, their share of the plantation work, and their homework is finished.

The greater perception of scarcity has also led to increased theft. A generation or more ago theft was uncommon or even rare. Nu'u, for example, tells of leaving a machete sticking to a tree in the plantation and retrieving it a couple of days later. Today nothing is left in the plantations unless it is well hidden, and the crops themselves are frequently pilfered. When the family goes to church or to some other village affair, one member must always stay behind to *leoleo fale*, or "guard the house."

Perhaps the most difficult change, the one that causes the most heartache and regret today, is the breakup of families. A generation ago families were still united, in good times and in bad. The village had not yet lost many of its most promising young people. Today migration is often expected and in many cases desired—yet it is also feared. Parents become separated from their children, friends are lost, and brothers and sisters scatter as they disappear into waiting airplanes.

MALE, FEMALE, AND CROSS-SEX ROLES

Males of all ages find more time to play or rest than females. In the late afternoons the young men and boys can usually be found relaxing or playing cricket on the village green, playing rugby on a sand flat exposed by the tide near the lagoon shore, or playing volleyball at the school grounds. A few young women join in the volleyball, but most remain at home, cooking and tending to the many children or the countless household chores. Even into advanced middle age, women are expected to keep busy (though not all do). Meanwhile, their husbands often sleep, play dominoes, or discuss the intricacies of the latest social or political maneuver, leaving their own household duties half-completed. Women sometimes express resentment towards men for this unequal division of labor. I was talking with a middle-aged woman named Fua one day in her house as she plaited pandanus-leaf floor mats.

"What does your father do?" she asked. She knew from photographs that my father was then over 60 and silver-haired, and she was surprised when I replied that he worked in an office.

"Samoan men," she muttered, "all they do is eat, sleep, and go off to play dominoes. Look at that great expanse of forest," she added, pointing to the mountain slopes that rise above the bay. "There's nothing up there but forest. Europeans don't sit around, they're always busy. If that was European land, it would all be plantations, cattle pastures, vegetable gardens. But Samoan men, they never do anything." She looked down from the mountainside to the mat in her hands, fiddled with it for a moment, and then went back to weaving.

Like men, women gain somewhat more control over their lives as they grow older. Even if a woman outlives her parents, however, she still may not fully control her own life until she is an elderly widow. There are exceptions, of course, when a woman rises to authority in her own household, her extended family, or even in village affairs. I know of no such cases in Vaega, however. A very few women even rise to national political prominence, but even though these women are exceptionally talented, they usually gain their initial opportunities through genealogical or marital relationships with powerful men. While women have less secular authority than men, they do occupy a position of elevated status over males, especially their brothers, within their own descent group. The relationship is marked by an attitude of respect and politeness, rather than a significant sharing of power. In this respect the position of Samoan women is similar to the pedestal of high status from which American women are now descending.

If a household is short of men, women and girls may perform all but the heaviest plantation tasks—in addition to their numerous household chores. As long as a woman is neither in an advanced state of pregnancy nor caring for a newborn infant, she will probably spend much of the early years of her marriage working alongside her husband in their plantations. This is a busy time, for not only must the couple support themselves and their elders, they usually need to clear and plant new land in anticipation of the many children that most couples desire.

Both men and women may work for wages, though men hold 60 percent of the country's wage jobs (GWS 1984a:234). There are few wage jobs that are exclusively male or female, but wage employment in Samoa closely follows the model of traditional Western gender roles. Clerks and general office staff may be either men or women, but the great majority of teachers, nurses, and secretaries are women.

Some individuals do not fit neatly into the society's male and female roles. In Samoa, males who affect what their society considers to be feminine behavior are called *fa'afāfine* (literally, "in the manner of a female"). The role of *fa'afāfine* is recognized and accepted in Samoan society (and in many other Polynesian societies). Though *fa'afāfine* are not common (there were no adult *fa'afāfine* residing in Vaega), they elicit little or no comment among other Samoans. Different individuals affect feminine behavior to different degrees. The most extreme, and hence the most visible, are transvestites. They dress in women's clothing, wear jewelry and make-up (in Apia), speak in a high falsetto, and use exaggerated feminine gestures.[13] At least some *fa'afāfine* become active homosexuals. *Fa'afāfine* also take on what the society considers to be women's work roles. Many *fa'afāfine* are store clerks (where they sell household goods and women's items), secretaries, or teachers. There seems to be no discrimination against them. Several have risen to the position of school principal, for example. *Fa'afāfine* associate with females, among whom they are favorite companions. Other people treat *fa'afāfine* as females, and in their speech they refer to them with female nouns.

Much rarer are *fa'atama* (literally, "in the manner of a male"). *Fa'atama* are females who affect what the society considers to be male appearance and behavior. I know only one *fa'atama* and have heard about only two others,

---

[13] Some of this behavior is strikingly similar to the exaggerated, effeminate behavior of Western stage transvestites. That stereotyped behavior bears even less resemblance to the everyday behavior of Samoan females than it does to Western females. Because of this, I suspect that some *fa'afāfine*, especially around Apia, have adapted a traditional Samoan transvestite role to a more recent Western model. This shows that *fa'afāfine* do not take on "female" roles so much as they create new roles for themselves that overlap in some respects with traditional female roles.

so it is difficult to generalize. *Fa'atama* associate with males, and people treat them and speak of them as males.

Among the individuals that I know, both *fa'afāfine* and *fa'atama* made the major changes in dress and personal style during their early teen-age years (i.e., during puberty), though the preference had already been apparent for several years. The one *fa'atama* that I know was a superior student in primary school, but quit at age thirteen rather than wear a dress, as the school administration demanded.

Merely doing work that is usually associated with the other sex does not indicate *fa'afāfine* or *fa'atama* status or excite comment in any way. Women attend to most of the daily cooking and child care, but a *matai* readily takes over these chores when his wife is away from home. I know two middle-aged women who were accomplished at fishing from a canoe, one at hook-and-line fishing and the other at spearfishing. The children of both women commented with pride on the fishing skills of their mothers. Most plantation wage workers are men, but women may work alongside them. When I was living in Neiafu village, on the southwestern corner of Savaii, I often watched the huge blue truck from the WSTEC cocoa plantation returning to the village in the evening with a load of day laborers crowded into the back. Among them were always several young women wearing colorful *lāvalava* over their work pants.

TATTOOING

A traditional mark of adulthood for both men and women is the tattoo. Samoans are the only group of Polynesians—and one of the only groups of Pacific islanders—who still practice the traditional art of tattooing. Most impressive is the men's tattoo, the proper term for which is *tatau*, from which the English "tattoo" derives (in colloquial speech, Samoans use the word *pe'a*). The men's tattoo is a series of dense, intricate, rectilinear designs that covers the entire body (except the pubic area), front and back, from mid-back to just below the knee. The women's tattoo, called *malu*, is a much sparser arrangement of similar motifs around the thighs and extending to just below the knees.

Buck (1930) records that tattooing of both young men and women was common into the late 1920s. I recall seeing no man and only one woman over about forty years of age with a tattoo (women's dress generally hides the tattoo area completely). After a hiatus during the late colonial years, the tattooing of young men has now regained its popularity, and a significant number of young village men now receive tattoos. It is still rare for a young woman to be tattooed. Since most young men receive their tattoos while in their late teens or early twenties, the resurgence of tattooing must have begun about the time of Western Samoa's independence. Whether the resurgence is due primarily to nationalistic feelings, however, I do not know.

The prohibition against tattooing came first from the missionaries, and later from the village chiefs, because of a Biblical injunction against making

Photo 16. Sala'i Fogalele and Vila Autafaga as they appeared when I first met them in 1979. Vila has hitched up his lāvalava to show off his new tattoo. Sala'i has no tattoo because he is the son of the pastor, and the Methodist Church does not condone tattooing.

marks upon the skin. Since villagers generally ignored the injunction for the first one hundred years after missionization, and do so again today, something other than religious devotion must have caused the relatively brief hiatus in tattooing.

The tattoo master is a highly skilled specialist. He is also well rewarded for his work, receiving money, fine mats, food, and other articles from the families of his young subjects, along with much ceremony and respect. Young men band together in small groups to be tattooed. This eases the financial burden somewhat, but the main purpose is mutual support. The tattooing itself is extremely painful, and the young men strengthen their individual courage with group resolve. Acting as a group also removes the stigma of drawing attention to oneself. Finally, when the tattoo master works on several individuals at a time, the surface area treated on each individual in one day

Photo 17. Tattooing implements.

is greatly reduced. In that way a process that could be completed in three or four days is spread out over three or four weeks—much to the relief of the subjects.

The tattooing is very painful not only because of the great area of the body covered, but also because of the implements employed. In order to cover a large area with dense, intricate designs, the artist hammers the ink into the skin with sharp toothed combs of different patterns. He makes the combs from flat, polished sections of boar's tusk, filed into rows of sharp teeth. The combs are bound to a wooden, metal, or turtle shell backing, which in turn is bound at right angles to the end of a short, thin stick.

I first witnessed the tattooing process at the home of Selesele Kalati, a neighbor in Vaega. When I entered the house, the artist was lining out the first strokes of his design on the back and chest of Selesele's son, Asotasi. Asotasi then laid down on a mat with a pillow under his stomach to flatten the arch in the small of his back. The tattoo master dipped the comb into ink made from kerosene soot and water, placed the comb in position with his left hand and then rapped the holding stick smartly with another stick that he held in his right hand. The blow drove the teeth of the comb into the skin where they deposited the ink. The master proceeded quickly along the line of the pattern, tapping out a smooth rhythm while one of the other young subjects wiped away the blood and extra ink with a rag. Several of Asotasi's cohorts sat closely around him, stretching his skin tight with their hands to maintain an even pattern and holding him still so he would not spoil the design by writhing. Others sat by watching, prepared to sing or play the ukulele to

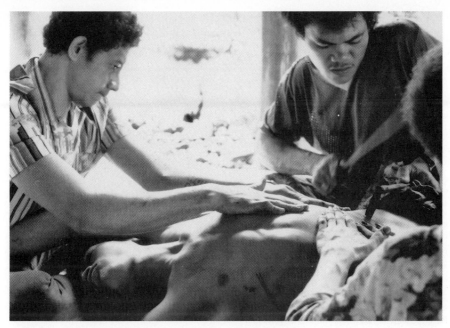

Photo 18. Asotasi Selesele under the hand of a young but expert tattoo master.

distract him from his pain. As the design grew, Asotasi maintained a stoic, unflinching silence.

When the first session was completed, Asotasi bathed in the cool fresh water that is piped down to the village directly from the mountain. After each of his cohorts was tattooed in turn, they bathed and then reclined together in the house, either swishing away the flies with a chief's fly whisk or retreating under a mosquito net if the flies became too troublesome. Only in the late evening when the flies quit their marauding did the young men venture onto the road, hobbling along stiffly with their *lāvalava* hitched up immodestly to prevent the cloth from rubbing on the day's fresh wounds. Youngsters and older men stopped to admire the work, while the girls giggled admiringly from a distance or called out, *'Ese lou mimita!* "What a show-off!"

Over the next three weeks the tattoos grew until only the young men's knees and the tops of their shins remained unadorned. That area is purposely left for last because it is the most painful. Since that area lacks a fleshy covering, the tattoo combs often drive right into the bone. Once the lower knees were completed successfully, the master added a small signature design around the navel, signifying that the tattoo was complete.

I naturally wondered what inspired Asotasi and the other young men to endure such pain in order to adorn their bodies. My inquiries turned up several reasons. The tattoo is quintessentially Samoan, and wearing one is a matter of cultural pride. Some people say that, according to oral tradition, the original purpose of both men's and women's tattoos was that the sight of the tattoo on areas of the body that normally remain covered stimulates the

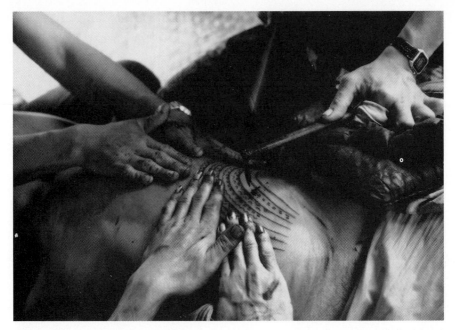

Photo 19. Asotasi distends his stomach and his cohorts stretch the skin tight with their hands while the tattoo master raps in the design.

romantic interest of the opposite sex. The tattoo ceremony also marks the beginning of adulthood. In addition, it brings a great deal of attention and praise to young men at a time in their lives when they normally get very little of either. Tattooing also gives the young men's families an opportunity to show that they can afford the costly ceremony. The tattoo was formerly a sign of chiefly status or impending chiefly status, as no *matai* was without one. But this traditional association must have less force today when none of the older chiefs have tattoos and virtually all of the young men become chiefs—with or without tattoos.

All of these factors induce young men to endure the pain of tattooing, but the single most important factor is the pain of tattooing itself. Young men adorn themselves with full body tattoos primarily to demonstrate that they can withstand the pain. Machismo is high on the list of desired traits among Samoan men, and tattooing is an excellent demonstration of courage and endurance. In addition to personal testimony, my evidence for this conclusion is that the young men eschew the use of any sort of painkiller or antibiotic during the tattooing even though these are readily available just down the road at the district clinic. The young men I talked to also had a devil-may-care pride in taking only minimal sanitary precautions during the operation. When one young man's fresh tattoo became infected, he would not hear of taking an antibiotic, even though I offered to supply it privately so he would not have to approach the nurses at the clinic. His only stated

Photo 20. Satufia's pastor, Ioane, stands amid his flock on Children's White Sunday. The children will form a procession to the church in Vaega where they and their families will join the people of Vaega in a special service featuring Biblical skits, recitations, and songs performed by the children. After the service the families will present the children with a fine meal. White Sunday was initiated by the missionaries in an attempt to at least temporarily reverse the normal order of service between children and adults.

concern was that the tattoo lines would blur if the skin were permanently scarred by the infection.

Some men see the emphasis on enduring pain as important not only to their own self-image, but also in the generally uneasy relationship between men and women. Men explicitly compare the pain of their tattooing (which, they note, continues for days or even weeks) with women's pain during childbirth. As one man told me proudly, "Women give birth, but men are tattooed."

CHILDREN

Everyone in the family pampers and coddles babies for about their first two years, but serious training for most children begins soon after that. I often saw my neighbors' many children marching home from the nearby coconut plantations in the evening, strung out like a line of tiny, ragamuffin porters. The oldest one was first, and they all carried a pole across one shoulder with as many coconuts on either end as they could bear. The oldest was a girl of fifteen, and she smiled coquettishly as she passed. She carried nearly a dozen nuts on either end of a pole, the nuts tied in bunches with thin strips of their husks that she had torn free with her teeth. The youngest and last in the line of carriers was a tiny girl of four who staggered along, sobbing under her load of two nuts.

Many families have a favorite child whom they spoil beyond the usual period of infancy. There is no formal name for this child nor an informal term of reference. *Tama pele*—literally "dear child" but perhaps better glossed as "favorite child"—is a usable descriptive term. The favorite child is usually the head of household's youngest son or grandson who is between about three and seven years old. The youngest daughter or granddaughter may be selected if there is no appropriately aged boy in the family. There is nothing subtle about the favored treatment of this child. He sits on the mat by his father's or grandfather's side at most meals, sharing the best portions of food that are served first to the head of the family while the other children eat separately. One of the most visible privileges of the favorite child is to accompany the *matai* to village council meetings or other formal affairs to sit quietly at the chief's side.

During my early residence with Nu'u's family his youngest son, Tauvaga, became so spoiled that he began ordering his older brothers and sisters, and even his mother, around like a little tyrant. Tauvaga was a real darling, though, a happy and gregarious little boy with a big grin. He often exaggerated his six-year-old bluff and swagger to the point of humor. I rarely saw his older siblings (and never his mother) even attempt to defy him while his father was present, though the strain sometimes showed in their faces. Fortunately for all of us, when Tauvaga reached about seven years old he decided on his own that he would no longer be a child, and he switched almost overnight to the role of an obedient, hardworking son. At that point Nu'u seemed to be grooming his infant grandson, my namesake "little Timo," as his new favorite.

During the time of Tauvaga's preeminence, Asiata Iakopo had taken his youngest grandson, Pati, as his favorite. With Asiata's tolerance and apparent encouragement, Pati became even more aggressive and insufferable than Tauvaga. A few *matai* had little daughters or granddaughters at their sides, but to my knowledge none were ever allowed to be as impudent as the little boys sometimes were. As one young mother told me, "In Samoa, it's hard to say no to a son."

From the time they enter childhood until they are old enough to have maturing children of their own, the lives of young Samoans are largely devoted to obeying and serving their elders. Nevertheless, children have many opportunities for sport and games. In the afternoons when their school was out, I often watched a group of children playing cricket in the yard across from my house, or swimming and splashing nearby in the shallow water of the bay. Their games were usually interrupted, however, and the children sent off on some errand. Children really come into their own on clear, moonlit nights. They congregate in boisterous groups along the village road, singing joyously at the top of their lungs, or playing wildly, safe for the moment from the demands of their parents and older siblings.

A Samoan family's greatest resource is its children. The only assurance of support that people have in their old age is a large plantation and several healthy and devoted children to work it. In these circumstances the villagers' desire for many children, and their emphasis on parental authority and respect for elders, are all understandable.

Young people in Samoa often say that they want to marry early so they can begin producing offspring as soon as possible, thus increasing the number of children they can have and speeding the time when those children will be old enough to support their parents. In areas of the world where infant mortality rates are high, parents usually want to have many children—hoping that enough will survive to support their parents in their old age. Better access to Western medicine has recently reduced infant and child mortality in Samoa, but most Samoan women still bear many children—sometimes a dozen or more. This is explained partly by their love for children, and by a time lag between rapidly falling mortality rates and the slower change of attitudes and expectations.

Birth rates also remain high for both medical and economic reasons. In addition to reducing health risks to the infant, Western medicine has also reduced the risks of childbirth to the mother. This prevents the removal of some women of childbearing age from the population, improves the general health and fertility of women, and reduces the health risks to the mother of giving birth. In spite of the higher survival rate of children, outmigration may mean that the potential economic contributions of some children are still effectively lost to their parents, just as if these children had not survived at all. Even though Samoan migrants as a group have a well-deserved reputation for contributing to their families back home, this support tends to decline over the years. Some migrants contribute little or nothing and are rarely or never heard from again, except perhaps at the time of their parents' funerals. My census of Vaega indicates that it is common for a family to have one or more children essentially "lost" in Apia or overseas. I have also attended village funerals where people returned from Apia or overseas for the first time in many years to pay their final respects and then quickly departed.

Finally, I suspect that the opening of several new but still mediocre economic opportunities to Samoan villagers in the past two or three decades has increased rather than decreased their desire to have many children. All of the old village duties remain. An elderly couple still needs family members to work the plantations, to fish, cook, carry firewood, weave mats, and do a dozen other chores. Children do many simple but essential household chores, so every household needs them. Households that have few or no children usually adopt one or two from their close relatives. As they grow, most children are quickly pressed into productive work. It is common, for example, to see ten- or twelve-year-old girls weaving mats in the house or sitting under the open water pipe beating the family's soapy laundry with a short wooden club. Boys of the same age are already walking inland with their fathers or older brothers to help with the lighter plantation work, and both boys and girls are pressed into service harvesting coconuts.

One of my most vivid memories of Samoa is hurrying home from the coconut plantations late one evening. As I rounded a bend, I saw a man and his young son walking down the plantation road before me in the twilight. The man was walking slowly without a burden, his arms swinging lightly at his sides. The boy struggled along thirty feet behind him with a ten-foot-long tree limb balanced across his bare shoulder, his head bent toward the ground. One small arm curled tightly over the branch to steady it. No one else was in sight. I did not want to overtake them and have to speak, so I stood and watched them continue down the long hill until they turned the corner onto the main road.

In addition to the obvious health risk and burden for the mother, there are other drawbacks to having many children. The children must be fed and clothed at a time when young couples are beginning to fulfill village and church obligations on their own account while still serving their parents or parents-in-law. Young couples with many children also find it difficult to pay the children's school fees. Some children are forced to drop out of school prematurely even though Samoans feel that a good education for their children is essential if both the children's and the family's future economic aspirations are to be realized.

While Vaega appears on the surface to be a strongly agricultural village, few residents pin their hopes for the future on the development of their plantations. Most families want to place at least one child in a good wage job in Apia and another one or two overseas—both of which require success in European-style education. The task of maintaining the family's plantations and looking after the parents thus usually falls to those who do not excel in school. Since no source of income is adequate or secure enough in itself, most families take a shotgun approach to financial success and old-age security, attempting to scatter as many children as widely as possible across the economic landscape. This shotgun approach is the Samoan planter's way of reducing risks by diversifying investments—a strategy that people all over the world employ in conditions of economic insecurity.

4/Village Life

While living in Vaega I tried to plan my research activities for the next day or the next few days. Since most of my own activities depended on those of my neighbors, I often asked them what they planned to do the next day. Unfortunately, the standard replies to my question were unenlightening: *Se'iloa* (literally, "Until known") and *Ta'ilo* (the equivalent of "Search me"), both pronounced while quickly raising the eyebrows and jerking the head backward for emphasis. It almost got to be a game between Nu'u and me. I pressed him one day for a more revealing answer until he finally said, *Pule le alofa o le Atua* . . . , "By the power of God's love, perhaps I might go up to the taro plantation tomorrow." Just as I began to integrate his response into my own precise plans, he added, "Or I might go fishing." Then he compounded my consternation by wondering out loud, "But it's not known whether Selesele might return tomorrow from his journey to New Zealand."

I knew that if they expected Selesele to return tomorrow, Nu'u and the other *matai* would sit around all day playing dominoes and waiting for him. They would wait to honor Selesele with a kava ceremony, or *inu*, upon his return to the village (and, not incidentally, wait for the gift of $2 or $3 that Selesele would give to each *matai* at the conclusion of the ceremony to thank them for honoring him).

Nu'u's reluctance to state any firm plans for the next day was not just indecision or a verbal nod to the supreme power of God. Since individual plans are so often preempted by unforeseen events, people rarely take the trouble to make them. This is partly a matter of preference—an attempt to mix up village activities and inject some variety into what for most people is a pleasant but otherwise rather uneventful existence. It is also a recognition of the importance of weather in the lives of farmers and fishermen. And it is an acceptance of the twin facts that virtually everyone must sometimes accede to the wishes of a higher authority and that everyone has roles in family and village affairs that often take precedence over personal plans.

Of course, villagers do make and carry out many plans, including long-range ones. The common belief that Samoans are carefree children of Rousseau—living in a tropical paradise of easy bounty, worrying little and planning not at all for the future—is a fantasy. For example, Samoan villagers buy and

Photo 21. Vaega orators playing dominoes. The orators and a number of untitled men are engaged in constructing a house for another orator of the village, but as the day wears on the dominoes game in a nearby house attracts more and more players.

gradually stockpile over many years the materials to build a new house (and thus prevent idle funds from tempting them or their relatives). They plant new coconut groves that will bear no fruit for five to seven years. They clear new plantations from the virgin forest in order to assure their children of adequate lands twenty years from now when the forests are gone. They educate their children with an eye to future employment and their own security in old age. They collect fine mats and raise pigs for distribution at the disinterment and reburial of the bones of a grandfather who died a generation ago. They faithfully serve their families and maneuver politically over many years to secure an esteemed *matai* title.

Within the boundaries of each person's authority and responsibility there are many different tasks to be done. One of the many attractions of village life is that village planters tend to a variety of affairs at their own pace rather than carrying an employer's burden every day, as wage earners must do. While the arena of authority that most villagers command is circumscribed by others of higher rank, village planters enjoy a responsibility and freedom of action within their own arena that is often the envy of their wage-working neighbors. Unfortunately, the planters' freedom of action brings with it very little material compensation, as the following episode shows.

CUTTING COPRA

The village leaders had just lifted the prohibition on collecting coconuts from the inland plantations for four days. On the first day, Nu'u, his oldest son, and his brawny son-in-law, Faleupolu, rose just before dawn. They walked immediately to the two plots along the inland road that they share with the families of Nu'u's sister and nephew. If they did not get there early to collect coconuts, the other two households would take all the nuts. The second and third days Nu'u and the two young men rose somewhat later. Again without eating, they walked two and a half miles inland and almost half a mile off the plantation road to the newer plot of nearly a dozen acres that Nu'u owns by himself.

Nu'u had cleared and then planted that plot fifteen years ago with seed nuts supplied by the Department of Agriculture. The nuts were no different from those he could have gathered from his own plots, but in those years the Department was paying a cash bonus for every 500 trees planted—one of the government's many coconut replanting schemes. Nu'u also enticed other village men to help him by allowing them to harvest food from his large taro plantation. In return for the taro, men carried the sprouted nuts to Nu'u's plantation and planted them in shallow holes. Nu'u later collected WS $87 in bonus money from the Department of Agriculture and used it to purchase roofing tin to build a second open-sided house. That house is one of only two tin-roofed houses in the village that was not built with remittance money from relatives working in Apia or overseas (and those two houses are among the least ostentatious in the village).

When school got out at one o'clock, Nu'u's three younger sons (ranging in age from nine to fourteen) and their eleven-year-old sister met the others in the plantation. Only Meaalofa and Nu'u's oldest daughter remained at home to do the endless chores, while seven-year-old Tauvaga roamed the neighborhood with his friends. In the plantation everyone collected fallen coconuts, slashing the brush and vines back with machetes as they searched. Some nuts had fallen to the ground as much as a month before and had begun to sprout. Tired of searching the brush for fallen nuts, the oldest boys sometimes threw great chunks of lava rock to knock mature nuts right from the trees.

In each part of the plantation they carried the nuts to a central spot where they husked them on a stick cut from the branch of a cocoa tree. The stick was sharpened at either end, and they carried it with them from one collecting area to another. They wedged the stick into the rocky soil at a slight angle for husking. Even the smallest boy could husk coconuts by jamming the nut onto the pointed stick and using his full weight to tear the husk off, strip by strip.

They wove large baskets from split green coconut leaves and filled them with the husked nuts. Nu'u or Faleupolu then inserted a stout carrying pole (easily cut from a nearby sapling) through the tops of two baskets. He jerked the 150-pound load to his shoulder and carried it along the rocky path to a thicket near the road. There he covered the baskets with brush to hide them and keep them cool. On the last day of the harvest, they would load the baskets onto a pickup truck that would carry the nuts to their house for WS $6.

For two days Nu'u worked alongside his children, moving rapidly and steadily with the expertise of one who has done the same work for nearly forty years. Since the family had not been eating well during the harvesting, he came down from the plantation early on the third day and went net fishing at low tide with some other *matai*. Later, after they had divided their catch and each had taken their share home, the men gathered again at the pastor's house for hot Samoan cocoa and a spirited game of dominoes.

On the fourth and last day of the harvest Nu'u did not go to the plantation at all. Instead, he put on a formal brown *lāvalava*, a striped sport shirt, and mirrored sunglasses and rode the bus to Gataivai to attend a funeral in his sister's husband's family. He took two fine mats and $2 to the funeral, but he did not fare well in the exchange. He had hoped to receive several fine mats and perhaps a pork shoulder but returned with only one fine mat, $1 "bus fare," two tins of herring (which we shared for dinner), and three strips of *maio*, the thick blubber cut from the back of a half-cooked pig.

After four days of collecting nuts there were still two, one-acre plots that the family had not harvested at all. The ground on those plots was mostly lava covered with a thin layer of soil, and many of the trees were old. The thick covering of brush there would not be hiding many nuts. During the following weeks, the children could collect nuts there after school for the family's daily food.

On the fifth day, when the harvest had been completed, we all gathered in the shade of the banana trees next to Nu'u's house to cut copra. Tapu, a serious boy of thirteen, was busy from morning until late afternoon cracking the nuts neatly in two with a blow from the back edge of a machete. Still holding the split nut in one hand, he quickly pried the two halves apart with the tip of his machete to spill the clear water from the nut, then tossed the two halves onto the grass where they spun to a stop in the sun with dozens of others. All over the village I could hear the sharp crack of nuts splitting under similar blows.

Nu'u and I and Faleupolu sat cross-legged nearby in the shade. Taking each half-nut in turn, we cut out crescent slices of white meat with our short, blunt-ended copra knives. Polevia, then a boy of fourteen but already beginning to show the strength that Samoan men develop from their plantation work, soon joined us. With a self-effacing smirk that is appropriate for one who is presuming above his age, he proceeded to cut copra with as much determination and speed as I. As the day wore on, two neighbors who had finished their own labors strolled over and sat with us for half an hour, cutting copra and chatting, and pausing occasionally to roll a cigarette from Nu'u's tobacco.

Cutting the copra out in slices with a straight knife is slow work, and I wondered why villagers did not use the special curved knives that workers

Photo 22. Selesele Kalati and his family cutting copra beside their house. Asotasi stands opening a coconut with his machete, and the top portion of his new tattoo shows above his lāvalava.

on commercial plantations use. With a knife that is curved to fit the shape of the shell, a worker can quickly twist and pry the meat from a half coconut in one piece. Commercial plantations in Samoa have used the curved knife for decades. Many villagers work on these plantations, and virtually all of them are familiar with the knives, yet they continue to use the slower, straight knife in their own work. I had heard development experts cite this as evidence of the villagers' resistance to change. Since I was then cutting copra with several village planters, I took the opportunity to ask them about the curved knife.

E le masani. "We're not used to it," one of the men replied.

"Which way is better?" I asked.

"The curved knife is better. It's faster."

"Could you get one of the knives if you wanted one?"

Masalo. "Probably."

"Then why don't you use one?"

Ta'ilo. "Search me."

So much for the direct approach, I thought. Deciding to try another tack, I asked, "Suppose you wanted to use the curved knife, what problems would prevent you?" My neighbor, Tauatama, had a ready answer to that question.

"Commercial plantations have trucks and large, hot-air copra dryers. With the trucks they can carry the unhusked nuts to the dryer and then split them open with an axe. We have to hire expensive pickup trucks or carry the nuts on our backs, so we husk them first. In order to pry the copra out quickly with the curved knife, they need the leverage of the husk. Once we remove the husk, the nut is too small to hold tightly, and we have to use the straight knife to cut out the copra."

"And another thing," Nu'u added, "the commercial drying ovens are made with 55-gallon drums, so the smoke from the fire doesn't touch the copra. That way they can use the shells with the husks attached to fire the ovens. We can't do that in our ovens because the husks make too much smoke. We can't afford the oil drums, so we use only the coconut shells to build a smokeless fire directly under the drying rack. With only the shells to dry the copra, we have to cut it into slices so it will dry faster."

"And for that you need the straight knife?"

'*Ioe*. "Yes."

When we had finished cutting, Faleupolu and the younger boys carried the heavy baskets of fresh coconut meat to the copra oven behind Lautafi Keka's house and fired the oven with the coconut shells we had collected. If the coconut-shell fire was prepared carefully and the copra turned several times during the night, the copra would be dry enough to sell by morning. Then they would pack the rubbery, brown, and sickly–sweet smelling copra into the coconut-leaf baskets again and carry them a hundred yards up the road to Asiata Iopu's tiny copra shed, behind his one-room store and post office. Asiata Iopu would weigh the baskets on his ancient balance scale, which read out weights at even hundred-pound intervals with surprising frequency. Using a mysterious shorthand method of multiplication, he would then arrive at a value for the copra. Most of the total sale price would go to cancel the family's credit account at the store. Asiata Iopu would count out the few remaining dollars in cash. Our load of copra should weigh over 500 pounds, which would earn about WS $60 (US $50). After cancelling the debt, that would leave the family perhaps WS $15 in cash to last the next month.

With the copra finally cut and loaded onto the dryer, we stopped for the evening meal. No one had been to the taro gardens or to the reef, so we ate boiled breadfruit and canned-herring soup that Meaalofa and her daughter, Tauma'oe, had hurriedly prepared. Nu'u sometimes praised his hard-working wife for her cooking, but I never heard him (or any other village husband) comment on the quality of his wife's cooking—only on the speed. As we sat down to dinner that night, Nu'u tried to enliven the tired group by exclaiming, "Meaalofa's cooking really is fast!"

After dinner Nu'u and I rolled over onto the mats where we had been sitting (one of the many advantages of Samoan-style living). Two kerosene hurricane lanterns burned in the middle of the open-sided house, each lantern sitting atop an empty salt beef keg so the soft yellow light would spread farther through the house. The four youngest children were gathered beneath the hurricane lanterns doing their school work, while Nu'u's first grandson, not yet a year old, played on Nu'u's bare back. Meaalofa, who never seemed to rest, stitched a torn school uniform that she held just inches from her face. Behind her in the shadows Nu'u's eldest daughter and her husband devoured the last chunks of boiled breadfruit and the last spoonfuls of thick, canned-herring soup.

We all listened idly to the radio announcer as he read the list of people who had received money orders from overseas, telling them to appear at the Post Office the next day to collect their money. Nu'u and Meaalofa were not expecting any money since they are among the few villagers who have no relatives at all living overseas, but they were still curious to hear who did receive money.

When the Post Office announcements were over, the farmers' educational talk show began. It started as usual with a cheery musical jingle. We had all heard the jingle many times before, but that night, still aching from the days of harvesting and cutting copra, the words cut more sharply than usual. The joyous, singing voices urged us: *Sali le popo, tau le koko . . .* , "Cut the copra, pick the cocoa, save your money so you too can buy a new car or pickup!"

At that the children looked up from their lessons. Faleupolu and Si'uli stopped chewing, their cheeks bulging with chunks of boiled breadfruit. Meaalofa stopped sewing, and Nu'u's perpetual smile faded to a grimace, as if he had just swallowed something disagreeable. All heads turned toward the radio.

Kīgā kaliga i legā mea! . . . Nu'u muttered angrily in the coarse, common dialect. "That makes my ears hurt! They just sit around the radio station telling us to cut copra. Who knows how many hundreds of dollars they get paid every two weeks without cutting any copra. It is only *we* who cut copra."

FISHING

Next to politics and the growing of coconuts and taro, the most important task of men is fishing, for fish is the villagers' main source of protein. A technique called *'upega,* or "net," is popular with the middle-aged *matai* of Vaega. At low tide a half dozen men set a V-shaped net in a shallow area on the inland side of the reef and then drive the small reef fish into the net where they become entangled. The men propel themselves through the water with an alternating frog kick still clothed in their *lāvalava*, though the *lāvalava* billow around them immodestly as they move through the water. Once the drive is completed in one area, they untie their canoes from the nearby coral heads and paddle to another area where they repeat the process.

No formal rule prevents untitled men from employing the same technique. Only men of some means own nets, however, and men of means quickly become *matai*, so an untitled man is unlikely to own a net. Nor is there any formal rule to prevent an untitled man from joining a group of *matai* in their net fishing. They just think it is undignified for *matai* to associate with untitled men, and presumptuous of untitled men to seek the company of *matai*. Consequently, the two groups go their separate ways.

After my next door neighbor, Tauatama, received a nylon net from some overseas relatives, he sometimes set the net in the shallows near his house. He directed his many children in their attempts to net the silver and blue crevalle jacks that feed on the small fry that school among the rocks near shore. When the jacks tear into a school, the small fry jump in unison for their lives, plopping back into the sea like so many silver raindrops to be attacked again as the jacks come slashing through the water behind them.

Younger, untitled men and teenage boys usually drive fish without a net. They surround a shallow area of the lagoon, and by shouting and splashing they drive the few fish within the circle into crevices in the scattered coral heads. Then the young men submerge and spear the fish in their hiding places. They often use this method—called *mata*, or "goggles"—on the mornings of village council meetings. On these occasions they divide themselves into two groups with perhaps a dozen-and-a-half young men in each. One group stays ashore to prepare the ovens and the breadfruit, if it is in season, while the other group goes fishing. The fishermen return in about two hours with enough fish to provide a simple meal for their assembled *matai*.

Though it is against both village and national law, the young men sometimes supplement their efforts on these fish drives (and at other times) with a potent fish poison made from a small vine that grows in the plantations. The vine is called *'ava niukini*, literally "New Guinea kava." First they pound it, like the ceremonial kava root. Then they wrap the resulting pulp in a leaf, which they carry out to the reef. The fisherman dives down and opens the leaf package, spreading its contents around the bases of coral heads where it quickly kills or stupefies the fish. Its effect on reef ecology is devastating because it kills all marine life, including the coral. Villagers are well aware of this problem. As with other village laws, however, as long as infractions are uncommon and discrete, no attempt is made to completely halt the practice.

Fishermen sometimes set gill nets overnight in the center of the lagoon or in channels through the reef. Less often, someone sets a net just off the seaward face of the reef. One younger *matai* in Vaega has over a dozen sections of net that he occasionally sets at night over the sandy shallows in the center of the bay. It is a grueling chore because he must tend his nets all night to prevent other fishermen from stealing the fish. His catch was not sufficient to entice him to set his nets very often. Villagers say that they no longer set fish traps because their catch is often lost to passing fishermen.

In many areas of Samoa fishermen make huge fish weirs, or *pā i'a*, of chicken wire strung between wooden poles that they drive into the lagoon sand. They build the weirs across narrow lagoons at nearly right angles to the shore, the long arms leading back to small holding pens. When mullet or mackerel are running these weirs are very productive. No one builds fish weirs in Palauli Bay anymore. The smaller nylon gill nets that people set now are not very productive. Perhaps increased silt runoff into the bay has changed the lagoon habitat so that fish no longer run there in large enough numbers to make the weirs worthwhile.

Matai often troll over the reef in the predawn calm. If the fish are not biting along the reef, the fishermen work the rocky shallows along the shore for silver jacks. Each fisherman goes alone in his canoe, paddling slowly with his left hand between the outrigger struts while trailing a short line in his right hand on the starboard side of the canoe. By jerking the line with his wrist he jigs the tiny, polished-shell lure, making it dance and flash just under the surface of the water. This genteel form of fishing is appropriately called *toso*, "to pull."

Off Vaega, the catch from these predawn excursions is usually no more than a few thumb- or palm-size spotted grouper (the technique is more effective in some other areas). Occasionally someone lands a small tuna or a jack. Since my house stood on the shore of the lagoon, I often watched the men return just after sunrise, gliding silently by on the way to their separate homes.

A few men troll for octopus in a similar manner, except that the lure consists of a polished stone weight with two pieces of cowrie shell covering its top and a short, barbless wooden tail with horsehair whiskers sticking out behind. Talopa'u Feleti, a thin, middle-aged *matai* of Satufia, showed me his octopus lures and described the technique to me. Once an octopus leaps on the lure, the fisherman must pull it smoothly but swiftly to the surface before it has a chance to grab the coral or the canoe with its many powerful arms. Talopa'u warned me that the lure should only be used on the shallow, inner side of the reef. The large octopuses that live outside the reef can upset a canoe if they succeed in getting hold of both the coral and the canoe at the same time.

No one in the village currently trolls for larger fish offshore, a practice they refer to as *tuli atu*, or "chasing bonito." Milo Faletoi had an outboard-powered catamaran in Satufia, and the master of the Wesleyan High School had one, but neither boat is now serviceable. Two men in Pitonu'u have similar catamarans. They go deep-sea trolling during the day and bottom fishing offshore at night. Very few Samoans still use the traditional bamboo poles and pearl shell lures when trolling for bonito. Most now prefer the spool reels and plastic squid lures that are part of the foreign aid package that comes with the new aluminum catamarans and Yamaha outboard motors.

The catamarans generally troll around fish-aggregating buoys anchored several miles offshore. The Fisheries Office placed these bouys as part of a Pacific-wide tuna fisheries development project. The buoys relax the need for luck and skill in tuna fishing, but the local tuna fishery still suffers from a lack of both experience and expertise on the part of the fishermen. The boats are plagued by frequent mechanical failures, shortage of spare parts and trained mechanics, and expensive fuel. Fishermen also complain that fish have become scarce because of poaching by huge tuna seiners. Local fishermen claim that these boats sweep the coasts on their way back to the canneries in American Samoa. This practice will probably halt, however. In 1988 Western Samoa began operating a high-speed boat (a gift from Australia) to patrol the waters inside its two-hundred-mile economic zone.

Photo 23. A newly constructed bonito trolling canoe, or va'aalo, *on the beach at Neiafu.*

In spite of these problems, much progress has been made in the last fifteen years in establishing a commercial fishery for the local market. Catches are still too small, however, to sustain many full-time commercial fishermen, and there are virtually no exports.[1] Nevertheless, by 1988 many of the early problems had been solved, and in June of that year tuna were very plentiful and very cheap in the Apia market.

A few of the younger village men sometimes try their luck at bottom fishing with hand lines just outside the reef during the day, with uneven success. Perhaps Samoan fishermen today are not especially enthusiastic about or skilled at hook and line fishing because they lack the many generations of knowledge and experience that their island brothers possess in the eastern and northern Pacific. Like most of the island groups in the southwestern Pacific, Samoa has never had a tradition of hook and line fishing (e.g., Bellwood 1979, Buck 1930:676). Hook and line fishing brings the villagers little success today, and they seldom try it. Commercial fishermen out of Apia sometimes have better luck far off shore in deep water, though they complain that catches are not what they used to be.[2]

The oldest man in Vaega, Asiata Fatu, claimed to have been a successful hook and line fisherman in his youth. Neither he nor any other man in Vaega,

---

[1] The statistics presented in ADB 1985, which appear to show a very successful and rapidly growing tuna fishery, are internally inconsistent and generally of dubious quality.

[2] There is no ecological reason for line-fishing to be conspicuously unsuccessful in Samoa. For example, see Louis Becke's story, "Reo, the Fisherman," an account of the fishing prowess of a Malayan transient in nineteenth century Samoa (Becke 1967).

however, now claims the title of *tautai*, or master fisherman. Asiata Fatu offered to teach me what he could remember of his fishing knowledge, but to my regret I had to pass up the opportunity to spend several pleasant days talking with him in his house, for I was then burdened by the demands of my economic survey and the seemingly endless task of mapping plantation plots.

In villages such as Neiafu and Taga which lie along the open, rocky coast of southwestern Savaii, men and boys often fish with bamboo poles and tiny metal hooks from shore or off the seaward edge of a reef at low tide. Using hermit crabs or other bait they are often successful, which is fortunate since launching and retrieving canoes is difficult in those unprotected waters.

A few fishermen on the south coast of Savaii still catch sharks in the traditional way. They lure a shark alongside their boat and then one man leans over the side and slips a stout, braided-sennit noose over its snout. As the shark glides past the boat, the fisherman slides the noose past its jaws to its dorsal fin and then jerks the startled and thrashing shark into a vertical position with its head out of the water and its teeth gnashing wildly until a crewman bludgeons it to death with a wooden club.

In the same area of southern Savaii, two adjacent villages maintain a huge sennit net for catching turtles. Teams of fishermen set the net from boats in the shallow water along the cliffs where lookouts have spotted turtles. While the boats gradually close the net, two lines of swimmers drive the turtles into it.

As people have learned new skills, they have lost many traditional skills. For example, there appears to be no one in either Vaega or Satufia who knows how to mend a fish net properly. The nylon nets they use soon become torn and useless from snagging on the sharp coral or are severed by the teeth of sharks. Many of these same fishermen claim that their fathers or grand-fathers were master fishermen who made and repaired their own nets.

As late as the 1930s the *matai* title of Nu'u held exclusive rights to a particular kind of fishhook used for catching jacks. The hook was made of a fishbone tied at an angle to a stick that was then connected by a sennit line to a bamboo pole (Buck 1930:490). Today my friend Nu'u Vili, who was born in the late 1930s and now holds the Nu'u title, is completely unaware of the technique. He notes proudly, though, that the family was traditionally known for its expert fishermen. With the availability today of metal hooks, nylon fishing line, ready-made nets from Hong Kong, and canned fish at the local store, village fishermen have little use for or interest in traditional gear employing fish bones, sticks, and sennit.

The most common method of fishing in Vaega today is individual spear-fishing—a modern variation of an old technique. Men between about eighteen and fifty years old paddle out alone or in small groups at low tide to spear small fish in the shallow water above or just inside the reef. Rarely, a few of the more determined or adventurous men spearfish over shallow patches of coral outside the main reef. The fishermen wear goggles and fire five-foot-long spears made of one-quarter-inch diameter reinforcing bar. The spears are powered by two short lengths of surgical rubber tubing that they tie to a short, Y-shaped stick. They tie the rubber to the stick with narrow strips of cloth, and tie the free ends of the tubing together with another strip of twisted cloth that fits over a notch in the blunt end of the spear. They also wrap the "Y" between the two arms of the stick with cloth to make a shooting platform for the spear, which they fire slingshot fashion.

Hitting a moving target with one of these slingshots while swimming underwater, often in turbulent seas, is a very difficult skill to acquire. I always marvelled that the men were able to hit anything at all with the slingshots (I could not). Not surprisingly, their common prey are small reef fish that dart above the coral or hide motionless in it, though fishermen sometimes bring down a larger fish as it swims, or chance upon one hiding in a crevice.

ON THE REEF AT NIGHT

By far the most productive fishing technique is spearfishing on the reef at night. Samoans still call this technique *lama*, after the burning coconut-leaf brands that once provided the light, though kerosene pressure lamps and underwater flashlights have taken their place. Night spearfishing is very productive because many fish sleep at night in the coral, while the darkness brings the crabs and lobsters out of their lairs to scavenge across the flat reef top. Catches are usually much larger at night than during the day. Because of the cold, the loss of sleep, and the increased shark danger, the young men usually restrict their night spearfishing to Saturday nights—in preparation for the big Sunday meal, *to'ona'i*.

When I first arrived in Vaega, night fishermen used kerosene pressure lanterns. On Saturday nights I often saw sixty or seventy glowing lanterns out on the reef that stretches across the broad mouth of Palauli Bay. Soon I joined the other young men night fishing. We tied the kerosene lanterns at a slight angle to the prows of our canoes so the light would shine down into the water, but we did not light the lanterns until we arrived at the reef. We paddled out in darkness in order to save the kerosene for fishing and to avoid attracting the small needlefish that sometimes school on the surface. The aptly named needlefish's pointed beak can inflict a painful injury if the fish comes flying out of the water toward the light.

After a careful check of our gear on shore, we gathered in small groups just inside the pass. Moonless nights were best for spearfishing, when only the red glowing ash of a cigarette revealed the position of another canoe. When a group had formed, we paddled silently but swiftly out through the pass at Satufia and into the open sea. Then riding more delicately on the swells in our small canoes, we paddled seaward along the outer edge of the reef.

Like most other group decisions, we chose a spot to begin fishing by consensus after a short conference. In this case my neighbor, Vila, led the discussion. Vila is an excellent fisherman, and handsome and confident to the point of being dashing. He is a leader among the younger men. The decision on where to fish depended on the prevailing wind and current, and on whether anyone had beaten us to the reef. There is no use beginning before the night is dark and the tide has ebbed, but since most of the fish are speared while they lie motionless in the coral, the first group to comb an area usually spears the most and the biggest fish.

Upon reaching a starting point on the outer reef, we lit our kerosene lanterns and fiddled with them for a moment until the mantles were burning brightly. Then, adjusting our goggles and grabbing our spears, we slid carefully over the side into the sea. We tied the short bow lines around our waists so we could pull the canoes along behind us as we swam and still keep our hands free for spearing. Each man's lantern only lit the reef brightly to a depth of five or six feet, and the coral heads cast impenetrable shadows. The lanterns gradually dimmed as we fished, and we had to stop frequently to pump up the pressure and clear the soot from the jets. When rain showers blew across the bay, the lanterns needed constant tending, and within a few months they began to rust away from the salt spray. When the tide had risen and our lights began to die, we pulled our canoes together in the calm water behind the reef to rest, sitting gingerly on the coral while the others smoked.

There was no overt competition or boasting during or immediately after the fishing, but there was a good deal of peering into each other's canoes, and both considerable pride on the part of successful fishermen and quiet embarrassment on the part of unlucky ones. Though there was little overt competition, neither was there much cooperation during the fishing. On the reef it is every man for himself. As in other collecting activities, individual skill, speed of movement, and covering a wide territory are the critical elements of success.

Cold and exhausted after more than three hours of diving, we prepared to leave the reef. Vila and his older brother, Tevita, casually passed a few fish into the canoes of their unlucky neighbors and we shoved off for home, riding on the flood tide directly over the coral. Fishermen often divide their catch between them, or at least even out their luck a bit, especially if they have been fishing from the same canoe. This sharing is more than a gesture of friendship and good will. They know that both lucky and unlucky fishermen's families are waiting to be fed, and in the fickle business of fishing, everyone has bad days. In this and other cases of sharing between families, the main purpose is to even out each family's successes and failures over time. The purpose is not to even out resources between families.

As long as the fishing has been moderately successful, a portion of the catch will also go to the owner of the canoe or net, if one has been shared between the fishermen or borrowed from another person who remained on shore. A successful fisherman may give a fresh fish to any adult who comes to meet his canoe—a subtle form of bragging on the fisherman's part and begging on the greeter's part. A successful fisherman may also send a few fish—either fresh or cooked—by the ubiquitous child courier to the house of his sister or another of his relatives, the circle of gift giving enlarging somewhat with the size of the catch. Unfortunately, a fisherman's catch seldom satisfies even his immediate family, so the catch is usually shared no further.

A good example of the villagers' keen interest in new technology is their rapid adoption of underwater flashlights. In late 1981 some men who had worked in American Samoa returned to the village with underwater flashlights that had been imported from Taiwan. A few months later stores in Apia began selling the lights. By late 1982, just over a year later, kerosene lanterns were rarely seen anywhere on Palauli Bay. All the fishermen had switched to flashlights. On Saturday nights the surface of the bay is now dark. Only a scattered, eerie glow reveals the positions of divers where the beams of their lights play across the reef like search lights announcing the bizarre undersea opening of a Hollywood movie.

STALKING THE WILD *MATAPISU*

Vaega women do not fish from canoes (women in some other villages do very rarely). Vaega women do not even take canoes out to collect reef animals at low tide. At Vaega the reef is too far from shore, and a Vaega woman nearly drowned not long ago when her canoe overturned in the surf and she was swept into the sea. Women from Vaega sometimes meet on the sandy mud flats off Pitonu'u where they sit at low tide, probing with short knives for little cockles, bent-nose clams, and tiny whelks. The women of Satufia and other villages that lie on the open coast often collect octopus, clams, cowries, and other mollusks, as well as several kinds of sea urchins along the flat reef tops and sandy shallows that are exposed along their shores at low tide. The women are often accompanied by their daughters, who learn these reef-collecting skills at an early age, but the young girls are never allowed to go alone.

Along the rugged coast of southern Savaii, far to the west of Vaega, I sometimes joined a party of women from Gataivai collecting limpets, a small, single-shelled mollusk the Samoans call *matapisu*. I went there the first time with a New Zealand friend, Pascal Brown. Pascal was a teacher at the Wesleyan school during part of my stay, and he is a perceptive and enthusiastic student of Samoan affairs. The limpets stick to the wave-swept rocks right at the tide line, so we set out to gather them with the women just before low tide. We all clambered over the slippery rocks at breakneck speed, pausing only momentarily between waves to scrape the volcano-shaped *matapisu* off the rocks and into little flat baskets that we hung on cords around our necks like purses.

After we had traversed a couple of miles of rocky shoreline, we settled in the shade of some coconut palms by a broad, black sand beach. There we sorted our catch, wrapping the limpets in small bundles made from the glistening leaves of bird's nest ferns and tying them at the top with pieces of vine that the women plucked from the underbrush. As we carefully wrapped our harvest, the women entertained themselves with ribald jokes, using Pascal

Photo 24. Woman digging clams at low tide on the sand flats of Palauli Bay. Children playing nearby take the opportunity to show off for the camera.

and me as the butts. In the proper company, Samoans find these suggestive comments hysterically funny precisely because they are so outrageous and so improbable. If there was any possibility of following up on the suggestions, they would be highly embarrassing rather than funny. The jokes elicited peals of laughter from the women—the cruder the reference, the wilder the laughter—but only uncomfortable smiles from Pascal and me. We had learned, however, that in this situation the *only* defense is a good offense, and the more offensive the better. Finally giving in to the crudity of the occasion, our own quick and vulgar replies sent the women rolling hysterically on the ground.

These expeditions were good fun for the women (and for the dedicated scientist). It gave them a chance to step out of the reserved and dutiful character that most of them portray at home. It was a chance for lighthearted banter (and for some, even putting on the fool). It was also an adventurous change of pace from the humdrum of household chores. The expeditions were serious collecting trips, however. The women did not allow the fun to interfere for long with the important business of collecting a delicacy for the big Sunday meal.

FUGAFUGA BY MOONLIGHT

Even on what seemed to me a rare opportunity for completely frivolous fun, I was surprised that people were so serious and energetic about collecting food. The shallow, sandy lagoon off Vaega is ideal for expeditions to gather sea cucumbers by the light of the full moon. These late-night adventures are called *tolo gau* after the variety of edible sea cucumber called *gau*, which is the main quarry in some other areas. I cannot comment on the desirability of the *gau*, but the *fugafuga*, which is plentiful off Vaega, is of more interest as an exotic marine specimen than as *haute cuisine*.

The *fugafuga* bears some resemblance to a section of coconut husk torn from the nut, which perhaps only coincidentally bears the same name in Samoan. But the sea cucumber is more the size and shape of an over-large zuccini squash, the size one discovers in a backyard garden after being absent for a few days. Lacking any sort of internal support, however, the *fugafuga*'s posture is rather saggy, like the zuccini's after it has reclined on the compost heap for a couple of weeks. Though saggy in posture, the internal texture of the *fugafuga* is more like the coconut husk. While the taste is pleasant enough, its raw flesh is so hard that it cracks and crunches when chewed, like the joints of chicken legs or the ruffled lips of the giant South Sea clam. *Fugafuga* live in burrows in the sand of the lagoon during the day, but they come out at night. When the sea is calm and the moon is full their plump, mottled-white bodies are easy to spot in the waist-deep water.

The only preparation for catching *fugafuga* is to gather a few companions together. In Vaega this is usually a small group of young mothers who have no husbands to watch over them, with perhaps one or two adventurous older girls, and rarely a young man. The group strolls along the road to the seaward end of the village to await the ebb tide. This sojourn is a treat in itself, for only *matai* are normally allowed about the village after curfew. The little party is all smiles as it approaches a few middle-aged orators who have gathered in the bright moonlight to patrol the road. The guards challenge them in a brusk but familiar tone.

"Where are you going?"

"We are going to *tolo gau*," the young women reply, with just a hint of gay insolence in their voices as they stride past the night patrol.

The women might sit on a lava outcrop above the water and talk for an hour or more, nearly oblivious to the mosquitoes that swarm on still, moonlit nights. When the tide is sufficiently low the young women wade slowly out into the waist-deep lagoon, peering into the shimmering water for the telltale shape of the nearly motionless and defenseless animal. The women have to pick the *fugafuga* up carefully, however, or scoop it up with their toes if the water is deep. When disturbed, the sea cucumber excretes a sticky white glue from its intestines. The lucky hunter squeezes the intestines out into the water and then deposits the slippery, headless lump in a fold of her *lāvalava* as she continues her search. The view is spectacular from the center of the lagoon. The stars are out and the full moon overhead silhouettes the distant mountains in sharp detail, but the women stride through the water with their eyes on the chase.

A DELICATE BLUE WORM

By far the finest prize of the sea is the fluorescent blue-green *palolo* worm. The *palolo* is a slender, reef-dwelling annelid (*Eunice* sp.) that has trouble finding mates in the labyrinths of coral. To overcome their isolation the worms all discard their rear, reproductive sections at the same moment each year. This usually occurs just before dawn on the seventh day after the full moon in either October or November. These stringy, writhing egg sacks then rise in unison to the surface where they soon disintegrate, fertilizing each other in the open sea.

My first view of the activities attending a *palolo* rising was a memorable one. We began our preparations in the evening at Nu'u's house, hurriedly fashioning small dip nets. The nets were very simple. The frame was a length of woody vine bent in a loop and tied with thin strips of *fau* bark. Over the frame we draped an old piece of very fine-mesh cloth and sewed it on quickly, leaving a slight bag to the net. When the nets were finished we wove several coconut-frond baskets and lined them with the same fine-mesh cloth.

I was awakened at about three that morning by crowds of people walking past my house, talking and laughing gaily. An occasional pickup truck, jammed with passengers and its headlights glaring, tried to muscle its way slowly through the throng. The people came from the inland side of Vaega, from Pitonu'u, Mosula, Palauli, and even farther afield—places where there are no coral reefs, and thus no *palolo*. They were all headed for the far side of Satufia, where a broad coral reef hugs a deserted and sandy shore. By the glare of the headlights I could see that the people were dressed in their finest shirts and prettiest *lāvalava*, and many wore flower garlands around their necks or a single flower over one ear. An impressive party scene, I thought, for a stodgy village like Vaega.

I rushed over to Nu'u's house to see what his plan was. He had come down with a bad cold and wanted to wait until the last minute, so I went back to bed. Nu'u finally woke me at about 5:15 A.M. We had overslept, so we hurriedly launched the canoe from beneath the tree next to my house and paddled furiously out toward the reef. The canoe was old and waterlogged. With two of us in it there was only an inch of freeboard, but we powered rapidly across the glassy-calm lagoon, passing a few other latecomers as the first glow of daylight appeared over the Tafua headland.

I was startled when we reached the pass. There must have been a hundred canoes bunched up in the shallows just inside the turn of the reef. The canoes were jammed together, outrigger to outrigger and three or four deep, with a man standing beside each one in the thigh-deep water. The men—all *matai* who normally wear somber browns and blues—were gaily dressed in flowered shirts and *lāvalava*. Some wore garlands of fresh flowers, and many sported smiles on their weathered faces. With one hand braced on his canoe, each man peered at the surface of the sea in the half-light as he scooped up *palolo* a few at a time and flicked them into a basket in the prow of his canoe.

I had never seen one of the worms before, so I quickly scooped up a few for a close look. They were tiny blue-green wigglers, no bigger than a pencil lead and from one to several inches long. The worms were segmented into millimeter-long sections, each with an almost imperceptible pair of blue legs attached. I picked up one of the less active fragments and popped it into my mouth. Up to that point I had been speculating about the attraction of the *palolo*—whether it was really its taste, or just that it is only available once a year. The taste was exquisite—somewhat like lobster, but much finer and richer.

Unable to secure canoes of their own, a huge throng of young men, women, and children had gathered on the forested shore west of Satufia. Groups of people sat impatiently under the trees and on the little arcs of white sand that are scattered along the shore between lava outcrops. A few young men walked out into the darkness periodically to search with flashlights for the first sign of the *palolo* rising. When it finally came a shout went up, and the entire crowd waded out through the shallow water to the reef and began scooping up the tiny worms.

Out in the bay the men were working quickly and methodically, scooping *palolo* as the current swept them off the reef. In half an hour the sun was up, though obscured by clouds, and the *palolo* stopped rising. The crowd of canoes and their handlers then began to spread out down current, netting the worms that had risen earlier and been carried by the rising tide into the lagoon. In another half hour the faint light of dawn had given way to the heavy gray of an overcast day, and the *palolo* were gone for another year.

Returning home, Nu'u and I immediately began preparing the stone oven by building a big fire and stacking lava cobbles over it. Soon Meaalofa and the rest of the family arrived from Satufia, carrying their prize in three co-conut-leaf baskets. They plucked fresh leaves from the breadfruit trees and wrapped a handful of worms in each one for baking. We had captured enough worms to fill thirty-six of these individual servings, and everyone was excited at the prospect of eating their fill of Samoa's greatest delicacy.

Before the *palolo* even went into the stone oven, however, we were visited by a couple of distant relatives from an inland village. The two women ap- peared at the house from the direction of Satufia, each carrying a basket like our own, and their *lāvalava* still dripping from the surf. They stopped to chat.

"Alas, we are only two," one of the women sighed, "and our catch is not so large as yours."

As they rose to leave a few minutes later, Meaalofa placed a dozen packets of *palolo* in a basket for them, over their feeble protests. I watched Meaalofa carefully as she prepared the gift, trying to discern any hint of regret in her expression or movements. I saw her pause momentarily, glancing from our baskets to theirs as if she were both weighing the relative amounts of *palolo*

Photo 25. Baked palolo *worms in the dish at top center and in the breadfruit leaf at lower left in which they have been cooked. At the upper left are baked green bananas, and on the right a baked breadfruit split in half. These provide starch to go with the* palolo, *which is very rich. At the lower center is* palusami, *made from young taro leaves and salted coconut cream, wrapped in a wild banana leaf and then a breadfruit leaf, and baked together with the other food in the stone oven.*

and calculating all that would be lost, and gained, by the gift. Then she quickly added three more packets to the visitors' basket. Faleupolu appeared and handed the women another basket containing seven breadfruit. In a moment the visitors were gone and we were dining on the finest gift of the tropical seas.

WOMEN'S ACTIVITIES

Village women spend most of their time working at home. They may take the bus to Salelologa to purchase household supplies or rarely to sell home products in the market. Women sometimes travel farther on family business. If an activity has an air of novelty or importance, however, it will more likely be reserved by their husbands.

In addition to their duties at home, several village women and the pastor's wife run a half-day preschool in a small European-style house across from the pastor's residence.[3] Like the assistants at the pastor's own school (which

---

[3] Since Methodist pastors are not assigned to their own or their wive's home districts, they are technically visitors, rather than members of the village.

may include men as well as women), the preschool teachers are volunteers. The congregation collects a monthly donation for them during the school year, amounting to eight or nine Western Samoan dollars per month for each teacher. Women also meet for organized group activities. These almost always include some form of work, such as weaving or cleaning the church and its grounds. The younger women sometimes play cricket, and they may even compete in tournaments. These are special occasions, however, whereas young men may occupy the cricket pitch every afternoon for days or weeks at a time.

Women are responsible for tending and harvesting three varieties of pandanus trees which they grow in the mixed-crop lands immediately behind the village. The long, narrow leaves of a pandanus tree grow in clumps, projecting like a stiff green mop from the top of a spindly trunk. The edges of the leaves are armed with sharp barbs, and the women must cut the leaves carefully from the trees. They tie the leaves in large bundles, which they hoist onto their backs for the walk home, leaving the pale white bases of the leaves projecting out over their heads and the dark green tips dragging in the dust behind them.

From these leaves a woman and her daughters strip the barbs, then roll the leaves into coils which they boil in a large pot over an open fire. Later, they unroll the coils and spread the now-golden leaves in front of the house to dry. When the leaves are dry, they scrape the leaves one way and then the other with a dull knife to make them more pliable, then roll the leaves into great wheels for storage. If the woman's husband is sitting idly in the house, he may help with this task, but when it comes time for weaving only women participate. The weaver splits the leaves into long, narrow strands which she then plaits together to make several kinds of mats, including sitting mats and sleeping mats, which are usually bordered with colorful yarn.

The most finely woven of these is the 'ie tōga, or "fine mat." Women use a special variety of pandanus with thin, pliable leaves to make these mats. In order to make a finer weave, they may also split the leaves in half, top and bottom, and scrape them before splitting them lengthwise into strands for weaving. Fine mats are easily recognizable by the long fringe of unwoven pandanus strands dangling from the bottom, and by the row of bright red feathers affixed just above the fringe. Samoans formerly traded for these feathers from Fiji, which thus involved men at a critical stage in the manufacture of 'ie tōga. Today the women sew dyed chicken feathers on with a hand-crank sewing machine.

By the villagers' testimony, the 'ie tōga is the most important artifact of traditional Samoan culture. It is also the women's major contribution to ceremonial affairs. Unlike other kinds of mats, the 'ie tōga has no utilitarian value. Its only value comes from ceremonial gift giving and exchange (or now occasionally from sale to someone who needs it for exchange). As an item of exchange, fine mats share one of the properties of money—there is no limit to how many a household can use. Thus, weaving fine mats can absorb any amount of women's free time.

Photo 26. Glueing red feathers to the bottom of a new fine mat, or 'ie tōga. After the glue has set, the feathers will be stitched to the pandanus leaf mat.

Women's daily activities are delineated partly with an eye on keeping the women close to home. Women also have their own sphere of importance outside the home, however. They have their own council meetings run on the model of the men's. Each woman fills a ranked position according to the rank of her husband. Muta Asiata and the other leading women call council meetings to organize the women's many public duties, such as dispensing medicine in the annual campaign to eradicate filariasis (a disease that causes the swelling known as elephantiasis), or inspecting village homes to maintain standards of hygiene. The women's regular duties include cleaning the church and its grounds, and "guarding" their Committee Building and the district's medical clinic. These duties not only serve the important interests of the village, they also bring the women together, away from their husbands and children, and give them some relief from their monotonous household responsibilities.

In Vaega the Committee assigns several women each week to guard their Committee Building both day and night. The purpose is not so much to prevent vandalism as to maintain a constant presence in the building, so that it cannot be taken over for other purposes. Women on guard duty generally spend their time weaving mats and joking with their friends. They are sometimes accompanied by one or two of their young daughters, who help with the weaving during the day. These girls (along with infants and toddlers) may also sleep with their mothers in the large building at night.

In one sense the Women's Committee acts like a labor union. By running

Photo 27. A woman displays a fine mat before presentation at a funeral. The donor family has written their name with a Magic Marker on the fine mat at the lower left so there will be no mistake in assigning credit for the gift. At the same time, they have crossed out the name of a previous donor written on the lower right of the mat. As the host family receives fine mats from a group of visitors, they roll the mats in a bundle and affix the visitor's name to the bundle, written on a piece of masking tape. Fine mats come in all sizes and qualities, and the practice of affixing the donors' names prevents errors in the host's later reciprocation of gifts.

their own affairs and establishing their own routines (like guarding the Committee Building), the use the power of the group to free themselves occasionally from their daily household routines, whereas their individual efforts would often be inadequate.

In 1983 the Women's Committees of Vaega and the other area villages began to guard the district clinic to prevent vandalism, rotating the assignment each week among the Committees of the surrounding villages. The "guard duty," however, immediately took on a holiday air. Dressed in the flowered *lāvalava* or full-length dresses that are the uniforms of their particular Committee, the women decorated the hospital and grounds each day with fresh flowers. They spent the days and much of the nights in the Samoan-style house that adjoins the clinic, eating and laughing and playing dominoes— idle behavior that is more characteristic of *matai*.

When I passed the clinic on my way to or from Satufia, one of the women always called out to me to join them for tea or a game of dominoes. When I politely declined the offer, a more ribald invitation usually followed, setting the women on their ears laughing. I knew better than to join a large group

Photo 28. Muamua Logova and Tufa Tu'ua sitting in the doorway of Tufa's house in Vaega. The house was built fifteen years earlier with money Tufa's husband earned working in New Zealand.

of women like that. Conversation would likely take the form of good-natured but highly aggressive teasing and taunting, called *ula*. Over the preceding two years I had learned to hold my own in these friendly verbal jousting matches, in which both men and women excel. I even fancied myself a clever opponent, having previous experience in the very similar repartee that enlivens high school locker-room banter. But I knew I was no match for thirty unabashed Samoan ladies!

SLEEP CRAWLING, CLANDESTINE AFFAIRS, COURTSHIP, AND MARRIAGE

Shortly after guard duty began at the clinic, the women were successful in stopping a case of *moetolo* (or more formally, *moetotolo*), which translates literally into English as "sleep crawling." As on this occasion, some "sleep crawlers" decidedly do not have the woman's consent. The excitement at the Satupaitea clinic was caused by a village youth who attempted to *moetolo* one of the nurses in her chambers. Whether the youth hoped to be received by the nurse (who is several years his senior), I do not know. But the clinic was guarded by about two dozen women that night, and the nurse's shouts quickly brought them running to her quarters. The young man was discovered but managed to escape, achieving nothing more than seriously shaming himself

Photo 29. Tava'e Tunaali'i, aged fifteen, and Lili Ropati, aged thirteen.

and his family and embarrassing his village, which is charged with looking after the clinic and its nurses. He also cost his family a steer and some other goods, which they paid as a fine the next day to the village council.

The young man had been in trouble before and had only recently been released from jail. Since he had chosen to act out his desires in the one situation where he was almost sure to be caught, I suspect that one of his motives may have been to bring down a punishment on himself and his family—a somewhat perverse desire that is not unknown among delinquents in Western countries. The young man left the village the same night, however, and I did not want to upset people by asking indelicate questions about matters that were far from my stated research interests, so I did not pursue the matter.

Young women are usually so closely guarded by other family members (including both younger and older sisters) that the only rendezvous possible with a young man may be when she and her chaperones are asleep. An adventurous suitor may creep into the girl's house—where she sleeps fully clothed and surrounded by her sisters and parents. In each of the many cases I heard about from the principals themselves (two males and one female), the young man acted on his own initiative. None of the meetings were arranged beforehand. In all of these cases the young man hoped that the girl would not object to his presence, at least not to the point of rousing the household.[4]

---

[4] I heard stories of forcible rapes or attempted rapes during *moetolo* (and at other times), similar to those that Freeman (1983:247) reports from police records, but I heard them only third hand.

In most cases, after the young man woke the girl, they just talked for a few minutes before she sent him away. One young woman of eighteen told me that young men visited her frequently because her house is right next to the road but separated from the rest of the village. She always sent the young men away quietly, flattered by the attention but unwilling nevertheless. On one occasion she was visited by a serious suitor, however. She did not send him away and she became pregnant. A few months later when her condition had become obvious, the young man approached the girl's parents and asked their permission to marry her, but they refused.

As on that occasion, the young man may attempt intercourse if he is brave enough (or desperate enough). The girl may or may not allow this to happen. According to both male and female participants, even if the girl does go along, she may feign sleep in order to protect her own sense of modesty and perhaps her reputation should they be discovered. If she is not willing, and if the young man persists, she has merely to cry out to set the entire household upon the intruder.

Other opportunities for sexual encounters before or outside of marriage come in the plantations. Girls and young women are virtually always chaperoned, however, so these opportunities are only slightly less rare, difficult, and dangerous than sleep crawling. For example, one day while I was in a village that I visited regularly on the north coast of Savaii, I met a burly young friend named Mona coming down the road from the plantations. He carried no basket of taro, and he was holding his right hand, the knuckles of which were swollen and bleeding. I was not surprised since accidents are frequent in the plantations. In response to my question, however, Mona smiled a vicious smile and told me that he had just broken the jaw of a young fellow he had caught sitting under a breadfruit tree with his 20-year-old sister. A bit hasty and overprotective, I thought, to break the poor guy's jaw just for sitting and talking with his sister. Mona knew better than I, however, that there was only one reason for a man and a woman to be alone together. And right he was, for nine months later his sister gave birth to twins. The girl's parents tried in vain to force the young man to marry her. He had been visiting from another village, and when he got out of the hospital he returned to his natal village.

These rare, clandestine meetings are usually seen by the girl as an integral part of courtship leading to marriage, rather than being overtly promiscuous acts. Young men, on the other hand, sometimes have a more cavalier view of these encounters. As long as both participants have finished secondary school (before which time any interest in the opposite sex is considered to be highly inappropriate), however, these secret liaisons generally do lead to marriage.

If the couple is discovered or if the girl becomes pregnant, their families may follow one of several courses. If the couple and their families all agree, the couple may begin to cohabit openly—that is, they marry. If one or the other set of parents opposes the marriage, they may send their child (usually the girl) away to live with relatives in another village. They take this measure partly to punish the child and partly to prevent a recurrence. Young couples often elope, usually to the home of the groom's relatives in a distant village. They return to the bride's family when her relatives have finally accepted the (common law) marriage as an accomplished fact.

Young couples frequently shift their residence several times between the wife's and the husband's families. Unless their prospects are notably better with the wife's family, however, they eventually settle permanently with the husband's family. This is done primarily because people almost always pass their family histories, *matai* titles, and the authority they confer to men, and families are very reluctant to pass that knowledge and authority to a son-in-law. Consequently, prospects are usually dim for the son-in-law if the couple remains with the wife's family.

Another reason young men prefer to settle with their own families is that by the time they marry, they have already begun to develop their own plantations on their family's lands and they do not want to give them up by moving in with their wife's family. If the couple does settle with the wife's family and develops plantations on her family's land, the husband stands to lose those plantations if the couple separates or if trouble develops between the man and his in-laws and the couple has to relocate. A young talking chief named Fa'atamala had been living with his wife's family in Vaega for three years when her parents evicted him. He had objected openly when his mother-in-law beat his young children, and they threw him out for his insolence. His wife and children went with him back to his family, but he lost his taro plantation in the process.

Elaborate American- and New Zealand-style society weddings are common in the Apia area, complete with printed invitations. Formal weddings are very rare in rural villages, however, where only pastors, the children of pastors, and very wealthy villagers marry in half-Western and half-traditional ceremonies. Common folks just begin to cohabit without any ceremony at all. At some later time, often after the birth of their first child, the pastor and the couple's families usually pressure them into undergoing a very brief marriage ceremony during the regular Sunday church service.

Several people told me that a prospective groom could avoid all the hassle and intrigue of clandestine courtship by declaring his honest intentions either directly to the girl's parents or through a trusted intermediary, accompanied by an appropriate gift of food. If the girl's parents agree, that constitutes a formal engagement. The couple may then be seen together in public without scandal. According to some people, she might even visit the young man alone at his house. I know of no recent case where this actually happened, but the same effect is sometimes unwittingly achieved by young Westerners in Apia when they invite girls from traditional Samoan families to go out to the movies. The girl replies demurely that he must ask her parents for permission. Unless the family is familiar with Western customs, both the girl and her parents may take the young man's request as a formal proposal of intent to marry, for a proper Samoan girl should never be seen consorting with a man for any other reason. Even if the parents allow the girl to go out, the couple will be

Photo 30. High school girls of Vaega and Satufia bathing at the spring on the grounds of the Wesleyan school. Since they are still in school, they are forbidden to show any active interest in boys. Most of them will marry in the first year or two after graduation, however, and begin raising children soon after that.

accompanied by one or more chaperones. This has the double advantage of protecting the girl from disrepute and financing a trip to the movies for her sisters, her cousins, and perhaps even her mother.

Since all unchaperoned encounters are clandestine, it is difficult from the public's point of view to distinguish acts of force from those of mutual consent. This causes very serious problems for a girl if she is attacked. People told me a story of a girl who had committed suicide after being attacked, and other stories about girls who, feeling humiliated and defiled, had accepted their attackers as their husbands. While I cannot corroborate these stories, their moral is clear enough. I made no inquiries into these matters and hence cannot estimate how common such acts are. Nevertheless, I know that several of my friends and acquaintances in various rural and urban villages became the victims of rape, attempted rape, and incest. In none of these cases did the victim report the crime outside a small circle of friends. When I asked one young rape victim why she had not gone to the police, or at least told her family, she replied that she did not want to "waste her brothers." She explained that if her brothers found out what had happened, they would surely kill the man who did it, and then they would go to jail for their crime.

Contemporary Samoans apply a familiar "double standard" toward unmarried males and females. Young, unmarried men are allowed (or even encouraged by each other) to have affairs (though only with unmarried

Photo 31. Suitors must be very cautious, for a young girl's brothers and other relatives keep a close eye on her.

women). The same activity is forbidden for girls, whose virginity and reputation are social assets as well as moral virtues. Most families go to great lengths to guard and restrain their young girls. In the face of such constant chaperoning, most girls have to actively conspire in order to meet privately with a lover or suitor. Giving birth out of wedlock is even more damaging than losing her virginity or gaining a reputation for looseness (and more telling than unsubstantiated gossip).

A girl's motives are undoubtedly complex in these affairs. Some escapades occur when Samoan parents grow lax or permissive in their supervision. Other episodes occur when girls and boys begin to actively assert their independence from parental and family authority. In other cases, engaging in clandestine affairs is a way of covertly rebelling against and striking out at that authority, rather than being an expression of freedom from authority. By engaging in sexual conduct that Samoans consider illicit, an unmarried girl demeans and shames not only herself but also her family. That is why her brothers, her parents, and even her sisters chaperone her so closely, and why they may severely chastise her and beat her and her lover for a transgression. By crossing forbidden sexual ground, Samoan girls can covertly express rebellious and hostile feelings that they are not able to express openly. One young mother told me that she had an affair and became pregnant because, as she said, "I wanted to do something to hurt my parents."

According to villagers, sexual escapades of this kind are an increasing problem. Young Samoans usually express feelings of anger and hostility toward their parents and other authority figures only indirectly, sometimes in ways that hurt their families indirectly by first hurting themselves. Engaging in illicit sexual affairs is one such form of expression that is available to both young men (through *moetolo*) and to young women, though primarily to young women. It is primarily young men who resort to the far more drastic act of suicide.

A SUICIDE EPIDEMIC

Suicides were rare in Western Samoa throughout the early 1960s. Then in the late 1960s and early 1970s the number of suicides began to climb rapidly. In 1976 the number of suicides jumped to twelve out of a total population of about 155,000 people. By 1981, there were forty-nine. Western Samoa and two other small Pacific states (Truk and Yap in Micronesia) had the unfortunate distinction of leading the world in youth suicides.[5] The rate of suicide among young Samoan males was nearly 2 per 1,000 individuals per year— ten times higher than the current "epidemic" of youth suicide in the United States. Thankfully, the numbers have declined in Western Samoa since the peak in 1981, but suicide is still common.[6]

Seventy-five percent of the suicide victims are between 15 and 24 years old, with an average age of 20 years. Two-thirds are male. Most suicides by young people in Western Samoa are "anger" or "rage" suicides.[7] Samoans are taught to love, obey, and respect senior members of their families, including primarily their parents, their elder siblings, and their in-laws. They also depend on these people for virtually all of their personal support. Expressing anger or open hostility to them is strictly forbidden.

These relationships are not free of stress or ambivalence, however. Many Samoan parents raise their children with measures of authority and physical punishment that people in the United States now frown upon in an era of increased permissiveness. Earlier generations of American parents more often followed a disciplinary style of "spare the rod and spoil the child" that is similar to current Samoan practice. Many Samoan parents believe that physical punishment is the quickest and most appropriate method for teaching children to behave properly. They also believe that parents who really love their children will discipline them. Older children, who often care for their younger siblings, may be even more severe than parents in the punishments they administer. Practices are not completely uniform, of course, among (or

[5] For excellent discussions of the problem in Micronesia, see Rubinstein (1985), Hezel (1985, 1987), and Polloi (1985).

[6] In the first half of 1989, as I write, the suicide rate has again jumped to near record levels.

[7] Bowles (1985) and Macpherson and Macpherson (1985) provide excellent data and discussions of this sad chapter in Samoan affairs.

even within) families. The norm, however, is more severe among Samoans today than among Americans.[8]

The relationship between parents and their children contributes to suicides among young people. The great majority of suicides in Western Samoa are triggered by an argument, rebuff, or scolding from a parent or parent figure, and less often by an older sibling or a spouse. While the triggering incident may appear trivial, it is almost always part of a long pattern of denial or rejection that results in feelings of repressed anger, worthlessness, hopelessness, and isolation for the child. These feelings are all magnified when the sources of the problem are the same family relationships that young people would normally rely on for their support.

Being unable to express their anger openly, lacking other sources of support, and feeling that physical punishment is a proper response, young people sometimes redirect their anger inward. In the process of physically punishing themselves, they indirectly inflict pain on the people they hold responsible. The family's feeling of guilt adds to the pain of their loss. That guilt is often multiplied by silent public censure, for in Samoa, as in America, the family of a suicide victim shoulders much of the responsibility for the act.

The method of choice in all suicides is drinking the weed killer, paraquat. The poison is very lethal, and there is no antidote or cure. Nevertheless, the victim's agony may be prolonged for days or even weeks, depending on the amount ingested. In the case of anger suicides, this has an obvious though grotesque advantage over other methods. The prolonged suffering allows the dying person to confront family members with his or her agony, witness their grief, and hear their declarations of love and repentance before finally succumbing to the poison.

There were no suicides in Vaega during my stay (or since). One young man, long resident in Apia, did kill himself with paraquat, and his family brought his body back to Vaega for burial. A teen-age girl in Vaega drank Clorox, but was stopped in the act and did not suffer greatly. Everyone in the village was alarmed, though, and thankful that no paraquat had been available to her. At the time no one suspected the cause of her problem, but later events showed that she was repeatedly the victim of incest by her uncle, with whom she was residing. The younger brother of a close friend of mine (not a Vaega resident) also killed himself with paraquat. All of these tragedies—the only ones with which I am personally familiar—follow the pattern I presented above.

The characteristics of Samoan family life help to explain why some people kill themselves (and why they use paraquat). Since these characteristics have remained relatively constant for many years, however, they do not explain the rapid increase in suicides of the late 1970s and early 1980s. The correlation of the suicide epidemic with the rapid modernization of the post-independence

---

[8] Samoan parents may physically punish their children, but they never condone injuring a child in any way (though this sometimes happens in Samoa, as it does in the United States).

era in Western Samoa is no accident. The desires and expectations of young people are changing very fast. Radios, movies, television, videos, and New Zealand-style education all give people new ideas and new dreams. Perhaps most importantly, the dramatic increase in overseas migration and travel has opened up a different, and in many ways very attractive, world of new possibilities. The closeness of that other world sometimes makes patience difficult, yet the actual pace of social and economic change makes the fulfillment of these expectations very unlikely. Rapid social change alone is not the problem. Suicide is uncommon in American Samoa, where change has been far more rapid and dramatic than in Western Samoa, and where half of the population is made up of migrants from Western Samoa. The real problem appears to be *uneven* change, specifically the lag between young people's growing expectations and the social and economic realities in which they live.

The two main objects of people's desire are wealth and personal freedom (what Samoan's call *sa'oloto*). The two are closely related. Very few parents of today's secondary school graduates ever passed beyond (or even finished) primary school. To these people, a high school education appears to be the ticket to a good job, a good income, and a measure of personal independence. The harsh reality is that the economy creates only one new job for every several secondary school graduates.[9] Those who do find employment currently earn annual incomes of only WS $1,000 to WS $3,000 (US $500 to US $1,500 at 1988 exchange rates).

Young people find that their rising expectations of personal freedom are just as difficult to fulfill. With limited (or no) economic resources, young people remain housed with and mutually dependent on their parents, siblings, and often other relatives. Consequently, they also remain subject to their elders' authority. These elders were born and raised in a different and far more traditional era. Their children now want and expect more personal freedom, yet both economic conditions and parental attitudes frustrate their desires.

A recent report by the Suicide Awareness Committee in Western Samoa places most of the blame for youth suicides on the "generation gap" (*Samoa Times*, 15 January 1988, pp. 15–16). The report cites four major factors that contribute to youth suicides:

1. "The inability to facilitate a two-way communication between authority figures and subordinates in a rigidly structured system. This leads to frustration and an inability to cope with unexpressed feelings."
2. "The strong control of authority figures expecting obedience and subservience. This leads to rebellion."
3. "Social commitments which encourage people to live beyond their means until they can no longer cope economically."
4. "The instability of families resulting in children with problems of insecurity, rejection and low self-esteem."

[9] No precise figures are available.

As a primary method of reducing the number of suicides, the report urges that "the government consider ways of equating wages with the prevailing standards of living in order to reduce economic stress." Fortunately, the public awareness campaign itself has reduced the number of suicides. On several occasions I heard worried parents say that they have to be more lenient with their children now, lest they run the risk of losing them. Thus, the epidemic of suicides is helping to achieve for others the increase in personal freedom that none of the individual victims could gain for themselves.

LOOKING FOR WORK

For the people of Vaega, the search for wage work usually takes them out of the village, often permanently. Povi, for example, is a taxi driver in Apia, bouncing around the city streets in a Toyota Corolla that has been beaten almost beyond recognition. Povi has a certain flair to him though. His sideburns reach down to his jaw and his hair curls away at the back of his neck. He returns to Vaega every few weeks to see his wife and children and to strut along the village road in his blue jeans. He is a member of one of the village's largest families, and though they own over 30 acres of prime coconut groves, there is little need for his labor at home.

Uosi is the adult son of one of the village's smallest and poorest families. They own one of the smallest acreages of coconut land in the village, a scant 4.3 acres, which is not enough to support himself and his young family. He has recently moved his wife and three children to Upolu, where he now works as a resident laborer at a government coconut plantation. When I met him recently on the street in Apia he was barefoot, his *lāvalava* was worn and soiled, and he hung his head slightly as he talked. He was the last of his family to leave Vaega.

Fili and Lili, lovely twin sisters, went to live with relatives in Apia when they finished high school. Fili found work as a clerk in a dry goods store, while Lili cared for her relatives' children and attended to the household chores. In 1984 Fili returned to Vaega with her new husband, but they have since moved to his village.

Laea is a technician with a modest salary, trained in New Zealand on a government scholarship. He is thoughtful and intelligent, and he does his work well. I like him because there is no hint of aggression in his easy laugh, and I trust him completely. At his work he often speaks near-perfect English, but he never spoke English to me (even at first when I was still struggling with Samoan). That is the rule with most Samoans, but while the others were simply protecting themselves from embarrassment, I always felt that Laea spoke Samoan to me for my benefit rather than for his. When I was in Apia I could always find Laea either at work or at the Return Service Association, where he spent all of his off-hours playing billiards and sipping from quart bottles of the local Vailima beer, his face and girth puffy from years of heavy drinking.

Like many other villagers of his generation who dreamed of and then achieved success, Laea has found that the reality falls short of his expectations. He lives in a small house near the crowded center of town, where he supports his family and his wife's parents on his modest salary, often hosting his own relatives when they visit the city. For years he has plotted an escape to New Zealand, but both he and his wife are ambivalent about leaving and they continually postpone their plans.

MIGRATION

Some people move to the city or overseas to escape the more circumscribed world of their family and village, but it would be a mistake to assume that all or perhaps even most young migrants choose to leave. Many are forced out of the village and away from their families by their desire to earn more money to support their parents, or to secure a better education and a better standard of living for themselves and their children. Samoan parents leave very few important decisions to their children, and the decisions concerning which children will migrate, when and where they will go, and what they will do are no exceptions. Some of those who want to leave will have to stay. Conversely, some of those who want to stay will be sent overseas or to Apia to seek work. These migrants may work for a few months or years and then return to settle in the village, but more often they settle permanently where the jobs are.

Kinship ties are critical for migration, which is an important reason for villagers to maintain active links with their extended families. In order for a nuclear family to send its first member overseas, the parents seek financial and logistical support from members of their extended families who have already migrated. The previous migrant arranges the immigration and work permits, pays the airfare, helps the new migrant find work, and lodges the newcomer.

Once a family's first migrant becomes established overseas, he or she can arrange for and support the next child. Pressure might come from the parents, but earlier migrants also want to sponsor new migrants. They usually miss their families and want other members to join them overseas. And as their own financial obligations increase, perhaps because of starting their own families, earlier migrants also begin to tire of supporting the folks back home. These first migrants then sponsor younger brothers or sisters who come to take up the burden with renewed vigor. Thus, the interests of previous migrants tend to perpetuate the flow of new migrants out of the village, just as each new departure makes the remaining members more dependent on support from overseas.

A SON GOES TO NEW ZEALAND

Many villagers have made their way to New Zealand and American Samoa. When Milo Faletoi's oldest son, Fauena, finished high school, Milo examined the options carefully since he was anxious to place his promising son in the best possible position. Fauena is tall, strong, and handsome, a straightforward and pleasant fellow, and a good friend. When Fauena finished school, he worked for a time in the family plantations and as crew on his father's fishing boat. Neither work provided a reasonable income for this capable young man or his family, so Milo began to look elsewhere. At one point Fauena applied to join the tiny national police force, which is a respectable but not very lucrative position.

Having few relatives overseas, Milo's options for his son's future seemed limited, until he struck a deal with another relative in Apia. Fauena worked for several months as crewman on his uncle's fishing boat, in return for which the man's own son in Auckland paid Fauena's airfare over and set him up in his household. Though embarked on a great adventure, Fauena was genuinely sad to leave his family and his village, and he confided that he would not have gone if the choice had been his alone. We were just as sad to see him go. I saw many of my friends and neighbors leave Samoa, and I experienced some of the loss that all of the villagers feel as their friends and relatives trickle away to distant lands.

Once in Auckland, Fauena quickly found work at a textile mill, monitoring a machine on the night shift. It was easy work, and with overtime he made nearly NZ $350 (US $300) a week, ten times what he could have made in Samoa. Fauena soon joined one of the Samoan churches in Auckland so that he could meet other young Samoans. Since the mill was an hour and a half by bus from where he lived, however, and since he wanted to save as much money as possible for his family, he was left with little time or money to spend. He contributed his share to the expenses of the household where he lived and sent NZ $100 back to his family nearly every month. He saved most of the rest of his pay for his triumphal return to the village. Through hard work, thrift, and some amazing good luck, Fauena managed to amass over NZ $8,000 in one year. Additionally, relatives and a few older migrants from his home village who were already living in New Zealand added small gifts of their own.

Fauena's return to Satufia was triumphal indeed! He built a modest, European-style house for his parents, and he handed out money to everyone who greeted him. Then late at night we gathered discretely in the flower garden at the house of a friend who lives on the inland side of Satufia village. There we sat in the moonlight, drinking Fauena's beer and entertaining ourselves with music from his new cassette player. The drinking was followed by a meal of a small pig that the host of the party had baked in Fauena's honor. Three weeks later Fauena returned to Auckland to resume his new life.

Photo 32. Fauena Milo and Panoa Umama'o in the author's house. Fauena has just returned from his first year working in New Zealand.

A HOMECOMING CLASH

Few migrants return as quickly or as successfully as Fauena. Tupa had been living in New Zealand for fifteen years. He returned to Vaega for the first time when his mother became ill. Tupa told me that he had wanted to return earlier but could not afford to. As a child he had been at the top of his class in school, so his family sent him to secondary school in Apia. When finished, he went to work in the family plantations. Before he returned to the house the first evening with a load of taro and a searing pain in his shoulder, Tupa knew that the life of a village planter was not for him.

His father, an important chief in the village, soon arranged for Tupa's passage to New Zealand. He left when he was only nineteen years old—the first of his family to migrate overseas. Today Tupa is a moderately successful member of Auckland's working class. At first he sent money regularly to his parents, totalling perhaps WS $800 (US $680) per year. Then as he married, had children, and fell behind on his house, car, and furniture payments, he stopped sending money. His father visited him twice in Auckland, presenting him with a *matai* title on the last visit. Tupa said that he did not want the title, but his father explained that Tupa needed a title so he would not be ashamed to participate in Samoan church affairs with other men who were *matai*. Though Tupa was sometimes unemployed and had trouble making ends meet at home, he finally returned to his natal village with WS $700 in cash and presents—enough to make a respectable splash with his family and childhood friends.

Out of respect for his father and for Tupa's status as a *matai*, the chiefs of Vaega received Tupa with a formal kava ceremony. At the conclusion of the ceremony Tupa distributed WS $75 to the chiefs to thank them for the honor. That night and the next day several other chiefs and a few chiefs' wives came to formal dinner receptions bearing gifts of food. To these guests he distributed another WS $127. Later that night when the guests left, he gave everyone in his family gifts of cash and clothing, and he gave his father WS $200 on top of that.

On the surface it appeared to be a successful homecoming, but underneath there was an air of tension and stress. The homecoming was a financial and emotional strain on Tupa. He felt ill at ease in the village he had left so long ago. The ceremonies made him especially uncomfortable. He was expected to play a central role in them, but because he had spent most of his life in Apia or in New Zealand, he was only partly familiar with the elaborate etiquette. He could not even sit comfortably cross-legged on the floor any more. Tupa said that the visit was hard for him because this was his first return and because he had recently become a *matai*. On his next trip, things would be easier. We were all so preoccupied with the events of his homecoming that we did not realize until late the second night how difficult the homecoming was for his younger brother.

Tupa had given WS $15 to each of his two brothers and to his brother-in-law. Su'e, the youngest brother, had taken the money straight to Salelologa where he got drunk with one of his friends. Su'e had been trying for several years to obtain his own permit to enter New Zealand, but because he had a minor police record he had never succeeded. Su'e was pleasant to me and to his friends, but he sometimes had the troubled look of a young man who was trapped in a barely tolerable situation. He sometimes beat his young wife severely, sending her fleeing to her parents' home in a western village. Perhaps Su'e realized that he would never make much of himself in the village, or perhaps he simply believed that one day he would leave the village and his stern father behind, so it mattered little how he stood in their eyes. He never put much effort or care into either his own affairs or his service to his family and village.

I was talking quietly that night with Tupa about his life in New Zealand when we were startled by the first cries of rage from the village green—the sounds of a fierce battle between drunken friends. Presently we heard sounds of scuffling on the gravel road, then horrid screams: *Fasi oti! Fasi oti! Fasi oti!* "Kill! Kill! Kill!"

A crowd of men dragged Su'e, thrashing and screaming wildly, toward the open house where we sat with his aging father in the full light of a gas lantern. When the mob reached the light outside the house, I could see Su'e's powerful older brother and several other relatives and neighbors struggling violently to hold him. Su'e was in a white rage, his face almost unrecognizable, thrashing about, kicking and swinging wildly at his captors and screaming "Kill! Kill! Kill!"

Suddenly Tupa leaped to his feet and rushed out of the house at his screaming brother, punching at his face with both fists, trying to knock his brother unconscious in a desperate attempt to stop the public humiliation of himself and his family. Su'e only redoubled his screams and his thrashing. His father and I sat motionless within the house, the old man rigid in stoic silence, and I petrified in sorrow and embarrassment. With a wave of his hand the old man ordered the mob away from his house. They dragged Su'e, still screaming and fighting, into the night.

It seemed like a very long time that the old chief and I sat together in silence. Then Su'e returned. He was guarded closely by a neighbor, but he came slowly, quietly, with his shoulders bent forward and his legs wavering beneath him. He was still quite drunk. His clothes were torn and dusty from the fight, and he was crying softly. He kneeled with his guard on the doorstep, facing his father across the expanse of bare concrete. I could hear the shuffling of feet on the gravel road outside, where his other captors stood ready, just beyond the ring of light. Su'e's head was bowed, but I could see that his face was flushed red and his mouth was swollen. He tried twice to speak, but each time began to sob. Finally, in short, nearly breathless phrases, he apologized to his father.

The old man looked away, then without expression he ordered his youngest son to leave his family and his village.

'Ave 'ese. "Take him away."

The audience was over. Su'e trembled, his eyes fixed on the cement floor.

Fa'afetai le 'ese, he whispered. "Thank you for sending me away." Then he rose slowly from his knees, and with his head still bowed, he and his guard backed out of the house.

We sat in rigid silence for twenty minutes. Then one of the village orators arrived to inform the old chief of the fine they would impose on him and his family.

At dawn the next morning Seselesele Tasi, the village's leading orator, appeared at the village green with a delegation of six other orators. Facing inland toward the village, he announced the standard fine for drunken brawling in the village: two large pigs and two ten-pound boxes of ship's biscuits. In addition to the fine, the orators banned Su'e from the village for one year, and on his return he was to pay another fine to the village. The friend that Su'e had fought with received a lesser fine. The orators then walked up to the old man's house where Seselesele Tasi shouted out the announcement again. Finally, they walked to the far end of the village where he repeated it once more.

Su'e's father was not in the house that morning to hear the announcement. He and Tupa and another of his sons had left long before dawn in a hired pickup for Salelologa, where they hoped to buy two cases of canned fish and two boxes of biscuits to pay the fine. Villagers are free to substitute a case of canned fish (worth WS $35) or a similar item for each pig (worth WS $50 to WS $100), and they can substitute two boxes of biscuits (WS $10 each) for each case of fish. A fine mat of any size (worth WS $8 to WS $30) could also substitute for a pig. This way the village maintains a standard fine but allows some discretion on the actual cost and composition of the payment, depending on a family's particular circumstances.

When the group left for Salelologa, they woke the rest of the household, who sat up and discussed the affair in animated tones for two hours until sunrise. By the time the men returned in the pickup, the village *matai* had long since assembled in a high chief's house at the other end of the village, where they waited to receive the fines.

There was no discussion of guilt or innocence, no probing questions or impassioned pleas. Like most Samoan affairs, the previous night's transgressions had been acted out in full sight of the village. There was no need for a trial, and the chiefs had already imposed the fine according to the village's unwritten standards for various offenses. Nor did the youths who had fought with each other appear at this formal proceeding. Unless there is a question concerning the facts that can only be resolved by direct questioning, the accused do not face the council in public—largely out of fear that their presence will spark violent reprisals from the aggrieved or their relatives. Unlike most Western systems of law, which emphasize the punishment of guilty individuals, the traditional Samoan legal system emphasizes the restoration of peace and at least the public expression of harmony between social groups.

After Su'e's rampage, harmony was restored and the village propitiated by the payment of fines. The *matai* of each young man's family first apologized to the village and then presented his payment to the other *matai* who were assembled around the inside perimeter of the house. The chiefs were far more sober than usual, and several of them made angry speeches about the unruliness of youth today. When the speeches were over, the *matai* divided the food and fine mats among themselves. By this time the group had regained its customary joviality, and the last biscuits were tossed around the house to the oldest men while everyone bundled up their share of the fines in a scrap of cardboard or an old basket and sent it home in the hands of a waiting child. The fines were thus divided among all of the village families, including those who had just paid the fines. It was the village's peace that had been broken, and the whole village must be recompensed.

Tupa left the next day for New Zealand, and the village returned to its usual peacefulness. Su'e had already gone to live with his wife's family on the other side of the island. We did not see him in Vaega for a long time. After several months had passed, when the humiliation and anger had faded, he returned quietly to his former position within his family and village.

THE RESTORATION OF HARMONY

Samoans give precedence to the restoration of peace and harmony rather than single-mindedly seeking "justice" by punishing the guilty. They emphasize harmony because once the immediate problem has been resolved, family and neighbors must return to cooperating as members of the community. In Western industrial societies most communities are so large, complex, and fluid in their membership that there is usually little need for restoring harmony between disputants, or between victim and criminal. Outside agents enforce the peace. But rural Samoan villages are relatively small, homogeneous, and stable in their membership over many generations. And since Western Samoa has only a tiny national police force, families and villages must take the initiative in maintaining social order.

Samoans must rely on one all-purpose institution—their kin group, or *'āiga*—for both control and defense of their members. An important advantage of this system is that individual disputants never have to face each other again, since their kin groups (led by their respective *matai*) can make peace without them and then enforce that peace on individual members. An important disadvantage of this system is that disputes between individuals can spread rapidly to involve large social groups. In these circumstances, the restoration of peace and harmony is essential.

Problems are always handled first at the lowest possible level of responsibility. If a problem occurs between members of a family, for example, the chiefs and other elders of that family will normally settle it among themselves. Very serious crimes such as murder are an exception, since they must be reported immediately to the police. Even in these cases, the traditional social mechanisms often operate alongside the Western-style courts—not because villagers adhere blindly to these traditions, but because the courts do little to restore social harmony and because the tiny police force cannot guarantee peace.

Their emphasis on peace and harmony may even cause the village to ignore a serious offense. For example, I was living in Ofe village on Upolu when a thirty-five-year-old, untitled man named Tuli returned from a three-week stint as a laborer in American Samoa. Tuli suspected that his unmarried brother had been sleeping with his wife in his absence. He flew into a violent rage, beating his wife severely as she ran through the village until she finally escaped into the pastor's house. Fortunately, Tuli's brother was out of the village at the time. Though adultery is an extremely serious offense in Samoa, and one that would normally be severely punished, the village took no action. People told me that as long as the crime was never publicly proven, peace might eventually be restored in the family. But if the village even charged the brother publicly with adultery, they feared that Tuli would try to kill him.

Complementing and reinforcing the traditional Samoan emphasis on harmony are the Christian principals of charity and forgiveness, which many Samoans hold very dear. Several times I listened to debates concerning the punishment to be meted out to offenders, and always there were calls for compassion in the name of the *lotu*, or "Church."

Traditional Samoan society was (and still is to a great extent) hierarchical and segmented into relatively autonomous and competing families and ter-

ritorial groups, with direct physical confrontation providing the ultimate resolution of disputes. If individuals and families do not constantly defend their
interests and prerogatives from encroachment, they will soon lose them. It
is in this often divisive and combative environment that Samoans develop
aggressiveness, sensitivity to insult, and readiness to pursue their interests
with force. In the same environment they develop their great appreciation
for and elaboration of counterbalancing, integrative social and political skills
and institutions, including their polite etiquette, their humility, their ability
to forgive, and their emphasis on the maintenance or restoration of public
harmony. A startling incident that occurred midway through my stay illustrates both of these extremes.

VIOLENT DEATH AND A PUBLIC APOLOGY

I had accompanied the village cricket team to Apia for the national tournament, but I suddenly became very ill and was forced into the hospital at
Motootua. None of my friends knew I was there, so I sent a message by the
taxi driver to the Methodist compound in the center of town, where the team
and several *matai* from Vaega were staying. To my dismay, no one came to
see me at the hospital. Luckily, by the next day the emergency had passed
and I was released. Still weak, I went straight to the Methodist center to
rejoin my friends. To my surprise, the large, Samoan-style guest house where
the team had been staying was completely empty. I searched around the
compound until I found someone who could tell me where the team and its
supporters had gone. My heart dropped as I heard the news. A fight had
broken out at the game. Some of our team had attacked the referee with
their cricket bats. The referee was dead. Fearing reprisal, the team and all
of its supporters had then fled immediately to Savaii.

I reached Vaega the next day. People were tense. No one talked publicly
about the affair, but several eyewitnesses recounted the events to me in
private. The team had not been doing well in the tournament, and they were
close to elimination. Perhaps in frustration, they reacted angrily when the
referee's calls repeatedly went against them. Then, incited by supporters
screaming "Kill the referee!" some of the players flew into a rage and beat
the referee savagely with their bats. A battle erupted immediately between
the two teams and their supporters, with bats swinging and rocks and bottles
flying through the air. "If the gentleman had not died," one man lamented,
"it would have been a great war."

I was shocked at the story, but not greatly surprised. During my stay in
Samoa I heard many reports of violence involving both players and fans at
rugby games, and referees were sometimes injured. I also knew that similar
incidents had occurred as far back the early years of the New Zealand administration, when a referee was killed in a cricket tournament near Apia

and a player was killed during a game in Savaii (Eustis 1979:89–91). And a *National Geographic* report on American Samoa in 1919 told how the local militia had to be called out to quell the frequent disturbances that erupted at inter-village cricket matches (Quinn 1919).

"How could players become so angry at a referee's calls," I asked, "that they would kill him?"

One of the chiefs who had participated in the general melee explained what had happened.[10] At first they were merely angered by what, in their frustration, they thought were bad calls. As the game progressed, however, they began to feel that the referee was deliberately favoring the other team. They objected angrily as their hopes of victory gradually slipped away. They thought that the referee responded to their objections by favoring the other team even more. They objected even more loudly. To many of the angry and frustrated team members and their supporters, the referee seemed not only to continue his favoratism, they thought by his manner that he began to mock and taunt them. Now feeling the additional sting of public humiliation, they reacted blindly and wildly. They had not intended to kill the referee. It was an unfortunate and regrettable accident.

The police soon arrested three players. A few months later the young men were convicted of manslaughter and sentenced to three years' imprisonment. According to the legal system that Western Samoa had adopted from New Zealand, the matter was settled. Yet this did not end the affair. The Western-style legal system emphasizes the punishment of those individuals who are directly responsible for a crime. This system recognizes little or no responsibility for repairing social relations that were ruptured by the crime. In Samoa, however, this approach alone is inadequate.

Samoa is a small society where even today most relationships are face-to-face. It can support only a tiny police force, and traditionally it had no police force at all. In these conditions, social groups must be responsible for both the internal control of their members and their own defense against external threats. Partly for these reasons, people organize into hierarchical groups with authoritarian leaders—the chiefs. Individuals act at the direction of (and hence implicitly by the authority of) their chiefs. Thus, a victim's group may hold the aggressor's group, and especially its chief, responsible for the acts of individuals. This was particularly so in the cricket incident, since the chiefs attending the game had incited the players to violence by shouting "Kill the referee!" Since members of the two village groups could not avoid interacting in the future, and since the incident itself had been the act of a formal social group rather than merely an act of individuals, the need to restore harmony could not be ignored.

In Samoa, harmony can usually be restored if the offending group performs a public act of apology and penance, called an *ifoga*. For these proud people, this act of humility and self-abasement is profoundly moving. To perform an

---

[10] This account also matches court testimony given at the criminal trial, which I attended in Apia.

ifoga, the chiefs of the offending group go before dawn to the residence of the highest chief of the victim's group.[11] There they sit cross-legged on the bare ground, silently bowing toward the house as each chief covers his head with a fine mat. They also carry with them many other fine mats, and perhaps money, which they offer silently as restitution for the crime.

Once seated with their heads bowed and covered with fine mats, the chiefs cannot move until and unless their apology is accepted. They may sit there all day. If the victim's group is not willing to forgive, they may attack the chiefs where they sit, possibly killing them. If and when the victim's group is moved by the display, however, they may accept the apology and the restitution by bidding the chiefs to rise and join them in the house. There, formal speeches renew the covenant between the two groups to live in peace and harmony.

Performing an *ifoga* requires extraordinary humility and courage. Accepting an *ifoga* requires tremendous compassion. Both groups do so in the name of their Christian God and their own brotherhood, and because they realize that to do otherwise is to invite continuous revenge and hostility between them.

In the months following the killing of the referee, the chiefs of Vaega made no public move to resolve the crisis. Few villagers travelled to Upolu during that time, and almost none appeared in public around Apia—not because they were afraid of retaliation, some said, but because they had no errands there at the moment. My questions about the possibility of an *ifoga* were answered simply with *Lē iloa*, "It is not known," but behind the scenes, negotiations were beginning.

By tradition, the chiefs of Vaega are not allowed to contact the chiefs of the victim's family directly. In order to avoid direct contact—which might incite more violence—they first approached their counterparts in the village of Afega, on the northwest coast of Upolu. Each village has such an historical relationship with a village on the opposite island. Vaega and the other villages of Satupaitea may negotiate with villages on Upolu only through Afega, which they described as their "doorway" to Upolu. Acting as neutral intermediaries, the chiefs of Afega then contacted the chiefs of the dead man's family.

Six months after the killing, word finally came that a reconciliation might be possible. Asiata Iakopo immediately began organizing an *ifoga*. Every chief in Vaega would go, with the exception of a few who had been involved in the cricket melee. The chiefs of Vaega then mounted an intense campaign to recruit other chiefs from the two adjacent villages of Satufia and Pitonu'u. They were all members of the same district, the Vaega chiefs argued, and all owed allegiance to the title of Asiata. In addition, since the other two villages had not sent teams to the cricket tournament, the Vaega team was "the district's team." By that logic (which did not find universal favor), all three villages were jointly responsible.

---

[11] As at traditional trials before the village council, the culprits themselves do not appear lest their presence excite the anger of the victim's relatives.

The lobbying paid off, and we left for Upolu with 125 chiefs, more than three times the number that could have been recruited from Vaega alone. Only one untitled man joined the group. The people of Afega received us cordially that night, but without fanfare. Still no agreement had been reached with the leaders of the victim's family, some of whom were reported to be incommunicado in a distant village. Negotiations must have continued through the night, however, for at dawn the next morning we in the rank-and-file received word to proceed. We immediately loaded ourselves and several great bundles of fine mats into chartered buses and headed out along the coast road.

The sun had risen nearly to the tree tops by the time we arrived. A crowd of people waited around the house. Asiata Iakopo descended first from the lead bus, his shoulders already bowed and holding a fine mat above his head. As he descended the steps, the leading chief of the victim's family immediately took his arm and led him straight into the house. The *ifoga* had been accepted.

At Asiata's back came the other 124 *matai* of the district, pushing quickly toward the house. I pushed through the open doorway at the front of the house with dozens of our chiefs. It was not until I entered that I realized how small the house was. It was a European-style house with board walls and cement floor, perhaps twenty feet by thirty feet and lacking any interior divisions or furniture. Perhaps 200 people pressed in around the house, trying to get a look through the bare window openings and the two doorways.

Nearly fifty Satupaitea chiefs sat in rows three-deep along the walls on the left half of the house, while the remainder shouldered their way to the doors and windows from the outside. A nearly equal number of chiefs from the host family sat in rows against the walls on the right half of the house, but physically separated from us along either wall by perhaps a dozen chiefs from Afega. So many men had packed into the house that we were practically sitting on each other's laps, yet only a few square yards of space remained unoccupied in the center of the floor. Facing each other from either end of the house sat Asiata Iakopo and the high chief of the victim's family.

As I surveyed the room, I was surprised to find that one of our chiefs, Solo (a fat, cocky man of modest rank), had broken formation, circled around, and entered the house by the back door. He was seated almost adjacent to the high chief of the referee's family, far from the rest of us. Knowing that in Samoa seating order expresses status relationships, I presumed that his presence there had symbolic significance, and I made a mental note to ask Solo about it later.

The crowd fidgeted and became silent. It was time for the leading chiefs to seal the covenant with eloquent speeches. Asiata offered apology and restitution for the crime. The opposing chief accepted. They both pledged peace and harmony between their families and villages. I had expected that because of his odd seating position, Solo would perform some small part in the exchanges that followed, but he did not. He merely sat hunched over, looking intently at the family's high chief. As the speeches proceeded and the fine mats passed, the tension in the room eased and the crowd that pressed in around the house began to relax. When the formalities were over, we quickly exited through the crowd and then departed on the buses. It was not until we reached Afega that I learned what peril we had been in.

As soon as the buses halted, I found Solo and asked him what the significance of his seating position had been.

"I had a pistol under my shirt," he said with a grin, "aimed straight at their high chief. If any trouble had started, he would have been the first to go."

I must have paled visibly. I had been in Samoa for a year and a half, and I was shocked at my own naiveté. I never saw Solo's pistol, but I believe that he really had one, for he had bragged about it to me several times before. It was a cheap little hand gun—what Americans call a "Saturday night special," and Samoans call a *fana gutu ono*, a "gun with six mouths." A friend had brought it from American Samoa some months ago and then given it to Solo as a present. As I looked around I saw many other men pulling knives out from under their shirts or out of the folds in their *lāvalava*. I saw all manner of knives: short paring knives and pocket knives, but mostly long, kitchen-carving knives. I saw one ancient chief (and one of the gentlest men I know) pull an enormous World War II Marine Corps pistol out from under his shirt. The frail old man could hardly lift the pistol. He handled it very gingerly with both hands, but when I asked, he confirmed that he would have used it if necessary. A few other men also claimed to have pistols. Now it all made sense to me—the strenuous efforts to recruit more men, the rush to jam as many of our own men into the house as possible, and the jostling for position around the windows.

"You mean you were all packing guns and knives?" I shuddered.

"Not everyone."

I asked Asiata Iakopo directly if he was armed.

"No," he said with a kind of foolish grin, "I have nothing."

"Did the people from the other side carry guns and knives as well?" I asked, recalling with horror the packed room and the scores of excited strangers crowding around the house and blocking all the doors and windows.

Ta'ilo? "Who knows?"

"But I thought we were supposed to just *ifo*, bend down, and *pulou*, cover our heads, and let them do with us as they pleased?"

"Yes, that is the *fa'a-Samoa*."

"If that is the custom," I asked Solo, "why did you all carry guns and knives?"

Solo shrugged.

"We might all have been killed!"

A feoti, e feoti . . . , he replied. "If we die, we die. Besides, the agreement had already been reached. Nothing could happen."

"What if some angry relative did not accept the agreement and decided to attack us anyway?"

"That is not possible."

Perhaps they did not expect it to happen, I thought. But coming from the

United States, I was accustomed to hearing about similar acts of half-crazed violence, and I could imagine it happening here. "What if some relative was overcome by grief and anger and tried to attack us? What then?"

"They would kill him themselves," Solo replied without hesitation, "to preserve the peace."

5/The Changing
Matai System

During sixty-five years of colonial domination, Samoans did appear to be culturally conservative. It is clearer now in hindsight, however, that their conservatism during that era was largely a protective reaction against European incursion rather than an expression of inherently conservative forces within Samoan culture itself. In the centuries before European contact, Samoan oral history recounts that Samoans adopted many important innovations from neighboring islands, including the plaiting of mats, the making of bark cloth, tattooing, the kava ceremony, and perhaps the chiefly *matai* system itself (e.g., Turner 1884:123, Buck 1930:658). During the first years of contact with Europeans, Samoans readily—even eagerly—adopted Christianity, literacy, and European-styles of education, boat building, and commercial trading.

Though willing to adapt, Samoans have always been selective in their acceptance of innovations. John Williams, the early missionary, reported that their decision to adopt Christianity was preceded by long and thoughtful debate:

> The chiefs of the different settlements held meeting after meeting to consult upon the propriety of changing the religion of their ancestors and the case was argued on both sides with a calmness that seldom characterizes debates in more civilized countries and with an acuteness that does credit to their senses (letter dated 1836, quoted in Va'a 1987).

Williams recorded the characteristically pragmatic view of a chief at one such deliberation. The chief contrasted the Europeans' material wealth with the Samoans' own simple goods, and then concluded

> that the God who gave them all things must be good and that his religion must be superior to ours. If we receive and worship him he will in time give us all these things as them (ibid., quoting from Moyle 1984:237).

Since colonial control of Western Samoa ended in 1962, change has been swift and dramatic.[1] In the political arena, for example, Western Samoans adopted the British, parliamentary style of government. In the late 1970s and

---

[1] Change has been even swifter and more dramatic in American Samoa during the last twenty-five years, due primarily to a flood of financial aid and government programs from the United States.

early 1980s they created a disputatious, two-party political system that is entirely foreign to the traditional Samoan method of reaching decisions by consensus. In 1981 government workers walked out in a lengthy and bitter nationwide strike. Nor were these political changes confined to urban areas and national politics. In 1982 the untitled men of Satufia village went on strike against their *matai*.

Thus, while Samoans may resist changes imposed on them from outside, they have also shown an ability to modify their culture from within in order to adapt to changing conditions. Some of the most profound, yet least known examples of this adaptive ability are the changes in customary land tenure and other parts of the chiefly *matai* system that have occurred over the last five or six decades in the rural villages of Western Samoa.

THE *MATAI* SYSTEM, CUSTOMARY LAND TENURE, AND AGRICULTURAL DEVELOPMENT

The *matai* system is clearly the foundation of the *fa'a-Samoa*, or the Samoan way of life. In this system, extended families reside under the leadership of one of their members whom they elect to hold the family's chiefly *matai* title. Traditionally, each extended family owns both a residential site and agricultural lands, just as it owns the *matai* title. Once elected to the family title, the *matai* gains authority over the resident members of the extended family and their labor. The *matai* also has authority over the family's land and other productive resources (such as canoes), and the produce derived from them. The *matai*'s authority is limited only by his responsibility to care for his extended family, by their power to remove his title if he does not, and by the overriding authority of the village council in all inter-family matters. The *matai* system is thus a social, political, and economic system organized around extended families. Under the direction of their *matai*, extended families own property together, work together, and share the product of their work among family members. To Europeans who came from countries with nuclear family–based systems, Samoa's extended-family system appeared "communal" or "communistic."

In the 1920s, the New Zealand colonial administration tried unsuccessfully to legislate a change from extended-family to individual control or "tenure" of land (see Pitt 1970:105–106). The immediate goal of the program was to increase agricultural production (and thus commercial exports) by destroying the "inhibiting influence" of the "communal" tenure system (and not incidentally to shake the foundation of the *matai* system itself). Samoans were angered by the New Zealanders' meddling in their affairs, and their anger contributed greatly to the growing Mau resistance against the colonial government (Davidson 1967:118–46).

The Mau halted outside attempts to individualize Samoan land tenure, but foreign opposition (much of it well-intentioned) to the traditional tenure system continued. At the end of the colonial period Farrell and Ward concluded that "economic well being . . . can be achieved mainly by a change in custom and tradition as they apply to the land" (1962:236). Today, Europeans and even urban Samoans commonly cite the traditional land tenure system as one of the major obstacles to agricultural development. Fairbairn writes:

> Inhibiting effects of existing land tenure, with its emphasis on ill-defined principles of "communal" ownership, are increasingly held to be a negative influence on development (1985:79).

Like most other aspects of Samoan culture, however, the conservatism of the land tenure system is more apparent than real. In fact, a change toward individual ownership has been taking place since shortly after World War I. This change is little known outside of the rural villages and has not been reported by previous researchers. The change to individual tenure is also without legal sanction. The nation's constitution charges the Land and Titles Court with adjudicating disputes over customary land and *matai* titles according to the traditional "custom and usage" of the Samoan people.[2] The Court thus officially opposes modification of the traditional land tenure system. Nevertheless, the change has proceeded to the point where villagers now control the majority of their lands as individuals, rather than as extended families.

The change in tenure is significant for two reasons. First, it shows that Samoans are not rigid or bound by tradition. They can and do adapt to changing economic conditions. Second, the new system increases the security of planters' land rights because it assigns ownership to the individual planters who clear and plant the land, and it assigns inheritance rights exclusively to their children. Because of this change to individual land tenure, insecurity of tenure is not presently a significant cause of low farm productivity, as it may have been under the traditional tenure system.

THE SAMOAN "FAMILY"

The *'āiga*, or "family," is the organizational base of both the Samoan *matai* system and its subsystem of land tenure. Thus, understanding their operation first requires an understanding of what a Samoan family is and how it operates. Samoans have a different and much broader concept of "family" than Westerners generally do, and this sometimes causes confusion among students of Samoan culture. The Samoan word *'āiga* is usually translated into English as "family" or "family member." The way Samoans use the term, however, more closely approximates the English "group of relatives" or "relative," because there is no qualification on how distantly the people are related. Samoans commonly use the word *'āiga* to refer to all those people

---

[2] The Germans first established the Court, and New Zealand carried it over to their colonial administration. Western Samoans subsequently incorporated it into their own constitution at independence.

to whom they are related by blood. They may also casually refer to people who become related to them only through adoption or marriage as *'āiga*. Samoans carefully distinguish such outsiders from their "real" *'āiga*, however, which includes only those people who share the same "body, bones, and blood." Family members can neatly excise outsiders and their descendants from the core group of blood relatives during disputes, even after the passage of generations.

The use of the term *'āiga* becomes more or less inclusive as the speaker's intent changes. The range of reference may shrink to include only those half dozen relatives who reside together under the same roof. It may expand to include the few dozen active members of a corporate family group that owns land in the name of a particular *matai* title. Even more generally, the term *'āiga* may refer to all of the hundreds of people whose line of descent can be traced to a common ancestor several generations ago.

The vague and varying use of kinship terms such as *'āiga* allows Samoans some flexibility in taking advantage of kin relationships. In 1982 my friend Fa'apuna bemoaned the fact that his children could not move to Apia to work or attend school since neither he nor his wife had *'āiga* living there. In 1983, however, Fa'apuna established a kinship tie with a distantly related man who lived near the center of Apia. When Fa'apuna travelled to Apia, he often took gifts of fresh taro to the man. In 1985 the strategy payed off when Fa'apuna's son got a job at the Health Department and the boy went to live with Fa'apuna's new *'āiga* in Apia. By 1988 Fa'apuna was proudly claiming the Apia man as a very close *'āiga*.

Imagine the added difficulty that Fa'apuna would have faced in establishing a patronage relationship with his distant relative in Apia if he had to approach the man as "my distant relative," rather than simply as "my relative." By not distinguishing between "near" and "far" relatives, Fa'apuna hoped to swing the conceptual and moral center of their relationship to a point where the Apia man felt an obligation to help him, just as he would a closer relative.

People in Vaega commonly use only three terms to designate more restricted subsets of *'āiga*. These terms, and the relationships they specify, are important because Samoans use them to structure people's claims to the social and material resources of their *'āiga*.

'Āiga potopoto (literally "relatives who gather together") refers to a title descent group whose members meet together to elect a new chief. Claiming membership in any title descent group depends on being able to trace descent back to a previous holder of the title (preferably the original title holder). People can trace their descent through any combination of male and female ancestors to claim membership. When considering the merits of different candidates for election to the title, however, people give more weight to descent through individuals who formerly held the title, and those individuals are almost always male.

Samoans group people according to their relationships to particular *matai* titles, so that two people might be related in different ways to different titles. Since people may trace their descent through any combination of males and females to gain membership, they may claim membership in several title descent groups at the same time. As Selesele Tanielu told me, everyone belongs to at least four different groups—that is, the families of his or her four grandparents. As people trace their lines of descent back further, the number of title descent groups that they may claim membership in increases exponentially. In order to activate a particular claim, however, a person must participate actively in and contribute materially to that group's affairs. This requirement necessarily limits the number of groups to which a person can belong. It also puts a premium on having material resources to contribute and having time away from everyday labors to spend participating widely in family affairs.

Within a title descent group there are two major subgroups, one called the *tamatāne*, or "male child" subgroup, and one called the *tamafafine*, or "female child" subgroup. Traditionally, only members of the "male child" subgroup were eligible to hold the title, while members of the "female child" subgroup held something of a veto power over their selection. That distinction is often ignored today, however, and members of both subgroups claim access to the title.[3] Membership in the "male child" and "female child" subgroups is determined in the same manner as membership in the larger title group— that is, by tracing descent through either male or female ancestors—but membership is traced to one of the sons or daughters of the original title holder, rather than to the title holder himself. All descendents of the lines emanating from the original title holder's sons are members of the "male child" group. Similarly, all descendents of the original title holder's daughters are members of the "female child" group.[4]

Individuals are thus "male child" (*tamatāne*) or "female child" (*tamafafine*) in relation to specific titles, not in relation to each other. A person may belong to the "male child" subgroup of one title and the "female child" subgroup of a second title. In contrast, another person may belong to the "female child" subgroup of the first title and the "male child" subgroup of the second title, but all four memberships are permanently fixed by descent. As the old chief, Toleafoa Tipa'u, told me, a person's membership in those groups comes from *le 'amataga*, "the beginning."[5]

Itūpaepae (literally "side of the house platform") and other variants refer

[3] There are three reasons that it is ignored today. First, because of political and economic forces that I describe later in this chapter, families are engaging in wholesale splitting and sharing of titles. In the process, many loyal members of the "female child" subgroup have received titles where they would not otherwise. This has, in turn, confused the claims of succeeding generations. Finally, the title splitting often accompanies and legitimizes the division of family lands among heirs. Since families do not want to distinguish between male and female lines for land inheritance, they may not want to for titles either.

[4] If the original title holder has younger brothers and sisters, however, they would originate the two lines. In that case, the original title holder's own children and their descendents would all belong to the "male child" subgroup. The original title holder's older siblings (and their descendents) are not part of the descent group that originates with this first title holder.

[5] Shore gives a different account of the *tamatāne/tamafafine* relationship (1982:91–95). He states that "the terms are inherently relational and contextual . . . in themselves, the terms are meaningless. *Tamatane* and *tamafafine* are relationships rather than concrete persons or groups."

to smaller branches of a title descent group. Each "side" originates with and takes its name from one of the individual offspring of the first title holder. Thus, if the original title holder had three sons, there would be three "sides" within the "male child" subgroup of that title. When a large title descent group fissions, as they often do today (see below), they split along the lines of these "sides." Each "side" then confers (or attempts to confer) its own title.

THE ANTHROPOLOGIST GETS A LESSON IN KINSHIP

Though useful to Samoans, the wide range of usage for kinship terms such as *'āiga* presents some difficulty for the anthropologist. I tried without success to elicit more specific terms to denote "nuclear family," "household," and "extended family."[6] I was surprised that Samoans did not use more specific terms to denote these subsets of "relatives." At first I rationalized that finer distinctions were important only to me, but not to them. This explanation seemed to follow from textbook discussions of "classificatory" kinship systems, of which Samoan terminology is an example.

Like the type-case of Hawaiian kinship, Samoans use only three principles for assigning kinship terms: generation, sex of the designated kin, and sex of the speaker. For example, all male kin of the parents' generation may be refered to as *tamā*, rather than separating them into "father" and "uncle," as we do. This does *not* mean that Samoans call all of those men "father," nor does it mean that they fail to distinguish between their "father" and their "uncles" in their everyday behavior. It means only that a Samoan's role behavior with all of those men is similar in certain respects and that a Samoan may refer to all of those men by the term *tamā*. A Samoan would normally only extend the term *tamā* to an uncle, however, if they lived in the same household and the uncle raised or helped to raise the person.

Samoan kinship terminology is called "classificatory" because it classifies a great number of people of varying biological relationships together under relatively few kin terms. By some accounts, people are thought to divide the world into more and more specific groups according to their particular needs and then give each of those groups a specific term to facilitate reference. Thus, Eskimos have many terms for different kinds of snow, Arabs for different kinds of camels, and Americans for different kinds of cars, because the particular distinctions are important in those respective societies.

Falling prey to the easy but fallacious reverse argument, I assumed that if Samoans do not use more specific terms to refer to subsets of their *'āiga*,

---

[6] People also sometimes use *tauusoga tamā, tauusoga tinā,* and *tauusoga matua*, which refer to parallel and cross cousins (see Milner 1966:258–59). A few people did recognize or accept other terms that appear in the recent literature on Samoa, such as *fuaifale* (Shore 1982:236), *'au 'āiga* (Shore 1982:62, Weston 1972:38), *pui'āiga* (Shore 1982:62) and *'aufale* (Milner 1966:32). They did not like the terms, however, and did not use them. As one middle-aged woman said with a shrug, *'Āiga 'uma.* "They're all *'āiga.*"

they must not be concerned with more specific relationships. That was a mistake. I gradually came to see that in operation Samoan kinship terminology is more often extremely particular, rather than highly general. The key came when I realized that Samoans almost never refer to or call people by their kin terms. Instead, they use personal names, or titles in the case of chiefs. For example, children never call (and rarely refer to) their father or their uncles as *tamā*. They use their proper names or titles instead.

Samoans only use the kin terms when they want to stress behavior that is appropriate to a certain kin relationship or when they need to point out the relationship between particular kin. For example, a mother tells her son to go shopping with his sister by saying *O 'oulua ma Sina e fai le fa'atau*, "You and Sina go do the shopping," referring to the boy's sister by her personal name. Then the mother admonishes the boy to *Va'ai lelei lou tua-fafine*, "Watch over your sister well." In this case she uses the kin term to emphasize the Samoan male's strong moral obligation to care for and protect his sister.

The Samoans' so-called "classificatory" kinship terminology does double duty, being capable of both extreme generalizing and extreme particularizing. The terms can be generalized to include more distant relatives, but in the context of social or political maneuvering, Samoans use the same terms in ways that describe highly specific genealogical relationships. For example, the term *tamā* could technically refer either to a person's father or to an uncle. During deliberations over the election of a new *matai*, however, my neighbor Paulava used the term *tamā* to refer only to his father. He reserved the descriptive phrase, *uso o lo'u tamā* ("brother of my father"), to refer to his uncle. Technically, the term *uso* could include cousins along with brothers, and the term *tamā* could include uncles along with father. By using them together in a descriptive phrase, however, Paulava limited their meaning to "brother" and "father," respectively. The distinction was critical because Paulava and his cousin were both competing for the *matai* title formerly held by Paulava's father (his cousin's uncle). Paulava's direct line of descent gave him a distinct advantage over his cousin in the election—an advantage that would disappear if "father" and "uncle" were lumped together under the term *tamā*.

The facility with which Samoans specify complex genealogical relationships with only a few kin terms caused me some difficulty—and occasional embarrassment. I often found it impossible to remember the chain of kin terms long enough either to visualize the relationship or write it down accurately. While attending the funeral of a chief named Tupa, I asked Lautafi Pemita who the man was who had just arrived with a bundle of fine mats. After only the briefest of pauses, Lautafi replied, "He is the child of the daughter of the sister of the father of Tupa." I had to ask Lautafi to repeat that three times, by which point he had began to doubt my intelligence. "Timo," he asked, "has your head gone off with some girl?"

I waited for a quiet moment in the funeral activities to figure out the relationship Lautafi had specified. I then discovered that he could have said very simply in Samoan that "Tupa is his *tamā*." Though technically correct, such a broad use of the term was not precise enough in the context of the funeral. Thus, Lautafi's actual use of the "classificatory" kinship terms did not indicate a disinterest in more specific distinctions, but a vital interest in the most particular distinctions.

CHANGING USE OF KIN TERMS

The system of kinship terminology that I described above includes some contemporary changes in usage along the model of English kin terms. Even Samoans who do not know the English terms are usually familiar with the English distinctions between, for example, "brother/sister" and "cousin" or between "father" and "uncle" or "mother" and "aunt"—distinctions for which there are no terms in Samoan other than describing the exact relationship. In addition, many Samoans (especially younger, urban people) have begun to use some English kin terms, even when they are speaking Samoan. Many rural people now also use the Samoan terms with English meanings. For example, people use the term *tamā* to mean only "father," rather than any "male relative of the parent's generation."

Some of the impetus for this change to English usage may come from a desire to adopt Western customs. It is not just coincidence, however, that these changes in terminology come at a time when Samoan economics is moving from an extended-family base to a nuclear-family base. English usage allows people to separate the nuclear family from the wider kin group. The shift to English usage thus provides Samoans with a neat conceptual tool for excluding their more distant kin from access to the economic resources of their own nuclear families. This is a social and economic distinction that English-speaking people have long emphasized, but which Samoans formerly minimized.

The change from a social and economic structure based on extended families to one based on nuclear families involves many aspects of Samoan life. In rural villages where land is the most important resource, the change is perhaps most profound in their system of land tenure. Even "profound" changes are sometimes difficult to see, however. I stumbled upon the new land tenure system accidentally while I was mapping plantation plots.

MAPPING PLANTATIONS

I began mapping plots after being in Samoa for about five months and after living in Vaega for about three months. I had learned Samoan well enough to ask permission at a village council meeting to begin that delicate phase of my research, but at that point I did not speak well enough to dive into intensive ethnographic research. Since land claims are of critical importance to a farming village, and since there are virtually no reliable written records concerning them, the variation in knowledge between different planters is of some interest.

Fearing that the chiefs would be preoccupied with family and village affairs, and perhaps reluctant to engage in what promised to be hard and monotonous work, I first hired a 35-year-old, untitled man named Gata as my assistant. The existing aerial photos and topographic maps were inadequate even for base maps, so we began from scratch mapping the plantation roads using a tape measure and a Brunton field compass. As we worked our way up the main plantation road, we marked the boundaries of the plots we passed. From those known points we then began to branch off into the surrounding bush, mapping boundaries of plots with the compass and a range finder.

After a week we had mapped about half of the main work road and a few adjacent plots. I decided to test Gata to see if he could repeat exactly the names and boundaries that he had given me on previous days. As we proceeded up the road that day, Gata pointed out boundaries and assigned names to the plots we passed. To my horror, many of the designations did not match his earlier statements! Sometimes the boundaries were ten or fifteen yards from the earlier points, and several of the owners had changed.

I thought I had caught Gata trying to stretch his knowledge or even fabricate information just to keep the job, but he looked sincere and puzzled over my apparent disbelief of some of his statements. As we continued up the road I pressed him for explanations. In my state of ignorance and confusion, I did not understand much of his explanation. As we discussed the problem it seemed that Gata was unsure of his knowledge, and it appeared that what he did know of plot boundaries was largely confined to those that adjoined the main road. He was also uncomfortable discussing the fine points of land claims and boundaries, which he said was the proper business of chiefs.

I returned to the plantations the next day with Milo Fa'alaga, an aging but still burly *matai* who had until recently been the village *pulenu'u*, or government/village liaison officer. First we went over some of the roadside boundaries that Gata had shown me, and then we remapped a couple of easy plots. In most cases Milo agreed with Gata's designation of boundaries and owners. When he disagreed, he seemed to have authoritative reasons. For example, he told me the particular history of tree felling, crop cycles, and the planting of individual boundary trees on a plot. As the day progressed, however, I noticed many of the same inconsistencies appearing in Milo's statements that had alarmed me earlier in Gata's account. Yet Milo appeared to be just as sincere and concerned as Gata had been. Finally, we sat down in a shady spot between coconut trees, and through a series of my tortuous questions and Milo's thoughtful and patient answers, he helped me figure out what the problems were.

SHIFTING BOUNDARIES

The solution to the problem of shifting plot boundaries was embarrassingly simple—embarrassing because it was a common type of ethnographic problem that I was supposedly trained to avoid. I had assumed that the English word "boundary" and the Samoan word *tuā'oi* (which I had been using) always refer to identical things. They do not. I had incorrectly assumed that if a particular coconut tree marked the boundary of one plot, it must also mark the boundary of the adjacent plot. Coming from the United States, where every square inch of land is carefully measured and its ownership treasured, I had not considered the possibility that people might not really care who owned the twenty feet of barren ground between two groves of productive trees.

The designation of plantation boundaries sometimes varied because the boundaries of adjoining plots were commonly marked by the trees that each owner had planted. Trees will not produce well if planted too close together, so the boundary trees of adjacent plots—whether planted specifically as boundaries or acting as de facto boundaries—were often many yards apart. In between the two sets of trees is a no-man's land.

In a Samoan village, only the crops have economic value. Plantation land itself usually has no value since it cannot be sold or used for other purposes, so villagers are normally unconcerned with determining the "owner" of barren strips of land between standing crops. Thus, when I asked different people, or the same person on different occasions, to point out the boundaries of adjoining plots, they sometimes indicated the "boundary" of one plot and sometimes the "boundary" of the adjacent plot. That still left the more difficult problem of who owned the plots.

WHO OWNS THIS LAND?

According to the literature on Samoan land tenure, each plot is supposed to be "owned" by a particular *matai* title that holds the land in trust for the extended family, which in turn "owns" and owes allegiance to that title. Blindly assuming that the system indeed worked that way, I concluded that one or both of my guides was in error when they named different owners with different *matai* titles for a single plot. As I eventually learned, however, both accounts were correct. The error was again in my own assumptions, and my exasperation was simply the result of the tenacity with which I held on to those assumptions.

In Samoa parents give their new baby a first name at birth, for example "Gata." The baby's last name is just the first name of the baby's father, or the father's title if he is a chief. For example, Gata Fa'amagalo is the son of the chief whose title is Fa'amagalo. If Gata later takes the title of Sasa'e, he becomes Sasa'e Gata, with his title name preceding his given name.[7] Sasa'e is the name of the title, while Sasa'e Gata is the name of the person who holds the title. As long as the meaning is clear in context, however, people refer to the individual with just the title name. For example, people usually refer to Sasa'e Gata simply as "Sasa'e."

When I asked who owned each plot, both Gata and Milo sometimes told me the name of a *matai* title and sometimes the name of an individual. For example, Milo said that one plot belonged to Na'i—a title. Another plot he said belonged to Na'i Fualaga—an individual. I did not notice the distinction at first, or think it important. To make matters worse for me, Gata and Milo sometimes named different people or different titles as the owner of a single plot. According to the literature on Samoan land tenure, that was impossible.[8] I asked Milo whether plots belong to *matai* titles and their extended families (as I knew from the literature they were *supposed to*) or to individual people.

"Both," he replied.

Milo finally helped me realize that there were two distinct tenure systems operating at the same time, but on different plots. Villagers follow the traditional, extended-family ownership system for some plots, but a new, individual ownership system for most other plots.

In the weeks that followed our discussion, Milo Fa'alaga and I continued the laborious task of mapping plantation plots. When we reached the newer plantations that had been cut since about 1965, Milo's knowledge of plot histories began to give out, for he had begun to retire from active plantation work at about that time. Three other men then helped with the mapping. The first was a 36-year-old minor orator. Though he was knowledgeable about his own family's plots, he was largely ignorant of his neighbors' plots. The second was a 43-year-old minor orator who had married into his wife's family from another village many years earlier. He did not even know all the boundaries of his own household's coconut plots (which had been cleared many years before he joined the family).

My friend and part-time assistant, Panoa Umama'o, a 34-year-old untitled man, also helped map the boundaries of a few plots. One of those boundaries enclosed a great expanse of virgin forest that Panoa had staked out for his own family by planting coconut seedlings at wide intervals through the bush. As we slashed our way through the dark underbrush, attempting to make sightings with the range finder by peeping between hanging vines, I reminded Panoa that Samoan custom requires him to both clear and plant the land if he is to claim it. Panoa replied with a good-natured chuckle, boasting that so far his tactic had been successful. Anyway, he said, he was supported by the village because he was only trying to grab forest land for Vaega before the neighboring village of Satufia did.

----

[7] Samoans like to say that they "take" *matai* titles, rather than "receive" them, which is more accurate.

[8] See O'Meara 1987 for a discussion of that literature.

My host, Nu'u Vili, escorted me around and through the remaining 140 or so plots, and I dedicate the finished map to him (see map, Figure 5.2). At 46 years old, and after 35 years of work, Nu'u was still an active planter. Since he owns nearly a dozen plots scattered throughout the village plantation land, he has personal knowledge of almost every area of village land. He had been the field leader of the village council's informal "land dispute committee" for many years. Nu'u was also one of the orators sent by the village council to traverse the taro plantations counting taro stems for the council's frequent planting competitions and quotas. In addition, Nu'u is a man of intelligence, integrity, and good humor.

Ever wary, though, I continually tried to catch Nu'u in some lapse or indiscretion. I had trouble telling one tree from another, especially in the coconut plantations. I was afraid that I might not catch an error from one day to the next, so I fixed florescent-pink survey flags temporarily at boundary junctions. This gave Nu'u a good laugh (more than once). Upon completing the roundabout circuit of some overgrown plots that we had begun three weeks earlier, he sat down to roll a cigarette while I clambered over the rocks and through the brush to meet him. Arriving where he had last held the white range-finder stake, I did not recognize the spot as a boundary junction. I challenged Nu'u (who was now reclining with a self-satisfied grin on a bed of fern leaves) to demonstrate that this was the same spot we had started from three weeks earlier. He motioned nonchalantly toward the coconut tree I was leaning on.

"What about that?" he asked, exasperated at my ignorance. After a quick search, I found the pink flag lying among the leaves at the base of the tree.

Together with Nu'u Vili, Milo Fa'alaga, and the other men, we mapped all of the 195 plantation plots and sketched the outlines of the village house plots (unlike the plantations, village house-site boundaries are in such dispute that Nu'u would not even approach most of them with the mapping equipment). Using the resulting map as a base for interviewing, I was then able to document the existence of the two different tenure systems, one traditional and one modern.

THE TRADITIONAL LAND TENURE SYSTEM

In the traditional land tenure system, any particular piece of land is owned by the extended family whose members first cleared and planted it. The extended family takes its name from the *matai* title under whose authority the members work. Thus, people say that the family's lands are "owned" by that title. Administrative control over family land can only be gained indirectly by acquiring the specific *matai* title which holds authority over those plots.

Members compete to be elected to the family title. Personal qualities are important, along with two other criteria. First is the service a candidate has rendered to the extended family and to previous title holders. Second is the person's line of descent from previous title holders. Individuals with direct male links to prominent earlier title holders have the advantage. Occasionally a family will elect an adopted member or a son-in-law, but only if they have shown exceptional service and if there is no deserving heir. Any adult who can demonstrate descent from a previous holder of the title *and* who maintains active service in the affairs of that title descent group is eligible to participate in elections. Families reach their decisions by consensus, however, not by majority vote.

Many more people belong to any particular title descent group than actually reside on and cultivate that family's lands. Whoever is elected to the title then moves onto the family house site (if he does not already live there) and immediately takes control of the family and its lands. One of the resident sons of the previous title holder usually acquires the title, and there are additional safeguards to protect the use rights of those people who have been working the land. Yet there is always the distinct possibility that a nonresident rival will wrest control of the family plantations from the current occupants. That possibility causes insecurity of tenure in the traditional system, which in turn may inhibit people from developing their plantations.

With the increase in cash cropping over the last century, almost all Samoans have come to want exclusive control over their own lands, both for themselves and for their children. They no longer want to share those rights with nonresident or even other co-resident members of their extended families, as required by the traditional system. Villagers have changed their tenure system for the explicit purpose of restricting ownership and inheritance rights. I will describe this new tenure system in a subsequent section, but first it is important to differentiate between potential and actual rights to the use of and authority over land.

CLAIMS TO THE USE OF LAND

Any member of the extended family has the right to use family land, but only if the member does two things first. He or she must live with the family, and he or she must serve the *matai* of the family. Anyone who lives with the family on family lands must also serve the *matai*. Family members who do both of these things have the unquestionable right to use family land. The *matai* has the authority only to direct where, when, and how they shall expend their labors for the benefit of the family.

People do not always live with their natal families, however. Even if they live in the same village and contribute to their natal family's affairs, nonresidents have no right to use their families' lands while they live with, and consequently serve, another *matai*. They only maintain the *potential* for doing so later. Trouble is likely to develop if a nonresident attempts to use the lands of his or her natal family without permission from the resident *matai*. If they do, resources under the authority of one *matai* would be used for the support of, and be at the command of, another *matai*. This would imply the subservience of one to the other. *Matai* guard their prerogatives jealously, and few acts bring swifter and more determined response than appearing to demean the status or challenge the authority of a *matai*.

If people want to use land of one family while living with another family, they must first ask permission of the resident *matai*.[9] Asking permission removes the possibility of offense, since it publicly acknowledges the true locus of authority. It also allows the requested *matai* to be magnanimous by granting the request. Chiefs almost always grant such requests.[10]

Nonresident members of a particular family contribute periodically to the welfare of that family. If they do not, they lose their membership rights. This is the second most important reason (in addition to love and concern for the members) why migrants usually send money and goods back to their families, often for decades. In doing so, migrants maintain active membership in their families, and thus retain both for them and for their children the right to return to Samoa and gain access to family land and family titles.

CLAIMS TO AUTHORITY OVER LAND

In the traditional system, any family member has the potential of gaining authority over family land. This potential is only activated, however, if and when the member acquires the specific *matai* title that has authority over that land.[11] Nevertheless, a *matai* who has no legitimate claim may press a claim anyway. For example, in Vaega there is a house site that belongs to the Tauleulu title. During my visit in 1988, one household already living on the house site asked the current holder of the title, Tauleulu Pusi, if they could build a modest, European-style house in front of their old house. Tauleulu consented. At the kava ceremony that accompanied the ground breaking, however, a high-ranking chief named Laupapa tried to halt the construction. Laupapa belongs to the Tauleulu descent group, but the two titles are unrelated. Because of his membership in the Tauleulu descent group and his high rank, Laupapa claimed the right to be consulted before anything was done with the land. Since he had not been consulted beforehand, he now demanded that construction stop.

This is an excellent example of what Samoans call *fia poto* behavior (literally, "want to be clever or smart")—that is, when a person presumes above his or her station. Both the village council and the Land and Titles Court had already ruled in several previous cases that the Tauleulu title alone has authority over that house site. Since Tauleulu Pusi is currently the sole holder of the title, his decision alone counts. Yet his distant relative, Laupapa, was not above risking a little bluff and bravado on the chance that he might succeed

---

[9] An unrelated person living elsewhere may also request the temporary use of another family's land.

[10] This "temporary" use of land is a leading cause of disputes over tenure since it may be advanced later as evidence of ownership.

[11] If two or more people share the title, the principal authority rests with the *matai* who resides on the residence site of that title.

in his illicit claim. Laupapa knew that because of his high status and the Samoan emphasis on maintaining harmony within the family, he was unlikely to be rebuked openly. If he played his bluff and succeeded in intimidating Tauleulu, he could gain a share of the authority over the land.

Tauleulu's response was polite, but firm. Having failed to intimidate Tauleulu, Laupapa then pretended to be conciliated "in the name of family harmony." By publicly declaring his willingness to let the construction proceed, Laupapa tried to create the appearance that he had forced the family to consult with him before starting the project. Then in the future he could recall that public act of "conciliation" as evidence that the family had accepted his claim to sharing authority over the plot—even though they had only been polite in rejecting his claim. If Laupapa and his heirs are clever, devious, persistent, and powerful enough, they could eventually wrest control of the plot from Tauleulu's line.

If Laupapa had a better claim to begin with, and if he had pressed his advantage with more diplomacy, he could have used the opportunity to demonstrate his importance and the power of his words. But pressing a nonexistent claim with more force than skill, he merely alienated the other chiefs. When the confrontation was over, I heard several chiefs grumbling, '*Ese le fia poto o lea ali'i!* "That fellow really wants to be smart!"

TRADITIONAL AUTHORITY AND THE LAND AND TITLES COURT

All family members have the right, if not always the courage, to express their views to their *matai*. The *matai* is not required to conform to those views, however. He has only the general responsibility to act in the family's best interest and to maintain family peace and harmony. He is not required to have prior consent from all family members before making a decision concerning family land (see Marsack 1958:19). Both the Registrar and the Judges of the Land and Titles Court affirm that the *matai* alone has authority over lands that pertain to his title, and he does not need the consent of other family members for his actions (personal communication 1983, 1984).

Confusion over this matter extends to the Samoan population. There are two prominent reasons for this confusion. First is the general social trends of fragmentation of extended families and individualization of economic activities and inheritance. Second is the far-reaching effect of a seemingly innocuous administrative procedure.[12] This rule requires the Registrar to accept and act upon a petition, oral or written, presented by "any interested Samoan." Registrars have generally interpreted "any interested Samoan" to mean anyone who claims to be an heir of the family or anyone who claims to have used the land previously. In some cases, the Court has even accepted

[12] From the Samoan Land and Titles Protection Ordinance 1934 (now amended as the Land and Titles Act 1981), section 82.

petitions from "interested" people who claim no closer link to a disputed plot or title than living in the same village.

The Court is well aware that this administrative procedure gives people a legal right to contest a *matai*'s actions where they have no traditional right to do so. In fact, the original purpose of the procedure—written during New Zealand colonial rule—was to lessen the power of *matai*. It has been successful in doing just that. The practical effect of the rule is that *matai* now risk legal action if they do not seek prior approval of their actions from other family members—even those who reside at a great distance. The Land and Titles Court's petitioning procedure has thus blurred the traditional distinction between potential and actual rights to the use of and authority over land. Much of today's uncertainty and insecurity over land rights thus results from conflict within the Court, rather than from any inherent uncertainty in the people's customary tenure system.

Members of the Court recognize that this rule is eroding the authority and dignity of *matai* (personal communication 1984). Unfortunately, the effect of the rule is not generally recognized outside the Court. Whether the public approves or disapproves of these social effects of the Court's actions is unknown. It is clear, however, that in addition to hearing disputes over land and titles, the Court is also a powerful force shaping Samoan society.

Many Samoans know how to use the court petitioning procedure to their advantage in situations where they would otherwise have little social power of their own. For example, court records show that a *matai* from Vaega petitioned the Court to halt plantings on a piece of land owned by his wife's family in another village. The Vaega *matai* claimed that he was the rightful owner of the land because he had cleared and planted the land while living temporarily with his wife's family years before. According to custom, however, land belongs first to the village. A person who does not hold a *matai* title from that village, and who does not fulfill his obligations to that village, cannot hold authority over that village's land. The Vaega *matai*'s petition thus had no merit under Samoan "custom and usage." The Court is bound by the Constitution to uphold Samoan custom, so the Court could not decide in his favor. Nevertheless, the law required the Registrar to accept and act upon his petition.

Upon receiving the petition, the Registrar had to order the respondent from the other village to appear at the courthouse. This was a penalty in itself since the court was an all-day bus ride from the respondent's village. At the courthouse the respondent was forced to meet with the Vaega chief who had filed the baseless petition (and who lives only an hour's bus ride from the court) to try to settle the dispute. If a settlement had not been reached then, the petitioner could have forced the matter to a full court hearing, even though his claim was groundless. In this way people use the Court as a weapon to harass another party, the original dispute having arisen over some unrelated matter. That was exactly the purpose of the Vaega chief's petition. He had been slighted by his wife's family, and though he knew he had no claim to authority over the plot, he used it as an excuse to harass them in court.

Based on my reading of hundreds of court petitions and on interviews with several judges and other court personnel, it is clear that a large percentage of petitions filed before the Court have little basis under Samoan custom. Many suits are malicious. Using the Court's petitioning procedure, the lowliest untitled person can confront the highest chief, and a remote relative can force the family *matai* to meet him in court. By forcing respondents to consult with petitioners who have no legitimate claim, the Court implicitly supports the petitioners and consequently broadens and obscures claims to land and titles.

THE NEW TENURE SYSTEM

Western Samoa's constitution directs the Land and Titles Court to judge cases according to the "customs and usages" of the Samoan people. This causes a problem in the current period of rapid social change when past "custom" often conflicts with contemporary "usage." The people of Vaega and the other rural villages of Western Samoan now use two different tenure systems—one traditional and the other new. Under the new system, people who clear and plant new land may claim individual ownership over that land. In order to separate the two systems, I recorded the following information for each of the agricultural and house plots in Vaega:

1. who first cut and planted the land, and when (knowledge usually going back no more than three generations);
2. who planted the existing crops, and when;
3. who now uses the land and harvests these crops;
4. who also claims the land and crops, but does not use them;
5. who previously had authority over the land, who has authority now, and who will gain authority over it when the current title holder dies; and
6. how people justify those claims to the use of and authority over the land.

I gathered this information during private interviews with the thirty-two *matai* residing in the village and with several untitled men and women. I asked each person about the general operation of the land tenure system, as well as about each plot to which they felt they had a claim. Contradictory or overlapping claims were uncommon, but when they occurred I recorded each view and checked them with a neutral third party. I only counted a plot as individually owned if all interested parties agreed that it was.

Strictly speaking, land is not inherited under the traditional tenure system. Extended families act as corporate groups, owning land in perpetuity. Individual members come and go while ownership remains with the family, in the name of the family's *matai* title. Since the 1920s, however, villagers have come to accept a new principle of inheritance that compliments the new principle of individual ownership. Under the new tenure system, the individual who first clears and plants land not only owns the land, he may now pass that ownership directly to his children, regardless of his or their *matai* titles. An

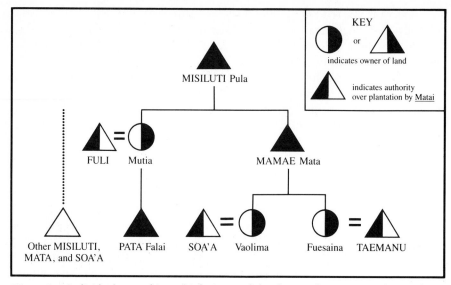

Figure 5.1 Individual ownership and inheritance of the plot "Leala." Matai *titles are shown with capital letters, common names without. Triangles represent males, circles represent females. Solid lines indicate direct descent. Equals signs indicate marriage between the adjacent individuals. The chart shows that ownership of the plot is inherited without regard to* matai *title names.*

example from Vaega will show how children inherit the lands of their parents even though they have different titles or no titles at all.

In the late 1930s a *matai* named MISILUTI Pula cleared and planted a piece of land that he named "Leala" (in the following discussion I will write *matai* titles with capital letters and common names without). He owned the plot as an individual, and when he died, his son, MAMAE Mata, and his daughter, Mutia, inherited the plot (see Figure 5.1). They each worked the plot together with their respective spouses and children. Mutia had one son, PATA Falai. MAMAE Mata had two daughters, Vaolima and Fuesaina. Now that Mutia and her brother, MAMAE Mata, have also died, their three children (PATA Falai, Vaolima, and Fuesaina) own the plot, while the three *matai* of those households (PATA Falai, SOA'A Pita, and TAEMANU Fatu) have nominal authority over the plot.

Even though MISILUTI'S three grandchildren now own Leala, everyday authority over the plot is shared between the *matai* heads of those three households—that is, by PATA, SOA'A (Vaolima's husband), and TAE-MANU (Fuesaina's husband). All three of these men hold newly created *matai* titles that have no previous history in their families or in the village. None of them holds the same *matai* title as the original owner, MISILUTI Pula, or the intermediate owner, MAMAE Mata. Three of the *matai* titles involved—MISILUTI, MAMAE, and SOA'A—are also held by other men in the village, none of whom use or claim any right to the plot. Thus, the plot "Leala" is owned and inherited strictly by the blood heirs of MISILUTI Pula without consideration of their extended family or *matai* titles.

Villagers recognize that such individual ownership and inheritance are contrary to their traditions (i.e., they were not used during the time of their parents and grandparents), and that this system has become established during their own lifetimes. But everyone accepts the validity of the new system, and nearly everyone claims at least one piece of land under the new tenure system. Villagers not only apply this new system to almost all newly cleared plots, but also to most of the older agricultural lands that their parents and grand-parents first cleared and held under the old system. Many families have even divided their ancient village house sites among individual heirs.

The change from extended family to individual land tenure is a long and continuing process, and village lands have become a mosaic of old, new, and altered tenures, as can be seen from the map of Vaega lands in Figure 5.2. The earliest explicit use of the new system that I recorded was in the mid-1920s. A man who is now an elderly high chief in Vaega cut and planted his own plot to grow cash crops to support his immediate family. Though he claims control over several extended family lands under the traditional system, he claims this one plot as an individual, by his "body," rather than by his *matai* title.[13] He says that when he dies, his children will inherit this one plot regardless of whether they acquire his *matai* title. The other family lands will go to whoever takes his title.

ADVANTAGES OF THE NEW TENURE SYSTEM

Everyone accepts and uses the new tenure system because it has several advantages in current village conditions. First, there is always uncertainty in the title succession. Second, since the extended family no longer works to-gether under one *matai*, parents want to assure that *each* of their children will inherit land for the support of his or her own nuclear family. Individual ownership and inheritance eliminates uncertainty by removing the interme-diate step of acquiring the family title. Instead, the new system awards a couple's lands directly to all their children. Traditionally, even though people lived and worked in extended families, they tried to favor their own children by passing their titles on to one of them. In order to do that, they sometimes circumvented traditional rules by force or guile. The important point is that under modern economic conditions, villagers feel that it is important to *assure* that their own children inherit their cash-crop lands and house sites, and they have modified their land tenure system accordingly. What they once could accomplish only indirectly, or by subterfuge, is now the social norm.

---

[13] The control of land is vitally important to villagers. Thus, the old chief and other villagers are quite explicit in distinguishing between the traditional and new tenure systems. They describe land owned under the traditional system as *fanua tau le suafa o*, "land appurtenant to the title of," distinguishing it from individually owned land, which they describe as *fanua tōtino*, "personal land," or simply as *fanua o a'u lava*, "land belonging only to me." In their words, extended–family land belongs to the family's "title," while individually owned land belongs to the person's "body."

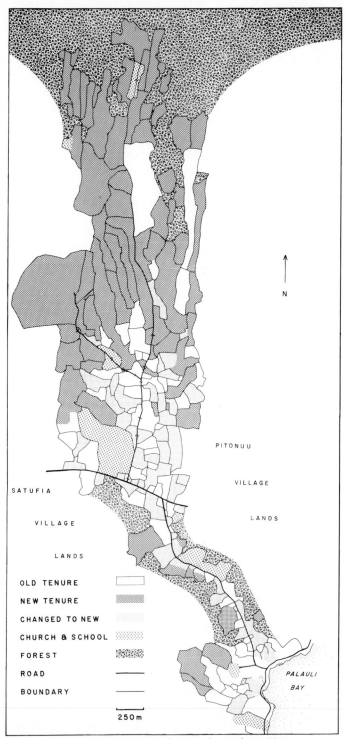

Figure 5.2 Map of Vaega plantation lands showing change from old to new tenure systems

The new tenure system is not yet the legal norm, however. This causes serious problems in the resolution of village land disputes before the Land and Titles Court. Conflict within the Court between the new and old tenure systems is especially important because it is jeopardizing the integrity of the new system, which villagers are creating as a useful adaptation to contemporary conditions.

Members of the Court ruefully agree that people increasingly claim land according to "un-Samoan," individualistic principles that should not be accepted in court. The judges publicly describe these modern practices as abhorrent, similar to the way conservative Americans view "creeping socialism." It is revealing, however, that in their private affairs at least some of these same judges claim plots as individuals under the new tenure system (personal communication). Numerous court decisions going back at least twenty-five years also support the individualistic principles of the new tenure system (court records, Apia and Tuasivi). Nevertheless, these court decisions—like the villagers' own claims—are usually couched in traditional terms.

LEGITIMIZING CHANGE

Villagers cite four principles from the traditional system to help them legitimize their new claims to individual ownership and inheritance. They apply these traditional principles differently than before, however, with the result that their new claims directly contradict the old system. The first rule that villagers cite to support the new system is: Land belongs to those who clear and plant it. Traditionally this principle meant that land belonged to the entire extended family (under the authority of the particular *matai* title) to which the people who cleared the land belonged. In the new system, however, people advance the same principle to justify their claim that land belongs only to those *individuals* who physically clear and plant the land, not including even a person's siblings if they did not share in the work.

The second principle that villagers have carried over to the new system is: A planter may gain authority over land that he (and perhaps his wife and children) cleared previously, but only when he also acquires a *matai* title. Until he acquires a title of his own, land that he clears remains under the authority of the *matai* he is currently serving. In the new system, however, control of the land passes to him as an individual by virtue of acquiring any *matai* title. Land is not vested in the title itself.

The third principle is: It is not possible to take the land of another without cause. Extended families formerly invoked this rule to defend their land against competing claims by other extended families, but today people apply the rule differently. Individuals now invoke the rule to protect their private cash-crop lands against claims by other members of their immediate families.

Fourth, Samoans still abide by the principle: *E pule le matai.* "The chief has the authority." This means that *matai* have final authority over virtually all matters affecting their family and their family lands. An untitled person still cannot legitimately claim authority over land.[14] Attempts to do so sometimes go unchallenged long enough, however, for the person to gain a *matai* title (which is usually not very long in modern Samoa).

Before the advent of cash cropping, there appeared to be little reason for conflict between a *matai* and his untitled men over the control of plots or over the disposition of crops. When planters produced only food to feed their families and to support family social activities, there was probably little divergence between the interests of individual planters and their *matai*. With the growing importance of agriculture as a source of cash (or in the case of subsistence production, as a way to avoid cash expense), conflict has increased. Villagers have consciously acted to reduce this new conflict by limiting the landholding group to a couple and their children, rather than the larger and less closely related extended family.

Following these four modified rules, individuals need only clear their own plots and gain their own *matai* titles for the system to be transformed from "communal" ownership by title groups to individual ownership. The new tenure system explicitly denies the traditional use rights of the extended family. It also denies the former claim of the extended family's *matai* to authority over land that is worked—and now owned—by other households. Those "communal" rights to family land and labor are at the heart of the traditional *fa'a-Samoa*, or Samoan culture. Their denial is thus a significant development in the individualization of rights in the modern *fa'a-Samoa*.

COMPARING OTHER VILLAGES

In 1984 I conducted similar research on land tenure in the villages of Neiafu and Malie, as well as spot checking other villages on both Savaii and Upolu. I chose Neiafu, on the southwest coast of Savaii, for several reasons. First, it was until recently even more remote and traditional than Satupaitea. Second, Neiafu was the village from which modern Satupaitea was recolonized many generations ago. Consequently, any major differences in land tenure that might have appeared would presumably have been adaptations to local circumstances, rather than originating from different subcultures. Third, Neiafu has more forest land available for clearing than Satupaitea. Fourth, the main cash crop in Neiafu is cocoa, which is more profitable than the main cash crops in Satupaitea, which are coconuts and taro. Fifth, I already had good personal contacts in Neiafu, and since it is the sister village of Satupaitea, my own *matai* title from Satupaitea was accepted in Neiafu as one of its own. Though the people of Neiafu did not know me before, I was thus able to investigate the sensitive question of land tenure quickly and without suspicion. My final reason for picking Neiafu was simply that it is an extraordinarily

---

[14] There is one exception to this rule. Upon the death or absence of the *matai*, senior heirs may exercise authority in the name of the vacant *matai* title.

beautiful village, even for Samoa, and I had been looking for an excuse to visit there.

The research in Malie was more difficult. I chose it mainly because of its proximity to Apia and because Pitt's earlier work there provided an important baseline for comparison (Pitt 1970). I had no contacts in Malie, however, and had established no reputation in the village. People are so sensitive about land issues that although I began (as I always did) by formally asking and receiving permission from the village council, a few people refused to talk with me. More often people were just wary. I was talking one day with a frail old woman in her house facing the main road. When I asked her who owned the house site, she gave me an animated description of the traditional tenure system. She waved her bony arm to point out the bounds of the land owned by the high title of Lapa, on which she said her family had been allowed to build its home. She did not know that her next-door neighbor had already been more candid. He had told me how the heirs of the Lapa title had divided the land among themselves many years ago. Each heir now holds individual authority over his or her own house plot and agricultural lands.

I waited until the woman had finished, then I said: "That's interesting. In Satupaitea where I come from, most families have divided their lands among the heirs, and they now own them as individuals." I then outlined the new tenure system and the reasons why people in Satupaitea favored it. She looked away, scratching her head.

'E te iloa mea nā? she asked. "You know about those things?"

I replied by raising my eyebrows, Samoa's energy-efficient version of a head nod.

"Oh. Well then," and she proceeded to tell the real story of her present claims to the land.

The three villages of Vaega, Neiafu, and Malie differ greatly in their degrees of Westernization, economic bases, and social histories. Yet all three villages accept and use the new land tenure system. I interviewed over eighty landholders in these villages and recorded the histories of land use and claims to authority for over 460 separate plots. Individuals now claim nearly two-thirds of these plots under the new tenure system.

ECONOMIC ORIGINS OF THE NEW TENURE SYSTEM

Colonial administrators tried several times to introduce individual tenure in Western Samoa, but without success.[15] Certainly these efforts had no effect on the more remote research villages in Savaii. I conclude that the villagers changed the tenure system themselves, on their own initiative. Villagers are quite explicit about their reasons for changing. They say that the primary

[15] See Farrell 1962, Pitt 1970, Holmes 1971, Powles 1979, and Thomas 1984 for summaries of these efforts.

cause is their increased access to and desire for income from cash cropping. They earn this income individually, and they want to control it individually as well. Asiata Iakopo explained it this way:

> *Aso ia* . . . In the old days there was no copra, no cocoa, no taro sales. Everyone worked together to help each other, but it is different today. Now people want to get the fruits of their own sweat in order to raise their children.

Ironically, a secondary cause of the change in tenure is that *parents* also want to retain the fruits of their *children's* sweat to support them in their old age. According to Samoan custom, parents support their children when the children are young, but when the children are grown, they support their parents. For example, almost all modern houses in rural villages are built primarily with remittance money sent by a couple's children living overseas. People increase the security of these investments by claiming the house sites as individuals rather than as members of extended families.

These new claims to land are also having a profound effect on the *matai* system itself. For example, I attended the formal meeting of an extended family in Vaega when they met to elect a new *matai*. They chose their new *matai* primarily on the basis of who was then living on the traditional house site of that title. It is traditional for a newly elected *matai* to move onto the house site of his title. In this case, however, one of the two main contenders had been born and raised on the site, and he had already built a European-style house there. The other contender lived in another part of the village.

The assembled family never entertained any thought of forcing the current resident to give up his expensive house to the other candidate. They knew that if they gave the title to the nonresident candidate, the man who already occupied the site could have prevented the family from meeting in his house. They said that it would be most unsightly for the family to meet anywhere else. The unavoidable result was that the man already occupying the traditional site got the title. The logic was overpowering, and all parties agreed publicly during the meeting. Nevertheless, the loser renewed the battle later in court, and the family eventually split the title between six contenders.

As Asiata Iakopo had said, all resident members of the extended family traditionally worked together under the direction of a single *matai* to feed, house, and clothe themselves, and to meet the family's social obligations. Today, however, individually produced income from both cash cropping and from wage labor is destroying the economic rationale for the extended family. For example, the construction and repair of traditional houses required a large pool of labor that was drawn largely from within the extended family. Today, modern purchased materials greatly reduce labor requirements while placing a premium on the control of the sources of monetary income. At the same time, competition over resources creates strife between extended-family members. As a result, the tradition of and the need for cooperation within an extended family may no longer be strong enough to contain intra-family rivalries. Villagers universally say that the immediate causes of dividing up old family lands are intra-family disputes over jointly held cash-crop lands.

Demographic changes have facilitated the reorganization of production from extended-family to nuclear-family units. Family genealogies show that a generation or two ago most couples had only a few children who survived to adulthood. Many couples were barren. Cooperation between nuclear families, or fragments of nuclear families, was necessary in order to pool a large labor force. With better medical treatment today, couples often have six to eight children who reach adulthood. With larger families, the need for inter-family economic cooperation is greatly reduced once the oldest children reach productive age.

At the same time, individual incomes remain low and subject to high risk. Thus, people still need to pool several individual incomes from different sources. They want to pool those incomes in such a way that they maintain tight control over them. Villagers have solved this problem by making the nuclear family the basis of production, by increasing the size of their nuclear families, and by claiming individual ownership and direct inheritance over land and other productive resources.

THE CHANGING *MATAI* SYSTEM

No matter how much nuclear-family "individualism" has grown at the expense of extended-family "communalism," most Samoans still uphold the principle that only *matai* can hold authority over land. A major reason for this apparent conservatism is undoubtedly that government law does not allow otherwise. But real conflict over the issue is also being defused because of a radical new development—the wholesale granting of *matai* titles. The number of *matai* has been growing rapidly over the last three decades, so that now most adult men hold titles.

In rural areas such as Savaii, 75 percent of all men 2 years and older are *matai*.[16] That is more than double the percentage of thirty years ago. This change alone makes obsolete the common argument that *matai* control inhibits the productive efforts of untitled men under their control. The great majority of adult men are now *matai* who control their own economic affairs. *Matai* titles are now proliferating so fast that the question of untitled men holding land, like the question of untitled men voting, will soon be a moot point. The real question that Samoans debate today is whether *women* will also share in this liberalization.

---

[16] In 1988 there were 8,200 individuals registered as *matai* in Savaii, or about one *matai* for every six residents. Roughly one-third of the population is twenty-one years or older, and half are male (*Samoa Times*, 19 February 1988, pp. 1–2). That means that one-sixth of the population—or about 8,200 people in Savaii—is male and twenty-one years or older (*matai* cannot register unless they are at least twenty-one years old). But not all *matai* registered in Savaii actually live there. Extrapolating from my records of Satupaitea *matai* in 1988, about 10 percent live permanently overseas. Another 15 percent live permanently in Apia or other places on Upolu, while very few *matai* registered on Upolu live in Savaii. Roughly 200 of the *matai* registered in Savaii are women. That would put the number of male *matai* living in Savaii at about 6,000—or just under 75 percent of all males aged twenty-one years or older.

The main reason for the proliferation of *matai* titles is the law governing the election of district representatives to Parliament. The law limits voting in these elections to registered *matai*. Members of the constitutional convention intended that law to forge an enduring compromise between traditional Samoan political organization and British-style parliamentary government. While the compromise has been successful, it has also caused a severe side-effect. Many candidates immediately perceived the electoral advantage of bestowing as many new *matai* titles as possible. Politically united families (and even whole villages) now commonly bestow dozens or even scores of new titles in preparation for an election. In some districts women, youths, and even children received titles without any, or with only peremptory, installation ceremonies.[17] I talked with some people who only learned about their new *matai* titles second or third hand, and they did not even know if they had been given high chief or talking chief titles.

Family members can elect people to their family titles at will. All that is required to stack an election is that no one in the family lodge a complaint with the Land and Titles Court or with electoral officials. Certain high titles also have the traditional power to create new titles and to bestow them freely, which many have done. Many influential chiefs abuse these traditional prerogatives for political gain, and some of the most honored and highest status *matai* lead the way. They reacted rapidly to the new election laws by subverting the *matai* system—their most fundamental and most revered social institution. This should be ample evidence that there is no "cult of custom" in Samoa today.[18] Instead, Samoans have shown their ability and willingness to adapt their culture in order to take advantage of new opportunites. In the case of elections, the opportunities are mainly political. In the case of land tenure, the opportunities are mainly economic.

As the population increases and as village society becomes more commercialized, competition for the control of economic resources also increases. Since *matai* still wield substantial power over untitled people, possession of a *matai* title is a critical asset in this competition. A conflict between two brothers, the sons of Ulusina, shows how the new political, economic, and social forces come together to make villagers change the way they organize their families, their land tenure and *matai* systems, and ultimately their entire society.

THE SONS OF ULUSINA

Ulusina is an old and infirm *matai* whose body is now crippled from a stroke. A few years ago his oldest son, who was then in his late thirties, was

---

[17] The law now prevents people under 21 from registering their *matai* titles.

[18] J.W. Davidson, the legal scholar who was the architect of the Constitution of Western Samoa, believed that the Samoans would put their revered *matai* system above political advantage. He could not be dissuaded from this belief even after the wholesale granting of titles before the 1966 elections (Derek Freeman, personal communication, 1989).

given the title of Solomua, which he shares with over twenty other men. The title bestowal was largely politically inspired, but the family accepted it because the old man was no longer active in directing their family's affairs.

Ulusina claims a large plot of coconuts and cocoa that he cleared and planted himself when he was a young man. Further up the mountain slopes the family works a large taro plantation that Ulusina and his two sons cleared from the forest, beginning in the late 1960s. The plot now contains taro fields, fallow grassland, and groves of cocoa trees. As Ulusina's younger son, Auva'a, matured and started his own family, he began to chafe under the authority of his older brother. They argued incessantly, especially over access to the valuable cocoa harvest. Ever since Solomua became a *matai*, he claimed the right to control the cocoa harvest and the proceeds from it. Auva'a bitterly resented Solomua's overbearing manner. The canons of respect prohibited Auva'a from challenging his older brother directly, so Auva'a retaliated indirectly by secretly picking and selling most of the cocoa harvest.

Solomua was infuriated, though not just by the loss of the cocoa. He felt that he was the *matai* of the family now, and he should control the labor and resources of the family. He considered his brother's actions to be an affront to his status as a *matai*. The two argued, nearly coming to blows. Solomua flew into a rage, but other members of the family prevented him from venting his anger directly on his younger brother. Solomua then grabbed an ax and charged off to the plantation where he began chopping down the cocoa trees. He was finally restrained and an uneasy peace restored, but the family feared an outbreak of greater violence between the brothers.

A short time later the high chief of their extended family proposed to give Auva'a and thirteen other young men *matai* titles, implicitly in preparation for the next year's elections. I sat with the family as they discussed the matter. Ulusina declared that he would not permit his son to accept the title. He and many of the other old men and women wondered out loud, "Who will remain to serve their *matai* when all the young men have become *matai*?" Ulusina's objections were finally overcome, or overridden, however. Most members of the extended family saw the offer as an opportunity to neutralize the dangerous conflict between the two brothers. And though none said so publicly, many were reluctant to oppose the interests of their high chief.

A few weeks later Auva'a and a dozen other insignificant young men received their newly created *matai* titles in a joint ceremony. Ulusina then divided his taro and cocoa lands between his sons, now both *matai*. The family and its lands had been split, the two brothers separated and appeased, and Ulusina was left with only children to serve his title.

THE PRICE OF MAINTAINING APPEARANCES

In order to satisfy electoral and court officials, and thus prevent a successful court challenge, the installation ceremonies for new "ballot *matai*" should conform to traditional standards. According to these standards, all leading members of the extended family should attend the ceremony to show their support. The other chiefs of the village should also attend, for this signifies their public acceptance of the new *matai* in village affairs. The host family should also distribute at least the equivalent of a small pig or a case of tinned fish and one or two fine mats to the guests for each new *matai* they install. Most title installations conform to these minimal standards, though some do not.

Once the individual has been installed, he (or rarely she) should also fulfill the public role of a *matai*. For example, new *matai* should attend council meetings and contribute to church and village affairs in the name of their new titles. These obligations can be very burdensome for a young man, especially since he often continues to serve the senior *matai* of his family as before. One 23-year-old man that I know well ran away twice to avoid being installed as a ballot *matai*. He finally succumbed to the political will of his wife's family, with whom he was then living, when his father-in-law directly ordered him to accept the title. His father-in-law mollified the young man by assuring him privately that he would not be responsible for making his own contributions to the pastor or for other village affairs. Instead, he said the young man could take his contributions from the general resources of the larger family.

In order to maintain the electoral status of new *matai*, the family and village should also treat the new title recipients as legitimate chiefs.[19] Thus, all of the rights, obligations, privileges, and honor of *matai* status are now dissolving rapidly into the wider population—ennobling younger and lesser people at the expense of the institution itself.

Traditionally, the rare recipient of a newly created title became the head of a new title descent group that had the right to bestow its title on subsequent generations. Today, thousands of "ballot *matai*" are receiving newly created or shared titles without the authority to pass those titles on to their children. I asked Milo Faletoi what would happen to those titles when the original bearer died. A pugnacious grin crept over his face as he reminded me that almost everything in the *fa'a-Samoa* is open to manipulation by those who are clever and powerful. His own orator title is ancient and highly honored in Satupaitea, so he is not personally affected by the problem. Nevertheless, he had already given the problem much thought. He told me that the recipients of minor titles dare not challenge the authority of the high chiefs who created those titles, but once those high chiefs die, the new chiefs and their families will surely try to pass their titles on to their children. "All things are possible," he declared emphatically, "for those whose words are powerful."

The *matai* system was the foundation of traditional Samoan society, and it remains so in modified form today. Thus, it is not surprising that many Samoans object to subverting the system for political purposes. They see that the *matai* system is now in danger of collapse. Yet there is also wide support for some of the consequences of the electoral maneuvering. The rapid spread of *matai* status is paving the way for the individualization of contemporary

---

[19] In the most flagrant cases, even this pretense is not maintained.

Samoan society. It is ennabling, speeding, and easing some of the social, economic, and political changes that many Samoans desire.

STOCKING A SMALL POND

One of the tragedies of large industrial societies is the insignificance and powerlessness that many people feel. To regain a sense of importance we create smaller and smaller social groups. We join clubs or gangs or professional associations, striving to find an arena where we matter, a small pond where we can feel like big fish. Samoans (especially Samoan men) have solved that problem with the *matai* system.

Western Samoa itself is a fairly small pond. The whole nation is no bigger nor more populous than an average county in the midwestern United States. Yet within that tiny nation is squeezed the entire apparatus of a modern nation. The country itself is further divided into districts, then villages, then extended families, and now into nuclear families—each with its own chief. One of the great successes of traditional Samoan society is the creation of a system where many people share a measure of dignity, power, and importance. As Holmes (1980) notes, this creates a broad base of individual support so that changes are likely to be incorporated into the system rather than overthrow it.

Nevertheless, the prestige and power of *matai* status must remain relatively scarce if they are to be worth achieving. By splitting and sharing titles among many people and spreading *matai* status far more widely than before, Samoans are approaching a critical juncture in their cultural history. In broadening the base of the *matai* system they may be adapting and strengthening it to serve them into the 21st century, or they may be creating a pointless and lifeless system where—by giving everyone something—no one gets anything.

The honor and power of *matai* status are significantly diluted today, but *matai* still bear their titles with dignity and pride. Low-ranking talking chiefs often told me of the great "weight" and profound "dignity" of their chiefly status. Lemaua is a kind but unaccomplished "ballot *matai*" whose own family ridicules him for his laziness, yet he often boasted to me: "In Samoan custom, power belongs to the chief." Now that the vast majority of adult men are chiefs, however, their power is usually restricted to simple patriarchy over their own nuclear families, and the tokens of their prestige are limited to politeness of speech from fellow *matai* and modest deference from untitled people.

INDEPENDENT INCOMES AND THE SHARING AND SPLITTING OF TITLES

The desire that people have for individual rights over cash-crop land and other resources has been changing both land tenure and the broader *matai* system since long before parliamentary elections began. The first documented title splitting occurred in the 1920s (Marsack 1958:7, and court records, Mulinu'u and Tuasivi), at the same time the change in land tenure began. The population was then at its lowest ebb following the devastating flu epidemic of 1918, so population increase cannot account for the changes. By the time the wholesale bestowal of titles for election purposes began in the early 1960s, both the new tenure system and the sharing and splitting of titles were already well established.[20]

Individuals want *matai* titles to solidify their control over economic resources. The system also works the other way around. Having gained personal control over sources of income, individuals can support their own candidacy for a title, even if no appreciable segment of the extended family is united behind them. Even the resident members of the title descent group no longer cooperate in production, and they rarely own land or other productive resources together. Instead of the extended family working to reach a unified choice, each contender can hold out for victory. The result is that today people are content to placate all branches of the extended family by dividing the title among several contenders.

A TITLE BESTOWAL CEREMONY

I witnessed an example of this process of compromise during the election and installation of new *matai* in a village near Vaega. The elderly high chief of the extended family had died two years earlier, and four different branches of the extended family had been fighting in court to win the succession of their respective candidates. A new *matai* is supposed to be elected by unanimous consent, but no branch would accept that a rival might receive the title while they remained without. The family finally agreed to bestow the title on all of the rivals. Each faction then held its own discussion to choose who would receive their share of the title. In this case there were no electoral reasons for sharing the title, it was just a matter of family pride—and the economic ability to support it. Once the line had been breached, other factions advanced their candidates as well. Until the installation ceremony began, we did not know who or how many people would receive the title.

The family sought out Asiata Iakopo to act as arbitrator. He is the leading member of the *tamafafine*, or "female child," subgroup of the title, which traditionally plays that role in title disputes. I went to Asiata's house two nights before the installation ceremony, when the leading orators from all the factions came to meet with him. The purpose of the meeting was to set a minimum contribution for receiving a share of the title at the installation ceremony. They agreed on the following standard:

WS $25 dollars
    2 large kegs of salt beef, or 1 large pig
    1 case of tinned fish or meat

---

[20] See Powles (1979:189) for a history of the early proliferation of *matai* titles.

20 loaves of bread
1 large pot of Chinese noodles
3 packages of cookies
1 large can of jam
20 pounds of ship's biscuits
1 large teapot of cocoa
50 breadfruit
20 *'ie tōga*, or "fine mats"
1 large *'ie tōga* (called the *'ie o le nofo*)

On the day of the ceremony, I joined a friend who belonged to one of the factions and we walked together up the gravel road to the village. His wife followed twenty yards behind us, carrying our share of the fine mats rolled up in a sugar sack under her arm. We arrived at the extended family's compound of houses amid a crowd of other visitors bringing fine mats, kegs of salt beef, cases of canned mackerel, tins of ship's biscuits, and cardboard boxes full of fresh bread from Salelologa. Young, untitled men arrived carrying the quarters and ribs of a freshly slaughtered steer on their shoulders. Two pickup trucks pulled up on the grass between the houses and more sweaty, smokey, untitled men unloaded two large roast pigs on crude wooden litters.

More guests arrived with gifts of fine mats and money, each group entering the house where their respective kin had gathered. When everything had been assembled and checked off by each faction, they brought it all together to the house where our group sat with Asiata Iakopo. He called five factions in turn, and told them to present each item on the list so that the entire family could see and count it. Some factions brought more than the minimum, others barely scraped by with smaller pigs and fine mats. While the goods were being presented, someone noticed that one of the big roast pigs had gone bad. It had been only lightly cooked the night before. The family that had brought it hurried it away, and the ceremony was delayed while they secured two cases of tinned fish to replace the pig.

When all the preparations had been made, we gathered solemnly in the central house of the compound. One hundred and ten *matai* sat in double and triple rows along the four sides of the house and spilling out onto the stone foundation and the grass outside. Twenty-seven of the *matai* were members of the title descent group that was conferring the new titles, and the rest were guests from the surrounding area.

When we were all seated, the candidates filed in. They each wore a fine mat as a skirt wrapped around over a cloth *lāvalava*. Their bare chests were shiny with sweet-smelling oil and draped with necklaces of flowers and paper money. The first candidate was a thin old man, a talking chief who came to receive his family's highest honor, probably not long before his death. He wore a large, very finely woven *'ie tōga* over his black *lāvalava*, with pieces of bright orange and red rayon cloth tucked under his belt. Around his neck hung a garland of red paper flowers and a necklace of New Zealand dollar bills tied at their centers to a strip of white cloth so they resembled little bows. Encircling the old man's balding head was a broad band of dime store pearls.

Five men had come to share a high chief's title that two other men already held. Three of the candidates did not live in the district. Two of those were completely unknown to my friend, who was himself a resident member of the family. One candidate had come from New Zealand. My friend's branch of the family was represented by a young, unaccomplished man of 24 years, his head bowed in humility on so great an occasion. He was the only adult male available to satisfy his widowed mother's desire for family honor.

The candidates filed around the perimeter shaking hands, first with the high chiefs who sat cross-legged at one end of the open-sided house, and then with the orators who sat along the front. The five candidates finally took their seats at the other end of the house where Asiata Iakopo sat alone. Then all five of the district's Methodist ministers entered, sweating profusely in their formal black coats and *lāvalava*, white shirts, and colorful striped ties. One after the other they led the house in song and prayer.

The highest ranking minister gave a combination speech and sermon on the exalted status and responsibility of *matai*, honored both on earth and in heaven. I had heard him give the speech before at another installation ceremony: " 'M' is for *matai* . . . 'A' is for *atamai* (intelligence) . . . 'T' is for . . ."

The five candidates then knelt in the center of the house while the five ministers stood before them. Each minister placed his palms on the head of the candidate who kneeled before him, while five chiefs did the same from behind. With their hands in place, Fogalele said a prayer over them. The entire assembly then sang another hymn, the leading minister delivered a final prayer, and the ministers departed.

As soon as they had left, the assembled *matai* began the long cycle of polite speeches, debate, and formal oration that carries a kava ceremony forward to the final crescendo of clapping hands and the ceremonious calling of the kava. When the last cup of kava had been presented, the five new *ali'i* filed out, depositing their fine mats, rayon cloth, and money necklaces in front of Selesele Tasi, the highest ranking orator in the district. This began the redistribution of goods and money.

Selesele announced that the five chiefs who had debated the right to give the formal kava speech would each receive one of the fine mats that the candidates had worn. As Selesele spoke, a bare-chested talking chief jumped from his seat to distribute the fine mats to their new owners. Selesele then apportioned the pieces of rayon cloth (a substitute for bark cloth *siapo*) and money garlands among the other high-ranking orators.

The local kin of the six high chiefs attending the ceremony honored each one by presenting him with a collection of special gifts, called a *sua*. The *sua* consisted of a single fine mat, a can of meat or fish, a small basket of cooked taro and meat, and either a small ceramic teapot of cocoa or a fresh drinking coconut, each adorned with a $1 bill. When the *sua* had been presented (and quickly whisked away), the dozens of younger men and women in attendance served food to all 115 seated *matai*.

With the meal quickly over, Selesele Tasi presided over the division of the goods and money that each candidate's faction had contributed. Young men carried all of the goods into the center of the house where the entire assembly could witness the division. Selesele allotted one keg of salt beef and one case of fish to *Sā Asiatā*, the Family of Asiata, and one of each to the army of untitled men and women who had prepared and served the food. Another keg of beef went to each of the traditional districts represented among the guests. He divided the remaining kegs among the high chiefs who represented the guest extended families.

The only items left in the center of the floor were the roast pigs and sections of beef, arranged side-by-side on coarse mats of woven coconut leaves. Selesele ordered that the pigs and fresh beef be divided among the remaining *matai* present, with large portions also going to each of the five pastors. The attendants immediately began to carve and hack the carcasses into traditionally prescribed pieces, their machetes crunching through bones and occasionally clanging off the oven rocks that had been stuffed into the pigs' chest cavities during cooking. Three mangy dogs slipped into the house and crept around the butchers, wolfing down stray fragments of flesh or lapping at the juice that ran through the mats onto the concrete floor.

As the carving proceeded, other young, low-ranking chiefs scurried around the perimeter of the house distributing portions of pork and beef to the sitting *matai*. Though the men worked at breakneck speed, both the division of meat and its distribution went strictly according to rank. They took great care with the portions they gave to the higher-ranking chiefs. As the distribution reached the mass of undifferentiated, low-ranking talking chiefs, however, the attendants merely hacked off lumps of pork or beef and handed them to anyone who was within reach.

With the division of goods over, the group quickly broke up to prepare for the final act. The 83 *matai* who were not members of the host title descent group moved to a house across the road. After a brief preparation, the host family's leading orators stepped out of their house onto the grass, and the visiting chiefs came out of their house and sat in a semicircle on the grass. The two groups faced each other across the asphalt road, the leading orator from each standing nobly with a long speaking staff thrust out before him in his right hand and a ceremonial fly whisk draped over his left shoulder.

The orator from the family's delegation spoke first, his chest bare and his ample waist girdled in a fine mat. After a short speech that was, like many other formal speeches, so esoteric as to be largely unintelligible to me (and to many Samoans), he began to announce the gifts. Each of the Asiatas received one of the large, *'ie o le nofo* fine mats. As the orator announced each gift, someone in the family quickly unfolded the fine mat and paraded it briefly for all to see, then took it to the high chief where he sat inside the house and laid it before him. As usual, each recipient protested modestly

Photo 33. The host family distributes fine mats to the talking chiefs who have attended the ceremony as guests. In this case it is the funeral of the high chief, Gasu, in Pitonu'u village.

that the others should receive theirs first. The orator announced that Selesele Tasi would receive $10, to thank him for conducting the division of goods.

Then the orator called the name of each *matai* waiting across the road. With each announcement, an untitled member of the family scurried across the road with a fine mat spread between his or her arms and handed it to the chief. Some guests also received small gifts of money, especially those who had come from a distance. The family's orator called each name in a loud, measured tone, while the other family members worked frantically in the house behind him to count and arrange the fine mats so that each man received an appropriate gift. People in the house often called out to the speaker, reminding him of someone he had forgotten or advising him to say this or that splendid thing. In reply, the spokesman for the visitors did not hesitate to stop the proceedings and argue—sometimes with humor and sometimes with force—for a greater gift for someone who felt slighted. With a final round of speeches, the bestowal ceremony was over.

One more act of the pageant remained, however—a kind of encore that was performed the following day. The candidate who had come from New Zealand was a mere untitled man when he arrived, so the village had given him no special reception. Now that he was a *matai*, the village chiefs performed a kava ceremony to welcome him. By this small stretching of Samoan etiquette, the new chief gained the opportunity to give away more money to the dozens of chiefs who came to honor him. The new chief also presented gifts, including a large donation of cash, to members of his host family. He also gave smaller gifts of a few New Zealand dollars to every adult who greeted him. Finally, he entertained some of the village *matai* at Taylor's bar and pool hall in Salelologa.

Altogether, the *saofa'i* had been a grand affair, fueled by the donations of five proud new chiefs and their families. But I could not help wondering how an extended family operates as a unit with seven equal leaders, each jealously guarding his own rights, privileges, and authority. The answer, as I learned, is that it does not. None of the men acquired authority over any new land or laborers by virtue of his new title—and little new authority over the members of even his own faction. Three of the new chiefs departed immediately for their homes in other villages or overseas. Except in honorific matters pertaining directly to the title, little had changed.

Formerly, the extended family united behind one candidate who had the social and political skills and the resources to *tausi le 'āiga*, or "care for the family." That person and his near relatives had to collect most of the food and goods needed to stage an installation ceremony that was appropriate in scale to the grandeur of that particular title. This could be a difficult burden to bear, and villagers say that the family was often "broke" when it was over. People valued a high title partly for the very reason that it afforded them an opportunity to demonstrate how *lima mālosi*, "strong handed," and *lima fōa'i*, "giving handed," a family was.

In modern ceremonies like the one just described, the families of several candidates contribute shares in a somewhat larger total of goods instead of one family providing everything. Each candidate now represents only a segment of the extended family, and each one's supporters help provide the needed goods. Eleven separate households contributed directly to my friend's faction of the family, and others contributed indirectly, so at least fifty or sixty households probably contributed to the entire ceremony.

The result was that many of the goods distributed at the ceremony were exchanged between the people who had collected them earlier, rather than one group providing the bulk of the goods. During the distribution of gifts, about WS $1,775 (US $1,500) of the original WS $2,350 worth of purchased goods, cash, pigs, and fine mats went to people outside the extended family. That amounts to an average expense of about WS $30 for each household that contributed to the ceremony. Most of that loss was in pigs and fine mats for which they incurred no cash expense. Contributors would soon recover even that small loss when they attended ceremonies staged by other extended families.

In contemporary circumstances, the title holder is usually little more than a ceremonial figurehead of the extended family. By sharing their titles among several candidates, extended families recognize (and sometimes increase) the already existing independence of their constituent households. Title sharing rarely (if ever) causes the breakup of an extended family that was formerly intact. Instead, the sharing of titles itself results from the earlier breakup of the extended family as a productive unit. Family members continue to help each other when they are in need, but they rarely produce or consume together. The extended family is still a social unit, but except for its (important) role giving mutual assistance, it has little economic function.

A *matai*'s social and ceremonial prerogatives were once symbols of the real authority he held over his extended family and its lands. An installation ceremony was the public investiture of that authority, and the ceremony itself was primarily the means to that end. Today, these titles are losing their power and material importance, leaving only an historical legacy to stir the hearts of men. Without a foundation of secular power, that legacy may also fade. Villagers continue to hold installation ceremonies, but the ceremonies have become largely ends in themselves—grand ceremonies that proclaim, rather than affirm, the importance of men.

THE CYCLE OF *TAUTUA* IS BROKEN

The traditional power of *matai* is based on two complementary principles: *pule* and *tautua*. The first is the chief's *pule*, or "authority," over the extended family's land and labor. The second is the *tautua*, or "service," of the extended family members to their chief. People traditionally gained material wealth, political power, and physical ease not by greater individual production or income, but primarily by organizing and then skimming off some of the labor and produce of those who served them. This system of authority and service is organized largely on seniority—those who are younger serve and obey those who are older. Ironically, this kind of system is stable only as long as the participants are sure that it will continue. As long as the system is closed and the cycle secure, young people perceive their service as a tolerable burden, knowing that one day they will, in their turn, command the service of others.

The cycle of *tautua* has been broken in the minds of many young people today. New technology and a market economy make individual production, profit, and accumulation of wealth possible. Many young people seek their futures in wage labor outside the village or even overseas, and they doubt that their own service will ever be repaid by a younger generation. In these circumstances, they no longer serve so gladly.

In 1962 Farrell and Ward wrote:

> A revolution in Samoan agriculture could be brought about that would raise the general standard of living and have ramifications in all sectors of the economy. But . . . to achieve such ends would require something in the nature of a social revolution (1962:237).

Samoan villagers have now accomplished most of that social revolution, not in spite of, but largely because of, their desires for larger and more secure farm incomes. Yet the agricultural revolution has not followed. From this we can see that traditional Samoan social institutions are not blocking development. The major obstacles lie elsewhere—in the economics of village agriculture.

6/*Su'e Tupe*:
Searching for Money

There is a chain of resort hotels called "Club Med" scattered around the world in idyllic tropical settings. The resorts offer to take vacationers "back to nature" and provide them with the perfect "antidote to civilization." One of the trademarks of these resorts is that after guests check in, they need no money. All of their food, drink, and recreational activities are either included in the purchase price or guests barter for them with beads (which they buy at the outset). The idea is to create the illusion, however thin, that guests have escaped to that mythical paradise where life is free and easy, where all wants are satisfied simply but luxuriously without the money-grubbing that characterizes the outside world.

The idea of such a tropical paradise has a powerful allure: simple people living simply, their few needs easily gathered by their own hands or purchased at the local trade store (a bit of tobacco, a bottle of kerosene for the lamp, a bolt of cloth from which to fashion simple clothes, a can of fish to eat on a stormy day). A paradise where people are so content that they ignore or even resist opportunities to make more money.

I have often heard people comment, after a brief visit to a Samoan village, how easy life is there. They did not realize that the ease was merely their own and their elderly hosts'. It is an ease made possible by the unseen labor of a dozen hands, and in the case of their hosts, earned through years of youthful drudgery. Expecting, perhaps, to step into a real-life Club Med, visitors are often shocked at the frank materialism that Samoans sometimes display. Consider, for example, the following event that occurred early in 1983.

Asiata Iopu, one of the high chiefs of our district and the owner of the largest store in Vaega, had been ill for some time. When he recovered and was discharged from the hospital, the talking chiefs of Vaega travelled to Apia as a group to visit him. Nearly thirty talking chiefs made the trip, and we each took a basket of food (including baked taro and a chicken) as a gift. Eight other chiefs who could not attend sent their baskets of food along with us. Seven of the highest-ranking talking chiefs contributed small roast pigs. We had all agreed on these contributions at a formal meeting the night before we left.

Asiata Iopu was staying at his son's European-style house in Apia. When we arrived at the house, Asiata and his two sons, who are both middle-aged chiefs, came out to receive us in an open, Samoan-style house next to the main house. Once seated, we immediately began a kava ceremony. Asiata's son, Leaoa, spoke first for the family. Selesele Tasi answered for the visitors, stressing our love and high regard for Asiata and our support for him during his illness. Asiata was then 79 years old, and though he walked with difficulty, he was usually strong. That day, however, the sickness showed in dark circles around his eyes, and he replied weakly, his speech choked by emotion. As he thanked us for our support, I looked out past him at the elaborate tomb that nearly filled the yard next to the house. I wondered if it was the emotion of our meeting or the fear of death that choked his words.

When the speeches were finished, we cleared away the sitting mats from the center of the floor and presented our gifts of roast pigs, chickens, and taro. A few of the men then cut up the pigs and presented a leg to each talking chief and the back and rib case to each of the high chiefs present. Younger members of Asiata's family served each of us a large bowl of beef stew with a fried egg on top, a glass of Kool-Aid, and the baked taro that we had brought.

After eating, Asiata retired and the rest of us sprawled out on mats in the meeting house. It appeared that the affair might go on all afternoon, and I had work to attend to in town, so I left the others to wait while Asiata's family prepared their return gift. I heard later that Leaoa came back out after about an hour. He stood in front of the house, posing with Asiata's speaking staff, which showed that he was speaking in an official capacity for Asiata. Leaoa called to each man in turn, including myself and a few others who were temporarily absent, as well as those who had not made the trip but had sent a gift of food. Leaoa presented WS $10 and a fine mat to the highest-ranking orators (those who had brought pigs), and WS $20 and a fine mat to Selesele Tasi for giving the speech. Everyone else received $5 and one fine mat apiece. Then he gave the entire group another WS $200 as a *fa'aoso*, a traditional gift given at the departure of a travelling party. The group later divided the $200, giving $15 to the village pastor, $10 each to the two pastors at the Methodist high school, another $10 each to the men who had contributed the pigs, and $2 to each of the other men. The few remaining dollars helped defray part of the group's transportation expenses.

Later that week when we had all returned to Vaega, Na'i Fualaga came around distributing the $2 to those of us who had not been present at the division, including Nu'u and myself. Another talking chief, Laumoli, came by later in the day with my fine mat, which he had accepted in my place when Leaoa called my name. I knew that Laumoli had also accepted my $5, but he did not offer it. I quickly mentioned the $5 before he had a chance to get himself trapped by either omission or falsehood, which would have embarrassed us both. He produced the money promptly from a fold in his *lāvalava*, but I think he was hoping that I did not know about it. He only had $4, though. He said that he had used the other $1 to make up his boat fare on the return trip because he had lost all of his money to one of the other chiefs in a poker game the night before. I told him not to worry about the $1, to which he protested halfheartedly.

The next day after church Laumoli came up to me and declared that he would give me the other $1 as soon as he had it. He said his family was angry with him for losing his money in the poker game, and they had scolded him for his "ugly" behavior. Laumoli changed the subject by remarking that I had been foolish to leave the affair before it was over.

"You should know the *fa'a-Samoa* by now. If the talking chiefs pay a formal visit on a high chief, the high chief must return the honor by giving gifts to the visitors."

I had been involved in perhaps a dozen similar affairs before that, and I was aware of what would happen. But in addition to having some pressing matters to attend to, I still felt embarrassed sitting around outside someone's house waiting for him to come out and give me a gift.

That night I strolled down to Satufia village to see Milo Faletoi. In good Samoan fashion I took the first opportunity to tell him what a grand trip we had made to Apia to visit Asiata Iopu. His questions and comments give an indication of what talking chiefs find important in these formalities.

Timo: Our trip to visit Asiata was *very* nice.

Milo: What did you take?

Timo: Seven small pigs, 38 chickens, and baked taro.

Milo: Who went?

Timo: All the talking chiefs of Vaega, plus Tavu'i from Pitonu'u, and another chief I don't know.

Milo: Where was it held?

Timo: At Asiata Solomona's house.

Milo: The one by the sports grounds?

Timo: Yes, the big, European-style house.

Milo: Who gave the speech for the family?

Timo: Leaoa.

Milo: What did they give you?

Timo: Most of us got a fine mat and $5, but some of the men got $10 and Selesele Tasi got $20 for his speech. Then we got $200 for the going away present. [Milo paused for a moment to calculate and then, scowling with displeasure, announced his evaluation of the trip.]

Milo: Bad.

Timo: Bad? Why?

Milo: You should have sent only four or five chiefs to represent you and left everyone else at home. That way you wouldn't have wasted all that money on travel expenses. Your trip would have been "square." As it is, when you came back you were "broke."

POOLING FAMILY INCOME

Milo and other Samoan planters are indeed interested in obtaining more money. The problem is that they often turn away from their plantations to search for income from other sources, including social ceremonies like the one for Asiata Iopu, but especially from wage labor. According to estimates available in the early 1980s, farm incomes were substantially *higher* than wage incomes. Yet Samoans flocked to the wage jobs and neglected their plantations.[1] One explanation for this seemingly uneconomic preference for lower-paying wage jobs might be that planters have to share their farm incomes with other members of their extended families (who together own the plantation land) more than wage earners do (wages being the product of individual labor outside the family or village). I checked this explanation by searching for differences in the way villagers share incomes they obtain from different sources.

My friend and part-time assistant, Panoa Umama'o, and I informally interviewed fifty-seven primary farm producers in Vaega, including members of every farm household. Only two people reported minor differences in the way income from different sources was treated in their families. Other than those two exceptions, everyone agreed that incomes from all sources are normally allocated for similar purposes and shared in similar ways within any particular household.

There are differences among households in how money is pooled and then disbursed, but these differences are due mainly to the differing age structures of households. As the members of households mature, the way they handle their family incomes changes in a regular pattern. Take, for example, the case of a young household whose head is still an active producer and whose children do not yet have major family responsibilities of their own. In this type of household, all of the members will generally deposit all of their income with the head of the household (who is almost always a *matai*). If the family is short of money or expecting a major expense (such as school fees), the *matai* might return an allowance of only WS $2 or WS $3 (or nothing at all) out of a WS $50 or WS $75 crop sale to each of his older sons "for tobacco." If the family has more money, the sons might get as much as WS $5 each. An average family would make a sale of this size roughly once a month.

When the *matai* of this household reaches 45–50 years old, his sons (or sons-in-law) take over most of the plantation work. They and their spouses already have several small children of their own to support. All members of the household still give their earnings to the *matai*, but now he usually gives each of them an allowance of WS $10 or WS $20. He keeps the rest to support himself, his wife and younger children, and his elderly parents if they are living. As a *matai*, he must also contribute to various village and church collections.

---

[1] For citations see Chapter One.

Type of Household as Reflected by Income Control

	I	II	III	IV	V
	keep all	give $5	give $10–20	keep $5	give all
Head of Household					
Matai	14	7	12	7	1
Untitled men	7	2			
Women	2				

————————————→   increasing age   ————————————→

Figure 6.1 Control and distribution of cash income in fifty-two Vaega farm households by type of head of household. In Type I (first column), the head of the household keeps all of the household's income. Heads of households retain less of their household's incomes as the age structures of the households mature through Types II, III, IV, and V.

By the time the *matai* is old and inactive, most of his children have either left the village, or they have set up their own, economically independent households within the village. At least one son (and less often a daughter with her husband) usually settles permanently on the family homestead to live with and care for the now elderly parents. These adult offspring now have large families of their own to support, while the *matai* does not. Consequently, they reverse the previous allotment of money. The aging *matai* now keeps only WS $5 or WS $10 for tobacco and other personal uses, and the son (or son-in-law) keeps the rest and manages the financial affairs of the entire family.

Families treat wage income much the same. The only major difference is that wage earners share fewer of the family's household chores than their homebound brothers and sisters. When relatives working overseas or in Apia send money home, they usually send it to one of the parents.[2] Since remittances from overseas are often larger lump sums than local incomes, villagers often earmark remittances for special purposes (such as building a new house or improving the old one). Otherwise, families pool remittances with other income.

Figure 6.1 shows the types of income-pooling arrangements for fifty-two village households.[3] In Type I households, the head of the household keeps all income. None of the twenty-three Type I households had mature offspring. The table shows that among the Type I households, there are fourteen *matai*-headed households. As these fourteen families mature, their method of cash control will shift from left to right across the table, changing them into Type II and III, and finally Type IV or V households. The nine untitled men who are heads of households will gradually receive *matai* titles of their own. When they do, their households will move up into the first row on the table, replacing

---

[2] Many migrants send at least some money directly to their mothers rather than to their fathers. They do this to express their affection for their mothers and sometimes also to give their mothers and her children first chance at the money.

[3] I have excluded four households: three nonagricultural households and one household that left the village during the survey.

older *matai*. There are no adult males in the two households headed by women. These women will not receive *matai* titles. As they and their children mature, however, their method of cash control will move across the table as well. The economic independence of a young household may increase somewhat when the husband receives a *matai* title of his own, but the title is more a means of explicitly recognizing and legitimizing the social facts and economic necessities that already exist within a family.

Wives, rather than husbands, often manage the household's daily finances. This is a delegation of responsibility, however. It does not imply that the *matai* has relinquished his authority over family finances. I am not aware of a single family in Vaega where a woman exercised real power over her husband.[4] Many wives seem even to lack much influence with their husbands, except in matters relating to their own relatives. It is common, however, for husband and wife to manage household affairs together, subject to the final authority of the husband.

PERSONAL TEMPTATION OVERCOMES FAMILY OBLIGATION

Individuals sometimes keep small amounts of income secret from the rest of the family. This may happen whether it is the offspring who normally hands the money over to the parent, or the parent to the offspring. Individuals rarely appropriate their regular income, such as wages or money from copra sales, in this way. On the other hand, I recorded several instances of young men who headed off to their family plantations in the morning, but worked for pay instead on a neighbor's land. They did not report that income to their families when they returned in the afternoon. Wage earners sometimes treat small bonuses in the same way. The head of a household sometimes keeps small cash gifts as well, and does not mention them to other members of the family.

Kilikiki, a 34-year-old untitled man with a wife and three children, explained how pooling and redistribution of money worked in his family. He normally sells the family's copra at Asiata Iopu's store. He takes the money that is left after the store debt has been cancelled to his father, the 64-year-old *matai* of the family. Kilikiki tells his father how much they received for the copra, how much had been deducted for the debt, and how much is left over. Then his father usually says "Give me $10." Kilikiki gives him the $10 and keeps the rest of the money himself. From that money, Kilikiki pays all the family's expenses.

Kilikiki said that if he earned $5 working for pay, he would tell his father and either give him $1 outright or his father would request $1 for tobacco. Kilikiki told me that "It is not forbidden to hide money from the *matai*, but it would be bad service (*tautua leaga*)." Then he added with a chuckle, "If I

---

[4] Since I did not investigate this question directly, there may be exceptions of which I remain unaware.

found $5 on the road, I would just stick it in my shirt pocket and not tell him."

In Apia it is not unheard of for family members to steal fine mats from their own (or a neighbor's) house and peddle them door to door. In the village young men sometimes sell family produce secretly and keep the proceeds. On one extraordinary occasion, a young man from western Savaii arrived unexpectedly in Vaega at my neighbor's house. His family had sent him on the bus to Salelologa to sell 100 pounds of dried cocoa at the government warehouse. The family could receive a slightly better price there than at their local village stores. The young man sold the cocoa for WS $85 and promptly spent the entire amount on a wild spree. Instead of returning home empty-handed, he moved in with his relatives in Vaega for a few months, waiting for the storm to blow over.

The young man showed in the next few months that he was not indolent. He worked diligently for his relatives. Though he was slightly built for a Samoan (perhaps 5' 8" and 150 pounds), I once watched him pass my house carrying two huge baskets of coconuts on a pole across his shoulder. He had walked barefoot a mile and a half along the gravel road from the coconut plantations to his relatives' house. He dropped the immense load behind the house and sat sweating and grinning while I counted and weighed the nuts. The two baskets contained 127 husked coconuts weighing 182 pounds. Ten minutes later he left again for the plantation, and he soon returned with another load of 124 nuts.

The important principle at work in all these examples is that families rarely have enough money to squander, and all members must contribute what they can to the family income pool. Vaega farm families usually do not have enough resources to set aside special funds for the entertainment of individual members. Temptation, however, sometimes overcomes the members' strong sense of family obligation.

REDISTRIBUTING FAMILY INCOME

In the families of Samoan planters, all members except the very oldest and youngest contribute significantly to household production and income. This does not mean, however, that all family members receive equal shares. The parents (especially the father) are usually the best dressed, the best fed, and certainly the most travelled members of the household. Babies are often pampered. Even very poor families sometimes buy expensive luxuries such as talcum powder for them. Once they reach the toddler stage, however, children receive much less attention from their parents. The primary responsibility for tending children shifts from their mothers to their only slightly older sisters (and less often, their brothers). While most households can afford to spend little money on children's favors, their school fees, materials, and uniforms are major household expenses.

As children grow older, they shoulder an increasing share of the household's chores and productive work. Each task is passed down the chain of command to the youngest person who is capable of doing it. As they mature, young men and women begin to do most of the hard work in the plantations and around the house, and they receive few favors. This is especially true for sons-in-law and daughters-in-law if they live with their spouse's family.

Samoan culture emphasizes the superior status and authority of all parents—and especially *matai*—over their children. The unequal distribution of goods within the family is an important way of demonstrating, protecting, and sometimes taking advantage of that status difference. Since mature offspring are the most likely to challenge their parents' authority, they are the least likely to receive favors or other individual consideration. The head of a household, who is almost always a male and usually a *matai*, consumes a larger share than any other member. It is uncommon, however, for a *matai* to abuse his position. There was variation among families in Vaega, but during my fieldwork period no family suffered economic hardship from a *matai*'s excesses, nor did I hear of any such incidents occurring earlier.

Samoan children learn very early to be strictly obedient to their parents and grandparents, as well as to be fiercely loyal to them and to the rest of their family. One demonstration of children's respect, loyalty, and love for their parents is the economic sacrifice they often make in order to give special gifts to their parents, especially their fathers. For example, children who live overseas are expected to pay for at least one extended visit by their father, and their mother if possible. And when the father returns to his village, he is expected to bring with him substantial amounts of food, household goods, and cash— sometimes enough cash to build an entire new house. These gifts come from all of the relatives, friends, and fellow villagers that the travelers meet during their overseas visits, but the greatest amounts come from their own children.

TIGHT BUDGETS

Perhaps because of their generosity, Samoan villagers have a reputation among outsiders for being "easy-come, easy-go" spendthrifts. Once again, the reputation is far from accurate. Because of the great difficulty of earning money, most families budget their cash incomes carefully, as they do their other resources. Villagers are extremely frugal in most of their affairs. For example, the head of the household locks the cash from copra sales in a trunk and parcels it out over several weeks. A family of ten that receives five cans of mackerel at a funeral would usually consume only one or two cans per meal spread out over several days. The family members share the one or two cans between them, eating the fish with taro or breadfruit.[5] Many times I

---

[5] One reason villagers like canned fish is that the flavor is quite strong, so a small amount can be stretched to feed several people. Contrary to popular opinion, few people actually prefer it to fresh fish.

have heard a man call out to a nearby child, *Mai se 'afi!* "Bring a fire!" The child goes immediately to the cookhouse and returns with a burning brand to light the man's cigarette, while he sits holding a ten-cent box of matches in his hand. I was gently chastised more than once myself for using a match to light my lantern when I could have sent a child to fetch an ember from a fire twenty yards away. The difference between levying a WS 20¢ or a WS 40¢ fine is enough to occupy a village council in a twenty-minute debate. Any time people hear of someone spending money unnecessarily, they click their tongues and wag their heads, then remark with genuine sadness, *Ma'imau lea tupe*. "The money was wasted."

In spite of careful budgeting, most families exhaust their copra money before the next harvest. When this happens, local store owners are usually willing to allow purchases on credit. In order to protect themselves, store owners limit a household's credit to between about WS $20 and WS $40, depending on the usual size of that family's copra harvest. The family cancels its debt with its next sale of copra. That is why most village stores both provide credit to their customers and buy copra from them. If they do not provide credit, they attract little business. If they do not buy copra, they have trouble collecting on the credit they have advanced. Store owners also want to buy copra because they earn a profit by reselling it in bulk to the government. Thus, if villagers do not sell at least some of their copra to a local store, the owner may refuse to extend them credit.

Since most villagers need credit at local stores, they are reluctant to sell their copra to the government (which pays about 10 percent more for it), or alienate store owners in other ways. Villagers are not completely powerless in these relationships, however. Many households have credit accounts at two or three village stores, and sometimes even at larger stores in Salelologa. Each of these store owners wants their business, and perhaps more importantly, wants them to pay their outstanding debts. This leaves a good deal of power in the hands of the customers.

Social obligations such as funerals or title presentations require larger outlays. But even at apparently extravagant social events, villagers try to watch their expenses very carefully, and they do their best to come out even (or preferably ahead) in the long run. The money and goods for these affairs are almost always pooled from many households. While the host family gives away these goods as gifts, the hosts are careful to remember whom they have obliged and by how much, hoping to receive reciprocal gifts in the future.

The host family appoints one of its members to act as a scribe at the funeral reception. The scribe sits beside the elders and records every gift that the family receives. Later on in the day, the family distributes to the guests some of its own resources and some of the gifts it has accumulated. Attention to the scribe's list prevents the unintentional slighting of guests. After the funeral, the leaders of the host family meet privately to account for all of the goods they pooled, the gifts they received, and the return gifts that they

Photo 34a. The host family receiving guests at the funeral of Gasu. His daughter and wife sit beside his body while his son, Selesele Misikupa (at the far left of the picture with the notebook) records the gifts brought by each group of visitors.

presented to their guests. They divide among themselves any goods or cash that remain.[6]

THE STRUGGLE TO SAVE

Most households in Vaega have a passbook savings account at one of the two banks in Salelologa, but many of these accounts are inactive or hold only a few dollars. Because of the constant demands on their meager incomes, villagers find it very difficult to save money. In an attempt to alleviate this pressure on individual incomes, villagers try to enforce group saving through their many formal and informal organizations. In this way they harness the social power of the group to insulate individuals from both their own desires and from the entreaties of their relatives. For example, the Women's Committee in Vaega periodically requires each of its members to contribute WS $10 (US $8.50), which the officers deposit in the Committee's savings account in Salelologa. These funds still belong to the individuals who contributed them, but the Committee prohibits their withdrawal except for authorized

---

[6] This procedure leaves the scribe in a position where it is possible to hide and then appropriate part of the group's common assets. Such accusations are often made, and judging from my inspection of several of these record books, with some justification.

Photo 34b. The widow Gasu, dressed in her mourning clothes on the day of her husband's funeral.

group projects. In 1983 many of the women had saved WS $50 in this way. For many households, that was more than all of their other savings combined.

The *taulele'a*, or untitled men of the village, had an even grander savings plan involving their cattle herd. In 1978 they received twenty-one cattle as part of the government's heavily subsidized Rural Development Programme. The villagers wanted to split the herd into smaller, individually owned herds, but there were not enough cattle to go around and the terms of the project prevented individual ownership. The villagers decided to increase the size of the herd for a few years. After they had repaid their 30 percent share of the project's cost, they would divide the herd among the village families.

During the following three years, the untitled men of Vaega had one of the more successful village cattle projects in the country. Together with the village *matai*, and under their direction, the untitled men created two large cattle pastures by fencing in many smaller family coconut plots. By late 1981, the herd had increased to between seventy and eighty head. But about that time the original fences began to deteriorate and the communal work group proved inadequate to maintaining them. At the direction of the chiefs, the entire male population of the village had to muster several times to repair the fences and search for the cattle that had escaped. They butchered a few of the young bulls and sold the meat to a store in Salelologa for about WS $250 each. Other times they sold the meat at a modest price in the village, or donated it outright to all village households. They deposited the income from the sales in the group's savings account in Salelologa. As the fences aged, however, the problem worsened, and by 1983 the herd was reduced to only a few animals.

The untitled men also raised money from within their own group by forcing every member to borrow a certain sum and then repay it a few weeks later with up to one-third interest. They call this *tupe fa'aola*, "growing money." By raising money in this way and adding it to their cattle proceeds, they were able to save WS $1,500 (US $1,275), or roughly WS $30 per person. They spent some of this money on group projects, such as purchasing bolts of red and white flowered cloth to make matching *lāvalava* for their cricket team. They also loaned money to individuals within their own group. Sometimes the council of *matai* or the Women's Committee borrowed money from them. One such occasion was when many of the village *matai* accompanied the pastor and his wife to the week-long, annual church conference in Apia. The untitled men extended these civic loans without interest. The group that borrowed the money repaid it by collecting a few dollars from each member after the next copra harvest.

The untitled men's savings account was severely depleted in mid-1982. Three of their group were arrested after the cricket fight and the group paid their legal expenses. Shortly after that, a few of the group's officers (who were also the oldest members of the group) used a large part of the remaining funds for private purposes, which did not excite the pleasure of the junior members.

The untitled men decide their business and other matters at their own council meetings, which they hold periodically in the home of one of their senior members. The recognized leaders at these meetings (and in all their affairs) are the half dozen oldest men, two of whom are in their forties. In contrast, the group's youngest members are just out of school. Asiata Iakopo's son, Eti, was the nominal leader of the group because of his father's supreme status and because he was one of the oldest members. When Eti received his *matai* title, he left the group to join the other chiefs. The council meetings of the untitled men are nearly exact replicas of the chiefs' councils. One of its explicit purposes is to provide a training ground for young men, where they can practice the delicate etiquette of village politics and sharpen their skills in the demanding arena of public oratory.

Individuals also band together informally to save money. As I mentioned previously, a few young men sometimes hire themselves out as a team to clear and plant taro gardens. My neighbor, Gafa, and his younger brother, and Nu'u's oldest son, Pulusi, joined together with some other friends to form a boxing team. They raised the few dollars they needed for entry fees and transportation to the local boxing arena in Sapapalii by planting taro for their neighbors. For several weeks before the fights they were up at dawn, jogging along the village road and looking very serious. In the evenings they would return from the plantations to spar in the clear area in front of Gafa's house, under the tutelage of his father.

Asiata Iakopo also instituted an informal Christmas savings plan among the dominoes players who regularly met at his house. Eleven regular players contributed WS 50¢ each week for several months. Monanu, one of the players, deposited the money for the group. In this case the group was apparently too informal to enforce regular saving. When I asked Asiata about it again, he laughed and said they had abandoned the project because too many people missed their weekly contributions.

INVESTING

Villagers are able to save some of their incomes, but they invest very little of their savings in developing their plantations. Their reluctance to invest in their plantations does not indicate a general lack of interest in or apprecation for the merits of investing, however. At least four Vaega households own land in the Apia urban area, and they consider it a good investment. Members of two of those households independently suggested to me that I should buy land there as an investment as well.[7]

Many villagers want to open trade stores when they manage to save several hundred dollars. They believe that this is a surer (and easier) way to wealth than cash cropping. Unfortunately, a village like Vaega can support only two or three tiny stores at the most, so this avenue is not open to most households.

Lacking more attractive and more productive investments, villagers spend much of their incomes constructing civic and religious buildings and improving their own housing. This willingness to build expensive European-style houses on village residential plots shows indirectly that insecurity of tenure does not prevent them from investing in their plantations. Court records show that disputes over house plots are ten to fifteen times more common than disputes over plantation plots (O'Meara 1986:152–55). Since villagers are not reluctant to invest large sums of money to develop relatively insecure house plots, they must be even less reluctant to invest far smaller sums to develop plantation plots that are more secure—if there were good economic reasons for doing so.

In their investment decisions, their control of household budgets, their attempts to save, and in their obvious materialism, villagers demonstrate a

---

[7] When I replied that foreigners cannot own land in Western Samoa, both of these village investment advisors suggested that I have a son by a Samoan girl and then put the title to the land in his name.

desire for greater incomes and an economic mindedness that contrast sharply with popular opinions of them. They have also shown a willingness to adapt to take advantage of new economic opportunities, both at home and overseas. Similarly, analysis of their changing *matai* and land tenure systems reveals no significant social impediment to agricultural development. I had suspected that Samoan planters were not so different from other people, and I believed that their limited enthusiasm for cash cropping would appear more rational if we had better data comparing their economic returns from agriculture with those from their other sources of income. In order to obtain that information, I began a year-long survey of household labor, production, and income in Vaega.

THE ECONOMIC SURVEY

By the time I felt prepared enough to begin work on the survey, I had been living in Vaega for nearly eight months. I was thus well acquainted with the people, and they with me. As I had done twice earlier, I began with a formal speech at a meeting of the village council. I sat at Nu'u's side, and when I faltered he whispered choice phrases to me or prompted me in the niceties of council etiquette. I described the purpose and general content of the survey to the assembled chiefs, and then asked their permission to begin the survey.

I already knew what the council's answer would be. Several days before the council meeting I had taken the precaution of sounding out my closest allies and the leading chiefs in private, as I had seen villagers themselves do. All assured me that "There's nothing to it." Asiata Iakopo told me to go ahead with the survey without bothering to ask the council. *E pule a'u*, he told me regally. "The authority is mine."

I needed more than Asiata Iakopo's permission, however. To succeed I needed the full cooperation of every household in the village for an entire year. I thought it best to present my request directly to the leaders of those households in the council of chiefs. As I expected, the council readily granted permission.

According to the previous literature on Samoa, each *matai* controlled the land, labor, and income of his extended family. When I was first planning my survey of village economics, I thought I would only have to keep track of thirty-three survey forms—one for each of the recognized extended families (thirty-two in Vaega and one in Satufia). Fortunately, I first took the precaution of running a trial survey for two weeks with four neighboring famlies. I immediately discovered—to my horror—that within these extended families even adjacent households did not cooperate in production, and they did not know each other's incomes. Each nuclear family (composed of father, mother, and their children) controlled its own resources independently of the others. This forced me to conduct the survey by households rather than by extended families. For the purposes of the survey, I defined a "household" as the

Photo 35. Tino Lama (at left) and Meaalofa Nu'u preparing "pancakes" and hot cocoa drink in Meaalofa's house. Though Tino is Nu'u's sister, and she and her children and grandchildren live in the same house with Nu'u, their households are economically independent. Only on special occasions such as this one, when some guests were visiting Nu'u, do the two households work or consume together.

largest residential group that knew each other's activities and incomes. Thus, I had to expand the survey pool at the outset from thirty-three extended families to fifty-six economically independent households.

The trial survey also allowed me to improve both the survey form and my presentation of it. When the trial was over, Tunaali'i Agafili helped me polish the language in the questions. That was no easy task, for the Samoan language has no words for English economic terms such as "income" and "expenses." Villagers readily understand the concepts, however, so we settled on common descriptive phrases such as "money gained" (*tupe maua*) and "money wasted" (*tupe fa'ama'imau*). I took the finished survey form to the government printers office in Apia and returned a few days later with 3,000 copies. An English translation of the form appears in Figure 6.2. A copy of an actual form in Samoan appears in Figure 6.3.

For the next three weeks I went from house to house through the village, chatting informally with people and explaining the details of the survey. Once understood, I asked the head of each household if he or she would participate in the survey. To my relief, everyone agreed. After three weeks of explanation, practice, and constant checking, recorders in all fifty-six households were able to complete the forms without difficulty. At that point we began fifty-two weeks of formal recording.

FAMILY NUMBER _____ WEEK NUMBER _____

1. How many adults worked in your coconut plantation all day? ....
   How many for a half-day? ....
   How many children worked in your coconut plantation all day?......................
   How many for a half-day? ....

2. How many coconuts were brought from your land today?............................
   How many small baskets?..................................
   How many large baskets? ....
   How many horse bags? ....

3. How many husked coconuts were sold today? ....
   How many bags of nuts? ....
   What were the expenses for that sale of nuts? ....
   How much money was received today from the sale of nuts? ....

4. How many pounds of copra were sold today?............................
   How many baskets of copra? ....
   How many bags of copra? ....
   What were the expenses for that sale of copra? ....
   How much money was received today from the sale of copra?........................

5. How much was paid to people who worked the coconut trees and copra?.........

6. How much was paid for a truck to bring the coconuts back? ....

7. What other money was spent today on making copra? ....

8. How many people worked in your root-crop plantation all day? ....
   How many for a half-day? ....

9. How many taro were pulled from your plantation today? ....
   How many small baskets?..................................
   How many large baskets?..................................
   How many horse bags? ....

10. How many taro tops were planted in your plantation today?..........................

11. How many taro did you sell today? ....
    How many cases of taro? ....
    How many small baskets?..................................
    How many large baskets?..................................
    What were the expenses for that sale of taro? ....
    How much money was received today from the sale of taro?..........................

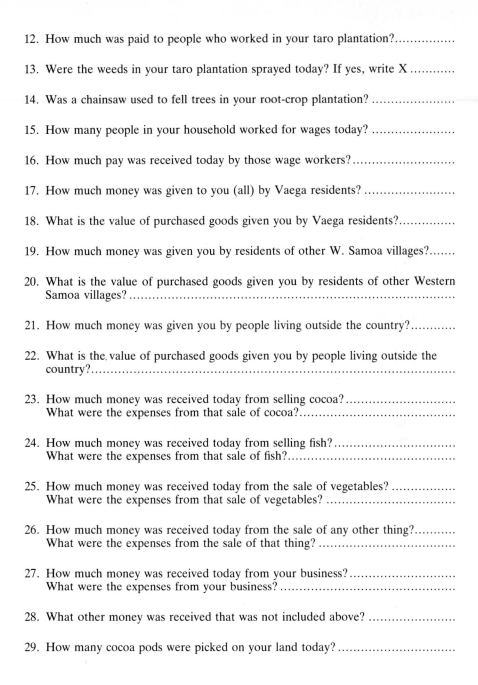

12. How much was paid to people who worked in your taro plantation?................

13. Were the weeds in your taro plantation sprayed today? If yes, write X ....

14. Was a chainsaw used to fell trees in your root-crop plantation? ....

15. How many people in your household worked for wages today? ....

16. How much pay was received today by those wage workers?...........................

17. How much money was given to you (all) by Vaega residents? ....

18. What is the value of purchased goods given you by Vaega residents?...............

19. How much money was given you by residents of other W. Samoa villages?.......

20. What is the value of purchased goods given you by residents of other Western Samoa villages? ....

21. How much money was given you by people living outside the country?............

22. What is the value of purchased goods given you by people living outside the country?..

23. How much money was received today from selling cocoa?............................
    What were the expenses from that sale of cocoa?.......................................

24. How much money was received today from selling fish?...............................
    What were the expenses from that sale of fish?...

25. How much money was received today from the sale of vegetables? ....
    What were the expenses from that sale of vegetables? ....

26. How much money was received today from the sale of any other thing?...........
    What were the expenses from the sale of that thing? ....

27. How much money was received today from your business?............................
    What were the expenses from your business? ....

28. What other money was received that was not included above? ....

29. How many cocoa pods were picked on your land today?...............................

Figure 6.2. English translation of the economic survey form shown in Figure 6.3. The spaces on the right-hand margin of the form have been omitted where the recorder noted activities for Tuesday through Saturday.

NUMBER AIGA ＿＿＿＿ NUMERA VAIASO ＿＿＿＿ ASO:

1. Pe toafia tagata matutua sa galulue i lou toganiu i le aso toa? ....
   Pe toafia i le afa aso? ....
   Pe toafia tamaiti sa galulue i lou toganiu i le aso atoa?.................................

2. Pe fia le aofai o popo masua na aumai i lou fanua i le aso lenei? ....
   Pe fia ato laiti?..
   Pe fai ato lapopoa? ....
   Pe fia taga a solofanua? ....

3. Pe fia le aofai o popo masua sa faatauina atu i le aso lenei?...........................
   Pe fia taga pop masua? ....
   Pe fia le aofai o tupe faamaimau ona o lena faatau atu o pop masua?..............
   Pe fia se tupe un maua mai i le aso lenei mai le faatau o popo masua? ....

4. Pe fia pauna o popo mago sa faatauina atu i le aso lenei?..............................
   Pe fia ato popo mago? ....
   Pe fia taga popo mago?..
   Pe fia le aofai o tupe faamaimau ona o lena faatau stu o popo mago?..............
   Pe fia se tupe un maua mai i le aso lenei mai le faatau o popo mago?..............

5. Pe fia se tupe na totogi atu ai tagata sa galulue i niu ma popo? ....

6. Pe fia se totogi o taavale sa aumai ai popo masau?......................................

7. Pe fia nisi tupe na alu i le aso lenei i le faiga o le popo?...............................

8. Pe toafia tagata sa galulue i lou maumaga i le aso atoa?...............................
   Pe toafia i le afa aso? ....

9. Pe fia talo na tasei mai i lou maumaga i le aso lenei?...................................
   Pe fia ato laiti?..
   Pe fia ato lapopoa? ....
   Pe fia taga a solofanua? ....

10. Pe fia tiapula na totoina i lou maumaga i le aso lenei? ....

11. Pe fia talo na e faatauina atu i leaso lenei? ....
    Pe fai pusa talo?...
    Pe fia ato laiti?..
    Pe fia ato lapopoa? ....
    Pe fia le aofai o tupe faamaimau ona o lena faatau atu o talo? ....
    Pe fia se tupe ua maua mai i le aso lenei mai le faatau atu o talo? ....

12. Pe fia ni tupe na totogi atu ai tagata sa fai le galuega i lou maumaga? ....

13. Pe na fana le vao i lou maumaga i le aso lenei? A ioe, tusi se "X" ....

14. Pe na fa'aaogaina se ili afi e pa'u ai laau i lou maumaga? ....

15. Pe toafia tagata o lou aiga sa fai galuega totogi i le aso lenei? ....

16. Pe fia ni totogi na maua mai i le aso lenei e na tagata fai galuega? ....

17. Pe fia ni tupe ua foai mai e tagata i totonu o Vaegā ia te outou? ....

18. Pe fia le tau aofai o oloa ua foai mai e tagata o Vaegā ia te outou? ....

19. Pe fia ni tupe ua foai mai e ni tagata mai nisi nuu o Samoa i Sisifo? ....

20. Pe fia le tau aofai o oloa ua foai mai e ni tagata mai nisi nuu o Samoa i Sisifo ia te outou? ....

21. Pe fia ni tupe ua foai mai e ni tagata mai fafo o le atunuu ia te outou? ....

22. Pe fia le tau aofai o oloa ua foai mai e ni tagata mai fafo? ....

23. Pe fia ni tupe ua maua mai i le aso lenei mai le faatauina atu o koko? ....
    Pe fia le aofai o tupe faamaimau ona o lena faatau atu o koko? ....

24. Pe fia ni tupe ua maua mai i le aso lenei mai le faatauina atu o i'a? ....
    Pe fia le aofai o tupe faamaimau ona o lena faatau atu o i'a? ....

25. Pe fia ni tupe ua maua mai le faatauina atu o laau aina? ....
    Pe fia le aofai o tupe faamaimau ona o lena faatua atu o laau aina? ....

26. Pe fia ni tupe ua maua mai le faatauina atu o soo se isi mea? ....
    Pe fia le aofai o tupe faamaimau ona o le faatau atu o lena mea? ....

27. Pe fia ni tupe ua maua mai lau bisinisi i le aso lenei? ....
    Pe fia le aofai o tupe faamaimau ona o le faiga o lau bisinisi? ....

28. Pe fia nisi tupe un maua mai soo se isi auala e lei lavea ai i luga? ....

29. Pe fia ni *koko* na tai mai i lou fanna ile aso levei? ....

Figure 6.3. Survey form in Samoan. A column of handwritten numbers at the far right summed up each day's activities. Names of paid workers were often listed on this form as part of the record.

Almost all Samoan villagers are literate, and most are fairly numerate. It did not take long to teach one person in every household how to answer the simple questions, such as "How many people worked in your taro plantations for the whole day?" or "How much money did you receive from overseas today?" During the year if the recorder was absent or tired of filling out the form, another member of the family was always eager to take over the responsibility. Because of this, and because I lived in the village and participated in its daily activities, the survey went very smoothly. Not a single household dropped out of the survey, and well over 99 percent of the 2,860 survey forms were completed.

I asked each household to answer the appropriate questions on the survey form every day except Sunday (when no work is allowed). Sunday evening after church someone from each household would bring the form to my house. Some of the recorders came to visit and brought their own forms, but most of the forms arrived in the hands of child couriers. Sunday evenings my house was often full of children. Some had brought a form, while others just tagged along as an excuse to visit me. The littlest boys and girls, hardly more than toddlers, stood wide-eyed behind the older children for protection. Cheeky little girls of eight or ten years sometimes flirted brazenly with me, the absurdity of which always brought roars of laughter from the other children.[8] The boys often tried to attract attention by strutting or showing off like little Tom Sawyers.

I checked each of the forms they brought, and if the form was filled out correctly I gave the child courier WS 50¢ (US 42¢) to take home to the recorder as a gift to show my appreciation for his or her help. If there was some inconsistency in the form, or if I saw that some item had been forgotten, I sent the form back with a polite note. Occasionally, I sought out a particular recorder that evening or on Monday morning to retrieve a survey form or to discuss something unusual that had appeared on the form.

When I began the survey, I had no idea whether people would cooperate or not. I did not want to jeopardize the entire survey by asking too many questions, so I asked only those questions that were essential to the research. The point of the research was to learn why villagers turn away from cash cropping at low levels of production. The villagers' own purpose in growing cash crops is to earn money and the goods it can buy. Thus, the critical information I needed from the survey was how labor and income in cash cropping compare to labor and income in other endeavors. I had to omit other questions about household economics, such as questions about expenses and receipts of subsistence items, because they were not directly relevant to the research problem. Still, when I pared my list of questions down to only the essentials of labor, production, and income, the form ran to just over sixty questions. Though long, the form is not difficult to fill out because fewer than ten questions were usually relevant for any one day. Also, all of the

---

[8] Older girls are much more demure because their flirting might be taken seriously.

Photo 36. Laloifi Milo with pre-school child. Laloifi poses in front of the European-style pre-school building in Vaega. She and the other pre-school teachers are volunteers, but the village contributes WS $6 to $9 to each teacher every month. Although it is technically a gift, even that small amount of cash is appreciated. The teacher's gift was recorded on the survey as wage income. In addition to serving as a volunteer teacher, Laloifi is one of the leaders on the Women's Committee.

answers were numerical, so once a person was familiar with the form, it was surprisingly easy to fill out.

As one check on the accuracy of the forms, I kept track of how often people recorded information on them. At first I stopped by the houses and looked at the forms on some pretext. Later on I realized that this was unnecessary, as I had unexpected help with the task. Anyone with a large family that includes many young and inquisitive children can appreciate how unlikely it is that a survey form would remain untouched for long in a Samoan house. By the end of each week most forms had been handled and smudged many times, often by inexperienced hands. And though I provided pencils with the forms, the recorder's search often turned up a different pencil or pen every day. The most surprising help in determining the frequency of record keeping came from the large, flying cockroaches that roam the nights in Samoa (as elsewhere in the tropics). These ill-mannered insects reach two inches long and they like to eat holes in paper and other household goods. Recorders sometimes had to write around these holes. At other times their previous writing was obliterated by an insect's gnawing. Relying on my previous archeological training, I could easily determine how often the form had been filled out by deciphering the chronology of bug bites, smudges, wrinkles, pen and pencil marks, and variable handwriting across a survey form.

Most people recorded information either daily or two or three times a week. Others relied more on their memories, recording the household's activities only once or twice during the week. This did not pose much of a problem since much of village life is so public. For example, if a family forgot to record the money they received from a travelling party, I had only to remind them of the event to get an accurate report of what they had received. More than likely, I had also taken part in the kava ceremony to receive the visitors, and had made a record of the gifts that each villager received. I had also built several crosschecks into the survey form itself. For example, a person might have recorded $2 from a sale of taro even though they had forgotten to enter how much taro had been sold.

As it turned out, people cooperated famously with the survey. Within a couple of months they had become so expert at filling out the forms that I began adding handwritten bonus questions at the bottom of the page. Every other week I alternated a question about the household's cocoa harvest with questions on fishing, weaving, and the feeding of domestic animals. By the end of the 57-week survey effort, village residents were so accustomed to the survey and so skilled at recording that I (almost) regretted stopping!

We did stop, however, and I took the completed forms to the new, government-owned computer office in Apia to be computer-coded and have the figures totalled. Most observers believed that plantation incomes were high relative to income from other sources.[9] But these preliminary figures confirmed what I had observed and what the villagers had told me: their incomes from farming were small compared to their incomes from other sources.

SOURCES OF MONETARY INCOME

Fifty-three of the survey households depended on their plantations for significant portions of their food and cash income. None of these "farm

---

[9] E.g., Lockwood 1971, Burgess 1981, GWS 1977, and Leng Wai 1978.

Vaega Family Income

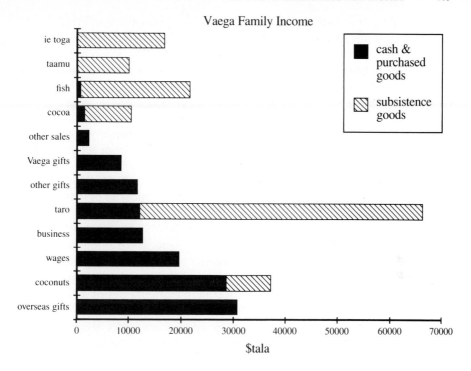

Figure 6.4. Sources of income for fifty-three agricultural households in Vaega. The chart shows the source of the largest monetary income, "overseas gifts," at the bottom. Other sources of income appear above it in decreasing order of the amount of monetary income earned from that source. The solid portion of the bars represents the amount of monetary income from each source. The hatched portion of each bar represents the value of subsistence items consumed directly by the household.

households" relied on their plantations, however, to provide all (or often even a majority) of their cash needs.[10] Instead, almost all farm households have at least one and usually several other important sources of money. Indeed, Samoan adults, especially *matai*, are continually engaged in what they call *su'e tupe*, "searching for money."

The results of the survey showed that as a group, village planters have six major sources of cash and purchased goods income (or "monetary income"). They also earn "subsistence income" by producing items for their own consumption. Figure 6.4 shows the respective values of net monetary and subsistence income (gross income minus direct expenses) by source for the fifty-three farm households in the survey.

Figure 6.4 shows that in spite of Vaega's reputation as a strongly agri-

---

[10] The households of the secondary school teacher and the owner of the large transport business did not earn significant incomes from their plantations. Their households are not included in the following summary of income data.

cultural village, the largest share of their monetary income came as gifts from overseas relatives. These "overseas gifts" amounted to nearly WS $31,000 (US $26,000), including WS $19,000 in cash and WS $12,000 in gifts of purchased goods. Most of these goods are common household items, food, and clothing, though flashy wristwatches and battery-powered cassette players are more noticeable.[11]

Next to overseas gifts, their second highest total of monetary income was from the sale of copra and whole coconuts (listed on the chart as "coconuts"). Most of that income was the WS $27,800 (US $23,600) from selling copra, for which they earned WS 5¢ for each nut processed.

In third place, village farm households earned WS $19,800 (US $16,800) working for wages.[12] Full-time wage workers earned almost all of that money. Temporary workers earned only about WS $1,500 of the total.

Three farm households together earned nearly WS $14,000 (US $11,900) from their small, family-run businesses—enough to make business income the fourth highest source of monetary income among all farm households.

Villagers sold 22 percent of their taro (a year earlier the amount of taro sold would have been far less), for which they earned a net of WS $13,100 (US $11,000), enough to gain fifth place.

The sixth major source of monetary income was gifts received from people living in other villages in Western Samoa (listed in the figure as "other gifts"). Vaega farm households received WS $11,600 (US $9,900) in cash and purchased goods from residents of other villages. Most of these were formal gifts that they received at a variety of public ceremonies called *fa'alavelave*. Villagers also received WS $8,400 (US $7,100) in gifts (including ceremonial gifts and informal sharing) from other households within Vaega. These "Vaega gifts" are an integral part of the larger system of ceremonial exchange. I have separated "Vaega gifts" and "other gifts" here only to prevent the counting of intra-village gifts as part of total village income.

As Figure 6.4 shows, villagers also earned minor amounts of cash from selling other products. Among these I have itemized cocoa, fish, *ta'amū* (the large relative of taro), and *'ie tōga*, or fine mats. The "other sales" category includes pigs, chickens, fruit, vegetables, and small amounts of virtually every other item of village produce. People bought and sold most of these items, and many services, within the village itself. Thus, while the village economy as a whole still has a large subsistence component, nearly every aspect of it has been monetized to some extent.

The fifty-three farm households earned a total monetary income of about

---

[11] I valued these gifts at their local prices, and I counted only cash and goods that actually arrived in the village. For example, the figures do not include the cost of airplane tickets and the support of travelers while they were overseas.

[12] To avoid double counting, this total includes only wages paid to farm households by nonfarm households. The difference is minor, however.

WS $120,000 (US $102,000) during the year of the survey.[13] That averages to about WS $220 (US $190) of monetary income per person per year.

SOURCES OF SUBSISTENCE INCOME

In addition to cash and purchased goods, villagers earned a sizable income from an array of subsistence goods. The survey recorded the amounts of the most important of these subsistence goods—for example, the number of fine mats or the pounds of taro produced. But we need to express these amounts in monetary terms in order to compare their values with the values of incomes from other sources. Since the subsistence goods were never sold, however, it is often difficult (and sometimes impossible) to assign them realistic monetary values. The main problem is that, except for copra and cocoa, there is little market for village products. Because markets are so restricted, prices change rapidly when villagers try to buy or sell more of some product than usual. Nevertheless, the only recourse is to assign average market prices to subsistence goods.[14] In this case, such an approach carries little risk since the purpose is only to give a broad comparison of the values of subsistence and monetary income.

Villagers consumed 11 percent of their coconut harvest as food for themselves, and they fed another 11 percent to their pigs and chickens. Assuming that these coconuts have the same monetary value as food and as copra, the village consumed WS $8,600 worth of coconuts.

Vaega households harvested and processed over 16,000 pounds of dried cocoa during the twelve survey months in 1982–83. They sold only 13 percent of the harvest, much of it within the village. Had they sold the other 87 percent of their cocoa harvest instead of consuming it, they could have received WS $9,100 for it. Villagers also bought cocoa at the Salelologa market, and they sometimes received dried cocoa beans as gifts from relatives in western Savaii. Thus, even though Vaega produced over thirty pounds of dried cocoa per person, the village is undoubtedly a net consumer of cocoa.

Cocoa was once the country's top foreign exchange earner, but cocoa exports have plummeted since independence. Both local government officials and international development agents frequently level severe criticism at village planters for what they believe has been a disastrous decline in cocoa production. The survey evidence from Vaega suggests that this criticism is unfounded. The government Cocoa Board estimates domestic cocoa con-

---

[13] The survey ran from the beginning of March, 1982, to the end of February, 1983.

[14] Since planters buy and sell almost all of these goods within the confines of the village, there is no significant difference between market prices and farm gate prices.

sumption at under 0.5 pounds per person, totalling only thirty tons, or 3 percent of the nation's estimated cocoa crop (GWS 1984b:158). This appears to be an extreme underestimate. I have no reason to believe that Vaega is exceptional in its consumption of cocoa. If Vaega's consumption rate was matched in the rest of Samoa, national cocoa consumption would equal nearly 2,200 tons per year, compared to average exports of less than 1,000 tons in recent years. By this estimate, local people are consuming roughly two-thirds of the cocoa crop, rather than only 3 percent as the government estimates.

The survey data from Vaega thus suggest that the drop in cocoa exports during the last twenty-five years was not caused by a drop in production, but rather by an increase in local sales and home consumption. To check this hypothesis, Panoa and I counted all of the cocoa trees in Vaega. We discovered that immature trees outnumber dead and abandoned trees by 50 percent, which suggests that cocoa planting has been increasing in Vaega, not decreasing.

Villagers consumed 78 percent of the taro they produced. Remembering the caution about limited markets, the monetary value of that taro was about WS $54,300. The caution is even more necessary for *ta'amū* (*Alocasia* sp.), the large, edible root crop related to taro. The annual harvest of *ta'amū* was about one-fifth the size of the taro harvest, or about 82,000 pounds.[15] Villagers sold very little *ta'amū*, however. Computing its value at a reasonable market price gives WS $9,800 for the crop.

During three survey weeks I asked the bonus question, "How many people in your household went fishing today?" The average for the village was 83 per week (117, 93, and 49) giving a very rough estimate of 5,400 half-days of fishing per year, including some shellfish collecting. I estimated that the average catch was worth WS $4. Subtracting the locally marketed fish gives a rough value of WS $21,000 for the subsistence portion of the catch.

During three other weeks the bonus survey question was, "How many fine mats did you finish weaving today?" The weekly totals were all quite similar (36, 44, 39), so using the mean to estimate a total number for the year is probably relatively accurate. By this method I estimate that village women produced 2,064 fine mats during the year. Mats vary in size and quality, but the great majority of them are roughly four by seven feet, with a local value of WS $8 in either exchange or sale. This gives an estimated market value of about WS $16,000 for all the fine mats produced in Vaega during the survey year. As the figure shows, villagers sold very few of these fine

---

[15] This is an estimate. Villagers often interplant *ta'amū* and taro, and the survey did not differentiate between the two. To separate them, Panoa and I counted all of the *ta'amū* plants in the plantations and then measured sample areas to determine the number of plants per acre. With this information I estimated that *ta'amū* acreage was one-fifth the size of the taro acreage. Village planters say that the yield per acre of *ta'amū* is about the same as taro and requires about the same effort to cultivate.

mats, or *'ie tōga*. Instead of selling them, villagers continually convert them into cash, pigs, and other goods through ceremonial exchanges.[16]

The value of all the subsistence items estimated from the survey data is nearly WS $103,000. If other subsistence items for which I have no estimates were included (such as breadfruit, housing, canoes, floor mats, and other household products), subsistence income would probably equal the monetary income of WS $120,000 (US $102,000).

COMPARING AGRICULTURE WITH OTHER SOURCES OF INCOME

The survey data show that agricultural incomes are lower than nonagricultural incomes in five critical respects. First, total monetary and subsistence incomes of village planters are drastically lower than total incomes of the rest of the nation's population. Combined monetary and subsistence income for the fifty-three farm households in Vaega was roughly WS $240,000, or WS $440 (US $350) per person per year. By comparison, the government estimated per capita income for the nation as a whole at WS $890 (US $712), just over *double* the income of Vaega planters.[17] But these government figures underestimate some kinds of income, especially subsistence and remittance income (see Fairbairn 1985, and O'Meara 1986:87). If the government figures were adjusted upward to correct these underestimates, national per capita incomes would probably be *triple* the per capita incomes of Vaega planters.

Second, even within Vaega itself, farm households earned far less than those families who relied on wage, business, or remittance income (because so few households are involved, the exact figures must remain confidential). Figure 6.5 shows the uneven distribution of monetary income among all fifty-five village households. The households with higher incomes are those with larger nonfarm incomes, not larger farm incomes.

Third, even among the fifty-three farm households, sales of agricultural products accounted for less than one-third of their monetary income.

Fourth, average incomes per day of labor also make nonagricultural pursuits more attractive than cash cropping. Within Vaega, the three small family businesses returned about WS $13 (US $11) per day of labor (this includes only the two store/copra traders and the home bakery; income from the large transport business was considerably higher). Average daily income for full-time wage employees was WS $7 (US $6) per day and WS $4 (US $3.40) for casual wage laborers.

The only cash crop that yielded a similar income was taro, which returned an average of WS $4.12 per day of labor. But like the wage labor market,

---

[16] Villagers exchanged these fine mats for "gifts," and I have already counted most of those gifts under other income headings. Thus, to prevent double counting, I will not include a separate entry for fine mats when computing total income.

[17] I compiled the national income data from government reports of gross domestic production (including subsistence production) plus remittances, foreign aid, and other transfers.

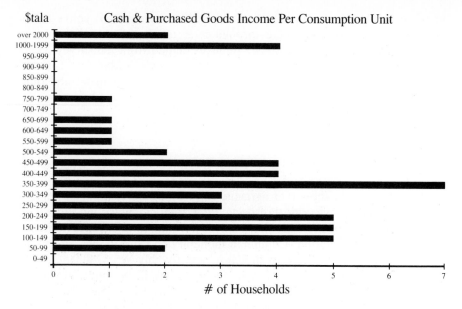

Figure 6.5. *Distribution of monetary income among all fifty-five village households. The vertical axis lists monetary incomes in WS $50 intervals. Each household's total monetary income has been averaged for the number of people living in the household, with each individual weighted by age to give the equivalent number of adult "consumption units."*

the taro market was very restricted. Thus, villagers could invest little of their labor in the production of taro for sale. My friend, Gafa, expressed the sentiment of most planters when he told me that the price of taro was "not bad, but the market is too small."

The villagers' only significant opportunity for earning money with their surplus labor was producing copra. To grow, tend, and harvest the coconuts and then process them into copra, villagers worked a total of 12,800 "adult days" during the survey year (where one day of child labor equals one-half day of adult labor). Children worked almost as many days in the coconut plantations as adults. Adults did virtually all of the processing, however, which consumed one quarter of the total production effort. With that expenditure of effort, the villagers' average income per adult day of labor was only WS $2.17 (US $1.84). When I asked Gafa his opinion of copra production, he replied, *Tīgāina tele* . . . , "The pain is great, but the return is small."

Finally, even these low average daily incomes overstate the incentive for planters to produce *more* cash crops than they do now. Because of what is commonly known as the "Law of Diminishing Returns," the product of each successive day of work will be slightly smaller than on the previous day (e.g., another day spent weeding will increase the harvest, but by less than previous days when there were more weeds). Even though a planter can increase his total harvest by working more days, the daily increments to his harvest become smaller and smaller as he works more and more. At some point the daily

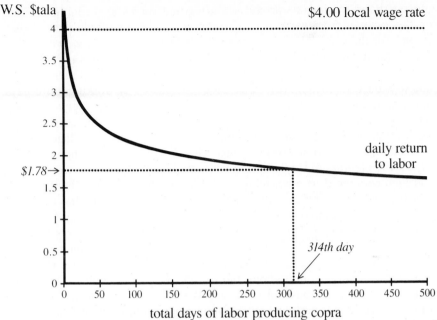

Figure 6.6. The relationship between the number of days a household works producing copra and the income they earn from each successive day of work. The graph shows that the average household worked 314 days and earned WS $1.78 on the final day of work. For comparison, the graph shows the local wage rate of $4.00 per day.

return drops so low that the planter turns away in favor of another activity that has become relatively more attractive. The critical question is, after how many days does the planter reach that point?

To answer that question, I used a computerized statistical technique known as two-stage multiple regression. The survey provided the amounts (and organization) of each household's agricultural labor and harvest for the main crop, copra. The plantation map supplied the acreage and productive potential of coconut trees worked by each household. Using these data, the computer program estimated a production equation for copra. The production equation is just a mathematical formula that shows how much copra villagers could produce from any particular combination of inputs (primarily land and labor).[18] Figure 6.5 shows one aspect of that equation. The graph in Figure 6.6 shows how much income the average household earned on successive days of work producing copra.[19]

The horizontal axis of the graph shows the total number of days worked. The vertical axis shows daily increments of income. The curved line illustrates the relationship between the number of days worked and the income earned on each successive day. The *height* of the curve above any particular number

---

[18] See O'Meara 1986 for details. I also estimated an equation for taro production, but it is less significant here because the market for taro is so restricted.

[19] When other inputs are held at their geometric means.

of days shows the income produced during that single day of labor. Adding up the incomes from each successive day gives the household's total copra income for the year, which is represented in Figure 6.6 by the *area* under the curve and to the left of the number of days worked. Note that the curve slopes downward from left to right. This shows that household members can add to their total income (the area under the curve) by working more days, but only so long as they are willing to accept the slightly smaller return that they earn from each successive day of work (the height of the curve).

If traditional social institutions and cultural values inhibit village planters from taking advantage of economic incentives in cash cropping, then we would expect the planters to stop working while their potential daily incomes were still high compared to other sources of income that are less affected by inhibiting traditions. But the graph shows that just the opposite has occurred. The average household in Vaega worked 314 adult-days during the survey year producing copra. The graph shows that the income they earned on that 314th day was only WS $1.78 (US $1.52), far less than the national minimum wage or the local wage for unskilled labor. The same conclusion holds not just for the "average" household, but for all village households. The highest return of any village household was only WS $2.60, earned by the household with the largest and best coconut plantations on its last day of labor.

Thus, the survey data show how woefully inadequate economic incentives are for cash cropping. Instead of finding a "pathetic" response to economic incentives, as Pirie and Barrett claimed (1962:76), the evidence shows a reasonable response to pathetic incentives. The villagers' response has been to direct their search for money away from their plantations and toward local wage labor, business, and overseas migration, where they see better economic opportunities.

7/The Economic and Social Importance of Sharing and Gift Giving

Sharing and gift giving are important for two reasons. First, many development experts believe that sharing and gift giving deter agricultural development, especially "in the more traditional societies such as Western Samoa" (Fairbairn and Tisdell 1985:138–42). The underlying argument is that since Samoans are often generous, they therefore lack the desire and the ability to accumulate wealth, which in turn impedes economic development. Second, many people believe that the continuing strength of the ceremonial system itself indicates that Samoan planters cling stubbornly to economically irrational traditions. A closer examination shows that the villagers' emphasis on sharing and gift giving is more an adaptation to their poverty than it is a cause of that poverty.

The survey data show how important gifts are as a source of income for village planters. The average farm household received one-sixth of its monetary income as gifts from people living within Western Samoa and another one-fourth from people living outside Western Samoa.[1] Most of this gift giving occurs at ostentatious public ceremonies called *fa'alavelave*.[2] In rural areas the most frequent ceremonies are funerals, title installations, and kava ceremonies to welcome chiefs who are either visiting or returning from overseas. Villagers also give gifts informally, usually through sharing with close relatives. The formal and informal systems are linked, since a household that receives a large gift at a ceremony often shares part of it with the households of close relatives.

INFORMAL SHARING

Polynesians constantly share small amounts of food with their relatives and less often with their unrelated neighbors. A fisherman on the island of Raiatea, near Tahiti in French Polynesia, once described this sharing to me as the "Tahitian icebox." He had just killed a huge sea turtle and lacking

---

[1] They received some of that overseas income at local ceremonies, for example at kava ceremonies to receive travelling parties coming from overseas, and at funerals where much of the gift distributions are funded by overseas relatives of the deceased.

[2] The term *fa'alavelave* literally means "entanglement," and Samoans use it to refer to any problem, disturbance, or trouble, including social ceremonies.

any way to store it, he divided it among his neighbors and relatives. While that was a very generous act, he knew that he would be on the receiving end another time. The same kind of sharing is common in Samoa.

In Vaega, neighbors also readily help each other in small jobs that require many people, such as cooking and serving food at ceremonies. At formal events, Samoan etiquette requires hosts to show their gratitude by giving these helpers a good meal and a gift of perhaps WS $1 or WS $2. But neighbors and relatives are just as ready to help each other without reward when making the stone oven early Sunday morning or in time of sickness. This informal sharing helps even out some of life's burdens and blessings, but the quantities of goods and services exchanged are relatively small.

Samoans value sharing very highly. They learn from infancy that to be *'ai'ū*, or "stingy," is one of the worst possible traits. They balance their positive emphasis on sharing, however, with a strong disdain for what they call *'aiafu*, "eating (or living off) the sweat" of others. As in other societies, there are some Samoans who are nevertheless willing to sacrifice their dignity for a handout. There were two such men in Vaega who lived mostly off the generosity of others. One young widower hung about the house of the pastor or the director of the Wesleyan school where he was sure to be well fed. The widower made his presence tolerable by his good humor and by running errands for those he patronized. Meanwhile, his children took their meals at his brother's house.

The other layabout in the village was a middle-aged man who held a job with the government. He did little or no work though, either at his job or in the village. His wife and young children worked hard to support the family, but they could not produce much. Consequently, the entire family often dined at the better-stocked home of the man's parents, where his wife and children acted as virtual house servants. While village households varied greatly in industriousness, only these two, or 4 percent of all village households (and 2 percent of the village population) received a significant part of their income this way.

FORMAL GIFT GIVING

Samoans often give gifts more formally to establish or maintain social relationships and to express their feelings. One example is the exchange of hospitality and material gifts between visitors and their hosts. Visitors arriving in a village bear gifts of food and minor household supplies to lighten the host's burden of caring for them during their stay. If the visitor's group includes a chief, a crowd of chiefs from the host village will welcome the visitors with honorific speeches and a kava ceremony. Once the ceremony is completed, the village chiefs expect to receive gifts of New Zealand dollar bills. The visitors count the money out from a briefcase, the delicate profile of Queen Elizabeth looking strangely out of place in the men's dark and calloused palms.

When the guests finally depart, they thank their host family with a heartfelt speech and with a gift of cash. The gift reimburses the hosts for the extraordinary expenses that they could otherwise ill afford. It also compensates them for their extraordinary hospitality, which has taken them away from their daily labors. The gift is *not* a payment, however. The mere suggestion of payment would offend since payment would imply that the host lacks affection and generosity. A hint that the gift is a charitable donation would also offend, for that would imply that the guests think their hosts are too poor to receive them. Failing to give a parting gift would have several troubling implications as well. It would imply that the guests are greedy, since they would have gotten something for nothing. It would also imply that they have not felt welcome. Perhaps most unsavory, it would imply that the guests believe themselves superior to their hosts, and hence deserving of their service.

When properly presented, a cash gift expresses the visitors' love or caring (*alofa*) for their hosts, just as the hosts' hospitality expresses their own love for the visitors. Samoans say that words alone are empty gestures. The gift physically "embodies" (*fa'atino*) their love—the size of the gift measuring the size of the love. Words convey the feelings, but the accompanying gift attests to their sincerity. Thus, guests do not give money in order to relieve their hosts' material needs, as would be the case with either a payment or a charitable donation. They relieve the hosts' material needs in order to express their gratitude and goodwill. The material gift is a means of expressing sentiment in order to fulfill a social end, rather than the gift being an end in itself.

But why give money? Most Americans would be offended if a house guest gave them a gift of cash after a brief visit (though we appreciate other tokens). But the Samoan and American circumstances are only partially similar. Even temporary guests in Samoa can have a significant impact on their hosts' financial budget, while temporary guests in the United States rarely affect their hosts' budget. If they do (for example, by staying for a long time), American hosts would also appreciate a financial contribution to the household, perhaps buying groceries or putting gas in the car.

Samoans find that money is useful as a medium of giving for many of the same reasons that it is useful as a medium of exchange. Money is easily stored and carried, and it is readily divisible. Most importantly among Samoan planters, however, money is something that everyone needs. Guests thus give the gift that is sure to please.

EXCHANGE OF GIFTS AND SERVICES

When gifts are not balanced by material countergifts, the imbalance results in requests for services and for deference, or in ill will. The system also works in the opposite direction. Villagers may take advantage of an imbalance of services to justify requests for material gifts (often requested in the form of a "loan"). Villagers usually do not try to even up their accounts with other people exactly. They prefer to maintain a credit that they can call on in time of need.

For example, Meaalofa is accomplished in the art of medicinal massage. She specializes in treating infants, and mothers frequently bring ailing children to her house. She massages the babies with scented coconut oil and sometimes with herbs. Asking for no payment, she is just glad to help. Sometimes a grateful mother will leave twenty cents as a gift to show her appreciation, but usually they leave nothing at all. One day a government official arrived unexpectedly to see Meaalofa's husband, Nu'u. The family quickly mobilized to prepare a fine meal for the visitor. Lacking fish or canned food, the only thing that could be cooked fast enough was a chicken, but there was no mature chicken around the house either. Meaalofa solved the problem by sending her young son, Lama, to request a chicken from another family. Instead of sending him to one of their neighbors or to her own nearby relatives, she sent Lama scurrying to the other end of the village to ask for a chicken from Pese, whose baby Meaalofa had massaged several times during previous weeks.

Matai also exchange gifts and services. Talking chiefs, for example, can request fine mats or sennit rope from their high chief, but in return the high chief can call on them to perform services. Talking chiefs also exchange gifts and services among themselves. When my new thatched house was completed, I asked Lafai Va'alele to build a food safe for me. Unlike most men his age, Lafai is still a full-time farmer and fishermen (and a part-time carpenter). He was then past 60 and though his age shows in his wrinkled face, his body is still lean and muscular. I provided the lumber, nails, and screen to Lafai, and within a few days the food safe was ready to install in my new home.

When I tried to pay Lafai for his efforts, he protested. He explained to me earnestly that fellow *matai* should not pay each other for minor goods or services. It was better, he said, to owe each other favors. "When you need something, you come to me. When I need something, I go to you." By exchanging favors, we created a social relationship between us that would work to our mutual advantage, as long as neither of us abused it.

I left the matter of payment as Lafai suggested, though I felt vulnerable because of it. Several months passed before he approached me for anything. I had just returned from Apia where I had bought two, twenty-foot rods of quarter-inch reinforcing bar, each cut into five-foot lengths for fish spears. At that time the nation's severe balance of payments deficit had caused shortages of many imported goods. The metal was difficult to find in Apia, and there was none at all on Savaii.

I gave away one of the new spears while I was still in Apia. Just after stepping out of the Morris Hedstrom store onto the sidewalk, I chanced to meet a distant acquaintance who expressed a need for one. While waiting for the ferry at Mulifanua later that day, I gave another spear to a fellow villager who inspected them closely, and one to his friend who remarked how difficult the metal was to obtain. Once aboard the ferry, I gave another spear to a young man from Vaega with whom I sometimes fished. By the time I reached the village I had only four of the original eight. As I descended the steps of the bus, Lafai was there to meet me. He asked for a spear straight out, but I gave him two, hoping to erase my debt to him. Others asked as well, but I declined. I finally reached home with one spear for me and one for Nu'u.

Several months later there was still no metal for fishing spears to be found in Savaii. Milo Faletoi was planning a trip to Apia, and I suggested that he search the stores along the waterfront. When he protested, I offered to pay for the spears, thinking that he just did not want to spend the money.

'*Aua te valea* . . . , Milo replied. "Don't be foolish. People on the ship would see the spears and beg them from me. Waste of money."

'*AISI*, OR BEGGING

In a memorable analysis of traditional leadership roles in the Pacific, Marshall Sahlins characterized the "big-men" of Melanesia as achieving success through "a profound measure of self-interested cunning and economic calculation" with their "gaze . . . fixed unswervingly to the main chance" (1963:289). In contrast, he characterized Polynesian chiefs as displaying the

refinements of breeding, in his manner always that *noblesse oblige* of true pedigree and an incontestable right of rule. With his standing not so much a personal achievement as a just social due, he can afford to be, and he is, every inch a chief (1963:289).

Contrary to Sahlins caricature, Samoan chiefs gain their positions almost entirely through individual achievement, and among them "self-interested cunning and economic calculation" are as prominent as among Melanesian big-men. The important difference between Samoan chiefs and Melanesian big-men is perhaps less in the fixedness of their gaze and more in the direction it is fixed. A Samoan chief's gaze is often fixed unswervingly on his neighbor's wealth, and he often sees his main chance in acquiring part of it.

Villagers employ several variants of '*aisi*, or "begging," to extract gifts from their relatives and neighbors. Sometimes these requests are quite direct. For example, early one Sunday morning I was sitting on an outcrop of lava beside the cook house with Mata, a middle-aged talking chief. We were folding young taro leaves to form cups and then filling them with coconut cream (an easy, chiefly kind of household chore), while Mata's sons prepared the stone oven nearby. Just then Vavae, a neighboring chief, cut through the yard on his way home.

Without bothering to greet Vavae first, Mata said casually, "Give me $2 to use for my *fa'alavelave*" (in this case, *fa'alavelave* could mean any "difficulty," from paying school fees to funeral expenses). Vavae halted and pulled a small roll of bills from a fold in his *lāvalava*.

"Here," he said, without expression as he peeled off two $1 bills and dropped them on the ground beside him, then turned and walked home.

Mata knew that Vavae had money because the Produce Marketing Board

Photo 37. Nu'u Vili preparing palusami *early Sunday morning. The wooden bowl in front of him contains cream squeezed from grated coconuts, which he pours into a cup of young taro leaves. He will use the breadfruit and wild banana leaves at his left to wrap the* palusami *for baking in the stone oven.*

had just paid Vavae for taro he had sold the week before. And at that moment, Vavae appeared to be returning from the tiny neighborhood store after buying cigarettes, so Mata guessed that Vavae had some cash on him. Since Mata and Vavae are neighbors, they are well aware of each other's affairs, and Vavae knew that Mata had no impending "difficulty." On the other hand, Vavae had exposed himself as fair game by walking through the village with money on him, when he could have sent a child on the errand instead.

Mata's *'aisiga*, or "act of begging," was not a case of what Samoans call a "weak hand" soliciting from a "strong hand," though that often occurs. Mata had also sold many bags of taro, but he had sold them to the YMCA. The YMCA had promised a much higher price than the government, but it had been several weeks since the shipment, and Mata had not been paid yet. Thus, the transaction between Mata and Vavae was between equals, one of whom had good luck and shared it on request with his neighbor, who temporarily had bad luck.

Social groups sometimes perform formal *'aisiga* to raise money or collect fine mats and other items for special occasions. Such groups may include the Women's Committee, the Chiefs' Choir, or even the *Sā Asiatā* (in this case, the holders of the Asiata title, together with their wives and attending orators). I never saw a formal *'aisiga* performed, but people told me that the group would proceed through the village, stopping in front of any occupied house to dance and sing. In return, the onlookers would give the group money, a fine mat, a bottle of scented coconut oil, or a particular item that the group was collecting. Groups conduct formal *'aisiga* only for special purposes, such as a recent one in Vaega that collected floor mats for the district medical clinic. The visits are unannounced, but people can usually see and hear the group coming, and they sometimes flee their houses to avoid contributing. Formal *'aisiga* now even travel overseas, where people refer to them by the euphemistic English term, "fund raising."

Among the least formal and most common kinds of begging is *'ai savali*, literally "eat walking." This is the practice mentioned earlier of passing close by (or even dropping in at) someone's house at meal time. If any food is out, the occupants immediately invite the passerby in to share it with them— whether the person is a two-year-old child wandering through the neighborhood or a white-haired chief on formal business. In Samoa, as in other parts of Polynesia, the universal greeting in this context is "Come and eat!"

Only slightly more subtle is the practice called *fa'asisila*, which means to "openly look at and admire" something in the hopes of receiving it as a gift. Recall that I lost several fishing spears to this technique as I carried them from Apia to Vaega. *Fa'asisila* is especially rewarding as canoes return from fishing—when the pride of the successful fisherman can be worked to advantage.

A common variant of straightforward begging is to phrase the request as a "loan" and then, often in spite of prior good intentions, not pay it back. A similar approach is to phrase the request for some item as a purchase and then not pay for it, or pay only a fraction of the agreed price—what I call "post hoc bargaining," or bargaining after the fact. In societies where people bargain over prices, the buyer and seller usually bargain directly with each other, and they conclude their bargaining before transferring the goods. In a Samoan village such crudeness is precluded by mutual respect, especially when the transaction is between chiefs, neighbors, or relatives. Instead of bargaining openly, the buyer usually makes a generous offer, which the seller immediately accepts. They defer payment, however, "until the copra is sold," or at some other time when the buyer expects to be able to settle the debt in full. When the debtor finally makes the payment, however, it is often much smaller than promised. But just as respect prevented the buyer from trying to reduce the opening price, respect now prevents the seller from trying to raise the actual payment.

I witnessed many examples of this post hoc bargaining. On one occasion a village *matai*, needing a contribution for a funeral, bought a large pig from my neighbor, Polofeu. The *matai* offered to pay WS $300 for the pig—very generous by village standards, but not excessive by Apia market standards. Some months later the *matai* had paid Polofeu only $100 for the pig. Polofeu seemed a bit chagrined when I asked him about his pig, but he conceded that $100 was enough. He would not press his neighbor for more.

There are scores of variations on this theme in Samoa, whether it is called "sharing," "gift giving," or "begging." Samoans are justly noted for their generosity, and they comply quickly and in good humor with most requests. But they are also practiced at dodging requests. Rejections are always polite. People have excellent excuses for denying requests so they do not injure their relationships with those who ask, or injure their own reputations for generosity. If a relative comes to beg a small pig for some social affair, most people, most of the time, will give one straight away. But if relations are strained for some reason, and no pigs are in sight, a person might also reply: "Alas, all of my small pigs ran off to the bush last week and they have not returned. Perhaps someone has stolen them?"

The practice of begging may have a negative effect on production. Like excessive foreign aid at the national level, it encourages an attitude of dependence.[3] People in all societies look to their relatives and neighbors in time of need, but Samoan culture puts more power in the hands of the offense than the defense, and the system is often overworked. The reason for the Samoans' emphasis on sharing is their determination to support those people who cannot support themselves. Like our own welfare system, this leaves them open for occasional abuse, and some people are allowed to remain unproductive or under-productive. The actual number is low in both cases, though the social and economic costs are significant.

Many Samoans perceive begging as a problem, and they are attempting to deal with it individually. For example, one reason people want to build European-style houses is that the occupants are less accessible and their possessions are more easily hidden from the eyes of their neighbors. In every society there are institutions that fulfill certain needs, but which also have undesirable side effects. In Samoa, begging is such an institution. What makes it an increasing problem today is that its advantages are greatest in a non-market, extended-family based economy. Its disadvantages are becoming more salient now that Samoans are firmly set—for better or worse—on the path of private ownership in a market economy.

Compared to most Westerners, Samoans emphasize the sharing of resources. Compared to most Samoans, Westerners place more emphasis on accumulating private property. But these differences in cultural emphasis should not obscure the underlying similarity of the people. When Milo Faletoi returned from a trip to New Zealand, he gave away WS $717 (US $531; just over half of the money he returned with) to his neighbors, first at a kava ceremony and then at a series of formal dinners. But he gave away the money in spite of his desire to keep it for himself and his family, not because of a lack of desire to keep it.[4] When Meaalofa gave the packages of *palolo* worms

---

[3] In the early 1980s, Western Samoa's Minister of Economic Development was asked by the local press about the nation's ability to repay its mounting foreign debt. He replied that "The good thing about all these development loans is that if you can't pay them back, they're just forgiven."

[4] By 1988 the people of Satufia had banned the kava ceremonies and formal dinners that village chiefs traditionally perform to greet other chiefs returning from overseas. Villagers felt that the social pressure to distribute money had gotten out of hand. They recognized that the money from overseas relatives was intended primarily to help their own family members and that the gift giving seriously dissipated these resources. Unhappy with their own tradition, they banned it.

to Nu'u's relatives, she did so in spite of her desire to keep them, not because of a lack of desire to keep them. Villagers realize that in their circumstances, hoarding would be disastrous for everyone in the long run. Their cultural emphasis on sharing is specifically designed to overcome that desire to hoard— a desire to which we give freer rein. Thus, the desire for personal wealth is common among Samoans in spite of their emphasis on sharing and gift giving. Conversely, sharing and gift giving are common among Westerners in spite of our emphasis on accumulating private wealth. Samoans like Milo and Meaalofa are familiar and understandable to us because of their personal similarity with ourselves in spite of the differences in cultural emphasis.

GIFT GIVING AT *FA'ALAVELAVE* CEREMONIES

Villagers participate in large, formal gift exchanges at public ceremonies called *fa'alavelave*. Most outsiders regard these ceremonies as ostentatious wastes of time and resources. Villagers themselves often complain of the burden that custom places on them. But social and economic conditions are changing in Samoa, and villagers are adapting their system of gift giving to take advantage of those new conditions. Villagers now often participate in the ceremonial system with the specific goal of gaining monetary income, in addition to their more traditional social goals. Guests at even very modest ceremonies may receive two or three dollars in cash or purchased goods, as well as food and perhaps a fine mat. When the alternative is spending the day slashing brush in the coconut plantations, *fa'alavelave* ceremonies present stiff competition for a planter's attention.

Village planters pursue both their social goals and their economic goals through sharing and gift giving. By combining the two sets of goals in one system, they can shore up one with the other. For example, people can apply their social (and political) leverage to gain material support, or they can give their material goods to gain social (and political) support. Thus, in any particular situation an individual's own economic and social goals may conflict, and their short-term goals may conflict with their long-term goals. In addition, different individuals and different families may come into conflict with each other as they pursue their respective goals. These conflicts add a good deal of emotional spice to the ceremonial system.

An important reason that village planters participate in *fa'alavelave* is that the ceremonies provide an opportunity for them to exchange their subsistence goods for cash and purchased goods. Gift exchanges are socially and ideologically distinct from the market sales by which villagers earn cash income, but the material outcome is often much the same. For example, a person may take two fine mats and WS $2.00 to a funeral. In return he or she might receive one fine mat, five tins of fish, and WS $1.00 for "bus fare." Materially, there would be little or no difference had they taken the one fine mat to the market, sold it, and then bought five tins of fish and paid the bus fare with the proceeds.

Samoans are quick to argue that gift exchanges are social, rather than economic, transactions. On the other hand, they are well aware of and concerned with the material outcome of gift exchanges. One indication of their material interest is that villagers readily judge ceremonies according to how well they make out in the exchange. For example, Panoa and I were lounging idly one afternoon when the bus stopped in a swirl of dust before the house. Nu'u climbed down from the bus and trudged across the grass to the house, his *lāvalava* and sport shirt askew from the long ride. Nu'u settled down beside us on a mat and reached for the cup of fresh cocoa that Meaalofa handed him. I had been in the plantation since early morning, so I did not know where he had gone. Panoa knew though, as usual.

"How was the funeral, eh Nu'u?" Panoa asked.

Nu'u shook his head and smiled sheepishly. *Gau*, he said. "Broke."

He had gone that morning to a funeral held by the family of some relatives in a distant village, taking with him two fine mats. He returned with nothing but the curried gravy and breadfruit in his stomach and three cans of mackerel rattling around in his briefcase.

"What about that Nu'u?" I asked. "Is it bad to give things at a funeral and then receive little in return?"

Tusā . . . , he replied, raising his eyebrows in an expression of unconcern. "All the same. Sometimes you get a lot, sometimes little, sometimes nothing. We don't give, just wanting something in return." Nevertheless, Nu'u was clearly dejected at the short-term imbalance.

Two weeks later Nu'u returned from another funeral. I came over to inspect the large basket he carried as Tauma'oe and Lama struggled to hoist it onto the house platform.

"How was the funeral?"

The two kids peeled back the layer of wilted banana leaves that covered the basket's opening, revealing a shoulder of half-cooked pork, several thick strips of pig blubber, and a half dozen greasy cans of fish.[5]

"Beautiful," he announced, smiling broadly. "Lots of food."

Because people pursue both social and economic goals in these ceremonies, the system is not so simple that people can just exchange one item for another (as they do in market exchanges). Generally speaking, guests give fine mats, small amounts of money, and (at some ceremonies) kava roots to their hosts. In return, host families give pigs, a few fine mats, money, and both local and purchased foods. The exact mix of gifts and countergifts depends on the type of ceremony and on the material circumstances of the parties. Host families try to give away more than they receive, or at least they try to appear to give away more. Just because hosts give away many goods on these occasions does not mean that they covet material possessions less than other people do. They give gifts to demonstrate their material wealth

---

[5] Samoans are very careful to cook all meat thoroughly before eating it. The pork distributed at ceremonies is only partially cooked because the recipients will recook it at home before serving it. Repeated cooking can prevent the meat from spoiling for two or three days.

and their generosity, both of which are in high esteem. They would gain no glory if either they or their guests did not really want the gifts.

Former hosts become guests at subsequent ceremonies hosted by other families. Acting as guests, they now hope to receive more than they give. Receiving large gifts demonstrates their high rank, since people give the greatest gifts to those of highest rank. When guests receive large gifts, it may also demonstrate their personal power, especially the powers of persuading and cajoling, in which talking chiefs try to excel. Of course, people also like to receive large gifts just because they desire the money and goods. Host families attract guests to their ceremonies by playing on these material desires. Some guests would come anyway out of friendship or obligation, but the promise of generous gifts attracts a throng.

Hosts and guests exchange gifts at a ceremony, but that is just the public portion of the event. Before the ceremony, neighbors, relatives, and friends often contribute to the respective stockpiles of both the guests and the hosts. Sometimes people solicit these contributions, other times people bring them of their own accord. When the public ceremony is over, both hosts and guests redistribute a share of their receipts privately to everyone who contributed to their stockpile earlier. Thus, some exchanges occur publicly while others occur privately. This allows the possibility of a family manipulating exchanges to portray a public image of generosity while actually achieving a net gain in resources.

A NEW TWIST TO RECIPROCITY

Reciprocity is a long-established practice in Samoan ceremonial exchanges. But new economic conditions now allow all villagers—hosts and guests—to gain economically from these ceremonies.

Two principles traditionally ensured that gifts were reciprocal, either in the short or the long run. The first principle is that high-ranking people should both give and receive larger gifts than other people. Gifts between extended families always flow according to rank. Villagers give no consideration to the recipient's economic need. While the recipients may consume these gifts as part of their daily fare, the gifts are not intended to, and do not, level incomes between wealthy and poor families. If a particular household needs charitable assistance, they must get it from other members of their extended family, not from the general public. For a household to seek assistance from outsiders would embarrass their entire extended family.

The second principle is that wealthy people should give larger gifts than other people. Ideally, rank and wealth go together, both depending largely on the number of supporters a person or family can muster. Families bestow their titles on individuals partly to recognize their talents and accomplishments, including their economic accomplishments. More importantly for the family, however, they bestow the title on an individual in order to formally bind him in obligation to the family, thus securing his talents and resources for the benefit of the group.

Sometimes an individual's (or a family's) rank differs significantly from his wealth. In those cases, the size of the gifts he gives varies upward or downward with his resources, but still within the range appropriate for his rank. For example, a wealthy high chief might give a large pig and a poor high chief might give a medium-size pig. The size of each gift depends on the donor's particular rank, current resources, and future aspirations. Later, each donor will receive a return gift that is roughly proportional to his original gift. All of this leaves much room for maneuvering and manipulation on both sides.

As villagers apply these principles in current circumstances, however, they may upset the balance of reciprocity rather than maintain it. Today, while status still generally follows wealth, wealth often depends on individual or nuclear-family effort, rather than on group effort, and families gain much of their wealth from a few members who live permanently outside the village. Many of those migrants still want to support their relatives back in the village and they want to achieve traditional status for themselves. Thus, when migrants return to the village for ceremonies, they feel obliged to contribute generously. But since they lack high chiefly status or an immediate presence in local social and political affairs, their village relatives do not feel equally obliged to reciprocate the migrants' generosity. The result is that migrants returning from both Apia and from overseas usually give much and receive little at village ceremonies. Their losses make it possible for the local host families to put on good public displays at little or no cost to themselves. As in the following example, some families now even profit from hosting funerals and other ceremonies.

Faletele arrived from Apia in a pickup truck to attend the funeral of his father, a high chief. It was the first time Faletele had returned to his village since he first left to attend school in Apia sixteen years earlier. Over the years he had risen to become a mid-level officer in a department store, and he earned a good salary. He brought with him four cases of tinned fish and 100 loaves of bread (worth about WS $240) plus WS $248 in cash to contribute to the funeral. This one gift cancelled 43 percent of the host family's monetary expenses and 28 percent of their combined monetary and subsistence-item expenses at the funeral, as Table 7.1 shows. Faletele deposited the gift with his family and then, having fulfilled his obligation, he departed immediately without receiving any return gift. This case is somewhat extreme, but even by generous standards he would have received only a cooked pig and a few fine mats, together worth perhaps WS $100 to WS $150. A few days later the host family received a gift from New Zealand of WS $275 for construction of a tomb. They did not reciprocate this gift.

Inspection of Figure 7.1 shows that the local host family ended up with net surpluses of fine mats, cash, and purchased goods. About half of that surplus they balanced by their own contribution of pigs at the funeral. Subtracting the value of the pigs, the local family of the deceased earned a net

Accounting of Funeral Receipts and Expenses

Value of Host Family's Receipts:			
Gifts retained from visitors:			
Fine mats (156 small, 4 large)	$1,356		
Cash	849		
Purchase goods (4 cases fish, 8 rayon cloth, 100 loaves bread)	280		
Subtotal		$2,485	
Cash received from overseas		275	
Total Receipts			$2,760
Value of Host Family's Expenses:			
Burial materials (casket, etc.)		$ 258	
Pigs provided at funeral (4 large, 2 medium)		450	
Gifts given after burial:			
Pig (1 large)	$ 100		
Cash	191		
Purchased goods	58		
Subtotal		349	
Lagi and tomb construction:			
Pig (1 large)	$ 100		
Fine mats (33 small)	264		
Cash	40		
Purchased goods (cement, etc.)	275		
Subtotal		679	
Total Expenses			1,736
NET INCOME			$1,024

Figure 7.1 Accounting of the host family's receipts and expenses at the funeral of a high chief. The accounting shows that the family received a net income of WS $1,024, which they divided among their three constituent households according to the number and size of pigs and fine mats each had contributed earlier.

profit of WS $1,024 from his funeral, largely on the strength of the two unreciprocated gifts from his children living in Apia and New Zealand. When the funeral was over, the local members of the host family divided the surplus between them, with shares going according to the number of fine mats and the size of the pig(s) each household had contributed.

I attended seven funerals (three in Vaega) and recorded the exchanges at three of them in detail.[6] The extreme imbalance in the gift exchange noted above appears to be the rule, not the exception. While custom dictates that a family should be "broke" after a funeral, the host family made a net profit at two of the three funerals I recorded, while the result of the third was unclear (due to charges of embezzlement). After another funeral that I attended (but did not record), a *matai* of the family boasted to me that they had ended with a surplus of WS $300. A few weeks later, the host family built an addition onto their European-style house, a sure indication that they

[6] Not all gift giving occurs at the funeral itself. Late–arriving guests may appear a week or more after the funeral, and gifts from overseas may arrive even later. At the funeral of a high chief, the talking chiefs of his district construct his tomb several days or even weeks after the actual funeral, and the family rewards them with fine mats and money. All of these late expenses are noted in Figure 7.1.

Local Host Family's Receipts

	fine mats	*cash*	*purchased goods*	*pigs*
Gifts retained from visitors:	156 (4 large)	$ 849	4 cases fish 100 loaves bread 8 rayon cloths	0
Overseas gift for tomb:	0	$ 275	0	0
Subtotal Values:	$1,356	$1,124	$280	$0

Local Host Family's Expenses

	fine mats	*cash*	*purchased goods*	*pigs*
Goods provided at funeral:	0	0	0	4 large 2 medium
Gifts given after burial:	0	$191	$ 58	1 large
Funeral expenses:	0	0	$258	0
Lagi and tomb construction:	33	$ 40	$275	1 large
Subtotal Values:	$264	$231	$591	$650

Total Value of Receipts:	$2,760
Total Value of Expenses:	$1,736
NET INCOME:	$1,024

Figure 7.1 continued.

had not suffered materially in the funeral exchange. Moreover, the funds for the construction probably became available to them because of the funeral, which drew in relatives from overseas and gave them an opportunity to further reaffirm their family ties by improving the family residence.

Consultation with other people confirmed that it is now common, though still shameful, for a family to profit from hosting a funeral or other ceremony. This is possible largely because they reciprocate gifts from urban and overseas relatives very lightly, if at all. The surplus from these gifts allows local families to be generous to their neighbors without dissipating their own resources, as they had to do in the past. Sometimes the local family reciprocates the generosity of an urban or overseas relative by giving him (or rarely her) a *matai* title (rather than a material gift), for which he must then provide even more money and goods. By participating as widely as possible in these ceremonies, other cash-hungry villagers gain a share of these funds.

A CHURCH DEDICATION IN SAVAII

One ceremony where the guests expect to give much more to their hosts than they receive in return is the public dedication of a new church. This ceremony is called a *fa'aulufalega*, which means literally "an invitation" to enter the building. The name is accurate, for a congregation extends invita-

Photo 38. Dedication of a new church at Sasina, on the north coast of Savaii.

tions throughout the archipelago and even overseas. Most other village ceremonies are hosted by a single family. A church dedication, however, is hosted
by the entire congregation and the supporting relatives of that congregation,
which usually includes most of the village. The dedication of a new church
is thus the grandest event that most villages ever host. Only the inauguration
ceremonies or funerals of the highest chiefs can match the size and importance
of a common church dedication.

At the first church dedication I attended (in Sasina district, on the north
coast of Savaii), virtually every family in the village was receiving guests. As
more and more relatives arrived from distant villages, host families began
dividing their ranks to receive different groups of visitors simultaneously—
one group inside the main house, another group in another house, and a
often third in the shade of nearby breadfruit trees.)

The guests had not come empty-handed. They arrived carrying many
bundles of fine mats and wads of money. As I watched, a twelve-piece brass
band escorted a large group of arriving guests through the village as the visitors
paraded their contribution of fine mats for all to see. The visitors continued
their procession to the principal residence of their kin, and the leaders stepped
inside.

Once seated inside the house, the visiting chief began reciting the
fa'alupega of the host's village—a ritualized list of the history and status
hierarchy of that village's chiefly titles. The host greeted him by reciting the
fa'alupega of the visitor's village. The visitor then began his speech, praising
the power and goodness of God, the beauty of the day, and the glory of

Photo 39. A local family receives groups of relatives who have come to celebrate the dedication of the church. The two leading talking chiefs of the family stand with the primary symbol of their office, the speaking staff, while one of the women of the family receives the fine mats the visitors have brought. In the background a young man carries a baked pig on his shoulder.

the occasion. He stressed the strength of their mutual bonds of kinship and affection, and his family's desire to help their relatives in time of need. Finally, he expressed his regret at the modest size of his group's gifts of fine mats and money—which they presented with a deliberately understated flourish.

The chief of the host family then spoke as eloquently in reply and immediately returned a third of the guests' own fine mats as a countergift. As a final gesture, the host presented another fine mat and a few dollars to the visiting chief to thank him personally for honoring them with his words. The guests then rose immediately, retiring to another house to eat, as the next group of visitors entered the receiving house. The hosts fed and housed all of their guests, some for several days.

By mid-afternoon the entire village was occupied by travelling parties. Dignified elders passed back and forth between the houses, followed by their wives or daughters carrying bundles of fine mats under their arms. Young men, stripped to the waist, carried roast pigs through the village on wooden litters or over one shoulder. Young women gathered in the smokey cookhouses to prepare bread, butter and jam, and curried soup for the masses. Restless children wriggled into every group, stared for a moment, and then departed in search of other diversion. Hundreds of conversations and fine speeches blended together in a hum of excitement, pierced occasionally by the screams of a slaughtered pig or the stentorian shouts of a tattooed man announcing (with great exaggeration) the gifts that his chief had just received.

On the surface, the exchange of gifts at a church dedication is similar to funeral exchanges, but the intent and the outcome are quite different. Guests come to celebrate the dedication of a new church, but they also come to help their relatives pay off the enormous debt they incurred in building it. Thus, unlike funerals and most other ceremonial exchanges, guests at a church dedication expect to leave with less than they brought.

In Samoa, businesses do not like to advance credit to individuals for mundane purposes. Businesses are especially reluctant to advance credit to villager planters who have only meager incomes and few assets. Local suppliers are usually eager, however, to grant credit to large social groups for special purposes, such as a funeral or the construction of a church. The greater volume of purchases by these groups is an important incentive for businesses to extend them credit. Just as significant is the public nature of the affairs and the social control of the group, which combine to ensure the repayment of the debt. And businesses know that as the guests arrive at a ceremony, they bring with them the means to repay debts quickly and completely. Today all churches in Samoa are built in Western style of imported materials. Thus, even a modest church costs many thousands of dollars. While much of that financial burden is relieved by guests at the dedication, the strain on village resources (and the resources of their overseas members) is still considerable.

As at other ceremonies, the host families at the church dedication thanked their guests by giving them gifts of food to take with them when they departed. Ideally, the highest-ranking orator present should have directed the distribution while the untitled men (or lowest-ranking orators if there are no untitled men present) carried out the orders. What actually happened was that nearly every orator in the vicinity stepped in to either advise the principal orator ("Don't forget that Fuimu is the representative of Palauli"), amend the original orders with orders of their own ("No, give that pig's foreleg to Polofeu, it's too small for Molimau"), or issue direct orders ("Five cans of mackerel and a chunk of beef for Manava!"). A half dozen orators shouted contradictory orders at the untitled men, who nevertheless jumped with alacrity to carry out the orders. The young men quickly arranged piles of food, and just as quickly rearranged them under a countermanding order. Some orators stood on the periphery and gave orders with no appreciable influence on the distribution.

Speed is of the essence in these distributions, for it demonstrates unerring competence on the part of those giving the orders and unerring obedience on the part of those carrying out the orders. Within minutes the young men chopped and sliced the half-cooked pig and cattle carcasses into pieces. They tore open cardboard boxes of tinned fish and pried open tubs of salt beef. They divided each into dozens of little piles on small coconut-leaf trays

Photo 40. The host family butchers and then distributes the baked pigs and cattle they have donated (in this case at the funeral of Gasu). The talking chiefs at the right of the picture bark out orders while the young, untitled men at the center and left of the picture jump to carry them out.

or fragments of cardboard packing case, each pile destined for a particular guest.

WASTED RESOURCES?

The construction work on the church had occupied the villagers part-time for many months, and they had incurred a sizable debt. The dedication ceremony itself had consumed much time and expense. Whether villagers contribute toward building a new church, refurbishing the old one, or merely supporting their pastor, most development experts look with disfavor on these projects, believing them to be a waste of productive resources that might otherwise be used to develop village agriculture.

Certainly *any* consumption of resources removes the *potential* of investing them for greater production in the future. The question remains, however, whether religious contributions are excessive, and whether the resources would otherwise have been invested in village agriculture. During the survey year, Vaega farm households contributed about 7 percent of their cash and purchased goods income to support their pastor, their local church, the national Methodist Church bureaucracy, the construction of a new church in a neighboring village, and several minor overseas causes. Though this church

Photo 41. Collecting money for the Methodist Church at the annual Mē services. The men seated at the table are all administrative officers from Apia. Fogalele observes at the rear left while the pastor and headmaster of the Wesleyan school, Samuelu Tupu (standing at left), records the donations and adds them together with a hand calculator.

giving is highly visible, as a percentage of income it does not seem extraordinary. The gifts sometimes are a burden to villagers, but I doubt the gifts are so onerous that they inhibit agriculture.

Neither the cash nor the labor donations are really being drained from agriculture. Returns from village agriculture are already so low and opportunities so limited that villagers prefer not to invest additional resources there anyway. Thus, the main economic effect of religious contributions is that village households forgo some consumption and some leisure. Whether outsiders like this system or not, Samoans have made it an integral part of their village life. If they want to change it, they can, just as they have changed other aspects of their culture.

NEW SUPPORT FOR THE "TRADITIONAL" CEREMONIAL SYSTEM

The newest and most powerful incentive driving villagers' participation in the "traditional" ceremonial system is their ability to exchange fine mats, pigs, and *matai* titles for large amounts of money and purchased goods from urban and overseas people. If only village planters participated in the ceremonial system, they would gain little material advantage over the long term from the reciprocal exchanges. But local business owners and wage earners as well as both urban and overseas relatives also participate. They tend to give more cash and purchased goods, while planters give more fine mats and pigs. The long-term result is that village planters are able to exchange their subsistence products for cash and purchased goods. Urbanites also usually give much more than they receive, which works to the net advantage of village planters. Villagers have very little power or influence over urban residents in most other matters. Villagers do control the traditional ceremonial system, however, and they often work it to their advantage.

Recall that the women of Vaega made roughly 2,000 fine mats during the survey year. These mats can circulate for many years without deteriorating, yet they do not pile up in the villages. Most households have no more than two or three on hand at any one time. Even wealthy, high-ranking households have only two or three dozen. Where do all the fine mats go? I have seen travelling parties leaving Western Samoa with as many as 3,000 fine mats. My guess is that a lot of closets in New Zealand and American Samoa are stuffed with fine mats. Thus, not all gifts from overseas are unearned. Formal travelling parties, or *malaga*, carry bundles of fine mats with them overseas (just as they do in Samoa) to give as gifts at ceremonies such as funerals, weddings, and church dedications. The travellers give fine mats, and they receive monetary gifts from their hosts in return.

Some of those fine mats were the direct product of the women's labor. They sometimes plait new fine mats for a specific trip. For example, I arrived at Milo Faletoi's house one night to find his wife, Valelia, and two young daughters plaiting an enormous fine mat by the light of two gas lanterns. Valelia explained that all of Satufia village was then preparing for a social visit to a village in American Samoa. Valelia worked continuously on the mat for several days in preparation for the trip. Milo also took many other fine mats that he had collected from earlier ceremonial exchanges, and a few other fine mats that friends and relatives from other villages gave him to take. Those mats were the indirect product of his and his family's agricultural, pig raising, and ceremonial activities. Thus, by giving fine mats when he travelled overseas, Milo converted his family's labor and subsistence products into cash.

Samoans express the traditional sentiment that these "gifts" are freely given, with no expectation of return or reward. Nevertheless, when the hosts are planning their return gifts, they pay very careful attention to the number, size, and quality of the fine mats they received from each group of guests. When Falanika was married in American Samoa, her family from Western Samoa gave the groom's family 300 fine mats. Leaders of the groom's extended

Photo 42. Talking chiefs of Satupaitea preparing to present the kava at a ceremony to receive their current Member of Parliament, Asiata Solomona.

family decided that $3,000 cash was an appropriate return gift. They explicitly chose that figure because $10 was then the market rate for fine mats in the city. The six branches of the groom's family each contributed $500 toward the total, and when they divided the fine mats among themselves, each branch received fifty fine mats.

Sometimes villagers organize travelling parties that coincide with a special need for monetary income. Several weeks before the national parliamentary elections, Asiata Solomona, then Satupaitea's incumbent Member of Parliament and a candidate for reelection, held a reception for over 100 *matai* of the district. He distributed food and money to all of the *matai* as a courtesy for their attendance. He got the money for the distribution from his salary, which the district chiefs judged a proper use of it since they had elected him to the position.

Asiata Solomona's competitor in the election was Asiata Iakopo. Asiata Iakopo had no salary to draw on to demonstrate his generosity to potential supporters, but he and his wife, Muta, had organized a travelling party to American Samoa. A man from the extended family of Muta's mother had married a woman in Tutuila several years before. The couple was still living with the woman's family and they now had three children. The explicit purpose of the visit was for Muta, her two sisters, and the chiefs of the family (Asiata Iakopo and Milo Faletoi) to "demonstrate" their kinship with the couple's children (*fa'ailoa le 'āiga*).

This is a traditional observance, which the travelling party carried out by presenting the family with 230 fine mats, including some very large and old ones (which are especially valuable). The group collected these fine mats from among the stores of their own five households and from contributions by their neighbors and relatives. One of Asiata Iakopo's principal talking chiefs, Lautafi Esau, joined the group, though he was not directly related to them. In return for "demonstrating their kinship" with the children, the family in American Samoa gave the travelling party twenty-four kegs of corned beef, thirteen cases of canned fish and meat, 110 packages of crackers and cookies, ten fine mats, one large bark tapa cloth, a few odds and ends, and just over WS $2,000.[7]

When the travelling party returned to Vaega, 100 chiefs from all over the district were waiting at Asiata and Muta's house to greet them with a kava ceremony. When the speeches and the kava ceremony were over, Asiata distributed WS $400, eight kegs of corned beef, and nine fine mats to the assembled *matai* and to the village pastor and the pastor at the Wesleyan school (who were not present). When the distribution was over, the assembled chiefs departed in two's and three's, and I listened to their evaluations of the ceremony as we walked together down the road. They all agreed that the rival candidates had to be generous because the chiefs look to see how well each candidate will *tausi le nu'u*, or "care for the village."

When the crowd had disbursed, I returned to Asiata's house. There the members of the travelling party divided the remaining money and goods among themselves, according to how many fine mats each household had contributed. These households in turn shared some of their receipts with the neighbors and relatives who had contributed fine mats to them earlier, again on the basis of how many fine mats each had contributed.

Both Asiata and Milo denied that the purpose of their trip to American Samoa was to solicit money and goods to help cover Asiata's campaign expenses. The trip had been planned for a long time, and the election was still more than a month away. Also, on their return they had given away only about one-fourth of their receipts. Nevertheless, the children they had gone to "recognize" were several years old, and they could give no other explanation for the opportune timing of the trip.

THE ENDURING CEREMONIAL SYSTEM

Like the modern *matai* and land tenure systems, the ceremonial system is far less traditional than it appears on the surface. The ceremonial system endures because Samoans have adapted it to their current needs, not because Samoans or their culture are inherently conservative. One reason the ceremonial system continues to flourish in Samoa is that villagers like the op-

[7] American Samoa has no import tax on goods from the mainland U.S., so prices are much lower there than in Western Samoa. Consequently, travellers want to take as many purchased goods with them to Western Samoa as they can, and hosts give their guests a high proportion of purchased goods, rather than cash.

portunity to exchange their subsistence goods (many of which, like fine mats and kava, have no other utility) for cash and purchased goods. Another factor is the recent increase in cash incomes, which allows more people to satisfy their status goals through public gift giving. Villagers also maintain the system because they profit materially from engaging their wealthier urban and overseas relatives in ceremonial exchanges.

Fa'alavelave ceremonies are important not only as foci for giving and receiving goods, however. Villagers also attend these ceremonies for socializing and for diversion. Ceremonies create an air of importance and excitement that interrupts the routine of daily life. In order to create a feeling of tension and excitement, villagers combine in a single public ceremony many of the things that matter most to them: family, food, money, competition in an open forum, a chance for men to display their knowledge and skill at oration, a chance to command and impress, a chance for women to take center stage for a moment as they display their fine mats, a chance for young men and women to meet and talk amid the turmoil of their labor.

These social and political affairs are the proper arena of chiefs, and when things are dull they sometimes sit around thinking of new opportunities to engage themselves. I recall going to the house of an elderly chief named Umusa one day and finding him sitting alone, drumming his fingers on the pandanus-leaf mat before him. Too old to work the plantations with dignity, he sat and stared out across the empty village green. Umusa directed our conversation to the many chiefly affairs that currently occupied him. During pauses he plucked frayed strands from the floor mats around him, as if he could not go on until everything was tidy. As he fiddled, he seemed to search the future for opportunities that would excite and stir his blood, for when he spoke again it was of a distant ceremony that he must attend, or an obscure court case that he must press. All the while he complained of the great burden that men of his rank must bear.

But *fa'alavelave* ceremonies are, above all, the public affairs of large extended families, and few Samoans are yet so wealthy that they can afford to withdraw from the mutual support and security system which is the ultimate foundation of the extended family. Nor is there any significant national insurance or social security system to take over that function of the extended family. Independent incomes and larger nuclear families have largely destroyed the productive necessity for the extended family. But because of the small size and insecurity of those incomes, most Samoans still look to their extended families for security.

The endurance of the ceremonial system may even be partly a response to the reduction of cooperation within extended families for production. Without the need for cooperation in production, people emphasize the social and ceremonial aspect of the extended family in order to maintain its solidarity, which is still important to them for security. Ceremonial exchanges provide frequent opportunities for people to demonstrate their own (and check other people's) ability and willingness to come to the support of their kin. As Nu'u once told me, "If we give generously now, when we have a *fa'alavelave* of our own, the house will be full." Those kin who fail the test may be coerced through gossip and other informal sanctions to reenter the system. If they do not, their relatives excise them from that particular social circuit. Thus, while nuclear-family households increasingly control their own incomes, Western Samoans continue to maintain the wider social network of the extended family in public ceremonies as a source of economic security, as well as an important source of pleasure, power, and prestige.

8/Conclusion

The ethnographic and economic data I have presented help explain many actions of Samoan planters that previously seemed peculiar or appeared to indicate that they fail to act in their own economic self-interest. For example, the data on copra production explain why villagers often leave coconuts on the ground unharvested—the income gained would not be worth the effort to collect and process them. The data also help explain why children do so much of that work—it is not worth an adult's time.

RESPONSES TO SOCIAL AND ECONOMIC INCENTIVES

Many observers have noted that while villagers usually produce fewer cash crops than they could, they will increase production temporarily to meet socially defined goals:

> Each village has gone through periods in the past when it did reach a much higher level of output: for example, during the construction of its church. But generally it did not sustain this higher level for longer than it needed to complete its particular project (Lockwood 1971:188).

From this observation, Lockwood and other researchers conclude that villagers respond better to social incentives than to economic incentives:

> The market incentive operates, but not to the same extent as in Western economies, or for the same reasons. In general the village community will work harder or longer for a greater surplus only when this is required to meet a specific end, e.g., building a new church, travel overseas, village ceremonies (Fairbairn 1985:304).

The evidence from Vaega suggests a markedly different explanation of the villagers' behavior. In response to the combination of everyday market and social incentives, villagers pushed the return to their labor down to WS $1.78 per day. Yet even at such a low monetary return, the added social incentive of renovating their church inspired the villagers to greater efforts. By the "law of diminishing returns," their increased effort must have pushed their daily income even lower, perhaps to as low as WS $1.50. That lower amount would normally be an unacceptable return, even for the cash-hungry villagers. But because of the added social incentive, they were temporarily willing to work for a lower-than-normal economic incentive. Once their goal was attained and the social incentive dropped back to its normal level, the $1.50 per day income was no longer enough to keep the villagers working at the higher level. Hence, they reduced their labor effort back to its equilibrium level where they earned $1.78 per day. While the villagers did increase crop production temporarily to meet a socially defined goal, that does not indicate that they respond better to social incentives than to market incentives. It merely shows that Samoan planters, like other people, respond to social incentives *in addition to* market incentives.

Other evidence from Vaega shows that planters respond strongly and quickly to attractive market incentives. At the beginning of the village economic survey, a private export company from Apia offered to buy whole coconuts at eight cents each—three cents higher than villagers would receive if they processed the nuts into copra. The villagers had just completed a major coconut harvest two weeks earlier, so there were not many ripe nuts in the plantations. But in response to the offer of a higher price with less processing labor, the high chiefs immediately approved an extraordinary session of coconut harvesting. During that week the people of Vaega worked more days in their coconut plantations than during any other week of the entire survey.

Friday evening a crowd of young men and boys gathered in the yard of the Wesleyan school to pack burlap bags full of coconuts. Many chiefs were there too, directing traffic and helping to fill and then load the bags onto the waiting truck. In contrast, chiefs normally do not participate directly in copra sales. More and more young men arrived, each carrying twin baskets of husked nuts slung on either end of a stout pole. The agent from Apia counted the coconuts one by one, inspecting them for size and quality. Just when he thought all of one family's harvest had been counted and bagged, a son or daughter would scurry up carrying a few more nuts to complete a final bag. Back in the village I saw one young man crawling on his belly under the wooden platform of his house—a place normally frequented only by pigs and dogs—trying to retrieve two nuts that had been overlooked.

The harvest that resulted from these extraordinary efforts was only modest since it followed the previous harvest so closely, and people were able to sell only about a third of their harvest as whole nuts. The remaining nuts were either too small, were already sprouting, or were damaged. The rejected nuts they processed into copra in the usual way. Thus, the return to their labor did not increase as much as the price might indicate. They were, however, anxious to sell more whole nuts at that price. In other words, it had not taken a particularly great increase in price to inspire them to significantly increase their production.

Outsiders often fault villagers for behavior that is commonplace in their own societies, the primary differences being only that the behaviors are acted out differently in different arenas by actors wearing different costumes. For example, to support their view that villagers are not "economic minded," development experts often cite the frequency with which newly opened stores and other businesses fail in Samoa. Most of these businesses fail because the owners extend too much credit to their customer-neighbors (partly because of social pressure and partly because owners lack business experience and skills).

It may be possible to infer from the high rate of store failures that Samoan villagers respond too much to social pressures, and are therefore, to some extent, not "economic minded." But this analysis implies a comparison with Western business owners, who presumably *are* economic minded. Yet in the United States, upwards of 50 percent of all new businesses fail within the first year, often because the owners themselves have accepted too much credit (from news reports of the U.S. Chamber of Commerce Annual Report for 1987).

In Samoa, businesses tend to lend too much. In the U.S., businesses tend to borrow too much. They fail at similar rates. Improvements could certainly be made in both countries, and development projects in both countries rightly focus on areas where improvements can be made. The error comes in assuming that differences in behavior derive from differences in basic desires or capabilities, rather than from differences in circumstances and skills.

People who believe that villagers are not economic minded frequently cite stories that show how planters subvert economic goals to social goals. A local development officer told me of a villager who had started a sizable cattle herd with a loan from the Development Bank. In spite of initial success, the herd soon dwindled because the man could not refuse the requests of his many relatives who each wanted a cow or two for a funeral. Finally, the man slaughtered all of his remaining cattle for a ceremony of his own, leaving him no way to rebuild his herd (and perhaps not incidentally, leaving him no way to repay his loan). Another local development officer told me of his exasperation with his rural relatives. He had given them three large breeding pigs and the fencing material to construct a holding pen. His relatives slaughtered all three pigs for the first ceremony that came along, and they used the fencing material to protect their flower gardens from the other pigs that roam the village.

Both development officers told me that the rural people did not realize the long-term productive value of their breeding stock. But Samoans have been breeding pigs and other animals and plants for thousands of years. They are certainly aware of the importance of breeding stock. They may slaughter their breeding stock anyway, but not without realizing the future consequences. Note that neither the recipient of the cattle nor the recipients of the pigs had any significant investment in the livestock. The pigs were free, and the owner of the cattle had paid only 5 percent down to the Development Bank, with 30 percent of the cost still due and 65 percent subsidized by foreign aid funds.[1] While it may not demonstrate great economic acumen, there would

---

[1] Even the donor of the pigs and pig fencing may have gotten them free. When I related this case to some villagers and asked for their explanation, they replied immediately that government employees often steal things like that from government projects, and then with a show of generosity give the things to relatives in a distant village. Guessing that the pigs might be stolen, the recipients then conclude that it is better to consume the evidence immediately.

be nothing unusual about treating the stock as windfalls and squandering the resource.

On the other hand, considering both social and economic costs and benefits, slaughtering the cattle and pigs may have been judicious decisions. The owners stand to make considerable social gains by giving away the livestock, and since the livestock were essentially gifts to begin with, on what grounds could the owners deny the requests of their relatives to share in the windfall? On the economic side of the equation, the benefits of retaining the animals for breeding stock were probably much less than the urban donors supposed. Village cattle mature very slowly, and they are often lost to theft, disease, and poor fencing. Because of the humid climate, the fencing itself requires constant maintenance. Once slaughtered, the cattle bring only a modest price.

The large breeding pigs are even more of a problem. They do not fit well in the (current) village environment even though they are a cross between a Samoan sow and a New Zealand boar. The cross-bred pigs are larger and their rooting is more destructive than pure Samoan pigs. Villagers also complain that the "foreign pigs" do not know how to forage for their food as well as local pigs, and hence they wander more. In order to realize the benefits of the breed, the new pigs must be raised in pens, where their owners must provide them with food and water. Diseases tend to become epidemic among the confined pigs (partly because their diets are not balanced), and veterinarian services are inadequate to handle the resulting problems. In addition, when the pigs are confined together, the filthy pens become a nuisance to the household. In contrast, village pigs require almost no effort or expense to raise. They wander freely, they rarely become ill, and their owners need only feed them a little coconut meat in the evening to fatten them and keep them domesticated.

Most village households already feed as many pigs as they can without confining the pigs to holding pens and growing additional crops to feed them. The addition of three fully grown, cross-bred pigs would thus force a household to adopt the far more difficult and expensive European technique of pig raising—unless the new owners just slaughtered the troublesome new pigs, took the windfall for what it was, and went about raising their village pigs as usual.

None of the above discussion implies that Samoans or other village farmers never mismanage or squander their resources. Building economic and social capital is no easier in Samoa than elsewhere. Villagers employ several different strategies in their economic and social affairs, and each of these strategies has its own risks and rewards. Just as in our own economic and social systems, strategies in one arena sometimes complement and sometimes clash with strategies in another arena. Not everyone who plays can win. Stories of villagers who extend too much credit to their neighbors or slaughter all of their breeding stock for a ceremony only show that in Samoa, as elsewhere, some people are wise and skillful and others are not.

LIMITED WANTS OR LIMITED PAY?

Some development experts believe that in areas like Samoa, village planters produce little because their modest labor efforts easily satisfy their wants, after which they have no reason to work more.[2] Such a hypothetical situation has been called "primitive affluence" or "subsistence affluence." According to this view, villagers who appear to be poor from our perspective are "affluent" from their own perspective. They are "affluent" not because they have great material wealth, but because their modest material desires are "rigidly determined by traditional or semi-traditional standards" (Fairbairn 1985:229), and because traditional norms and attitudes direct people's attention to social or spiritual goals, rather than to the material goals that are thought to grip the Western world.

I have heard both local Samoan officials and expatriate economists suggest this explanation for underproduction in village agriculture. In fact, the government's recent copra and cocoa pricing policies seem to be founded on the belief (or perhaps the rationalization) that if the government were to raise the prices it pays for crops, village planters would be able to satisfy their limited wants more easily, and would thus produce less.

There is some evidence that might appear to support this conclusion. Employers in Western Samoa do sometimes complain that it is difficult to keep workers. A commercial farmer near Apia told me that his workers leave because they work only for small target incomes—the price of a radio, for example. After reaching that target, the worker quits, his "limited wants" satisfied. I observed the same kind of work behavior in Samoa, but from talking with the workers it is clear that the cause is not limited wants.

One obvious reason that people quit their jobs prematurely is the combination of poor working conditions and low wages. Two less obvious problems also contribute. Curiously, the first problem is caused by the shortage of wage jobs itself. Since wage jobs are in very short supply in Western Samoa, workers might be expected to try to hold on to them. This is undoubtedly true for most workers, especially those holding skilled or high-paying jobs. But I have seen cases where just the opposite is true for the menial, low-paying jobs that make up the bulk of local employment opportunities.

Menial workers gain little or no status from their wage jobs. The jobs can be very tiresome, often dangerous (health and safety precautions are virtually nonexistent). Some managers also take undue advantage of their workers. For example, employers sometimes force employees to work overtime without pay, or they steal their employees' insurance premiums instead of remitting them to the government. For their part, employees retaliate against management by not reporting for work, by stealing materials and sabotaging equipment, and by other indirect reprisals.

---

[2] Fairbairn's analysis (1985) is founded on the assumption that village farmers limit their production to culturally imposed, traditional standards. On page 335 of the same volume, however, he argues in favor of an infrastructural "bottleneck" explanation for underproduction.

Since jobs are in short supply, only one or a few members of a household may be working at any time to support the family, while other members remain unemployed. Because of the need for cash to support the entire family, those who are working can keep very little of their income for themselves. And because of the Samoan emphasis on intra-family sharing, workers usually share with their unemployed siblings what little pay they keep out of the general household pool. I have seen these workers tire of supporting their families and simply quit their jobs. This forces one of their unemployed siblings to find work (often in the same firm, and even in the same position), taking up in their turn the burden of supporting the family through menial wage labor.

Another factor that causes wage workers to leave their jobs prematurely is—surprisingly—the financial poverty that drove them to seek the job in the first place. By necessity, the vast majority of rural Samoan families produce much of what they consume, including not only their food and their household items, but even the houses themselves. Families also need cash, however, and anyone who is not needed full-time at home may seek wage employment. Sometimes the press of finances causes members who *are* needed at home to seek wage employment as well, or it forces people to accept employment in poorer conditions or for lower wages than they would accept in better times. When this happens, two equally important forces soon combine—one to force and the other to allow early retirement.

First, in a wealthier, more commercialized society, a wage worker's response to a leaky roof would probably be just the opposite of the village planter's response. Unable to repair the roof himself, or seeing that his time is worth more than the wages of a repairman, a well-paid employee would work overtime in order to pay a specialist to repair the roof for him. In Samoa, very few villagers earn enough to be able to hire someone else to attend to their household tasks, so the villager will eventually be forced to retire to make the roof repairs himself.

Second, as workers earn more, the financial crises that forced them to seek work ease, allowing them to return home to fulfill their former duties. Also, the longer they work in wage employment, the more urgent their subsistence chores become. A man can neglect his gardens and postpone re-thatching his roof or repairing his canoe only so long. A woman can neglect her weaving and her other duties only so long. The longer these subsistence jobs are left undone, the more urgent they become, until finally they can be left no longer. Meaalofa's brother, a young chief named Lafai Misi, needed WS $50 and five fine mats for an upcoming church dedication. His wife could make the fine mats, but as a full-time planter with a large family, he had no money to spare. To earn the money, he decided to seek wage work at the Nelson Plantation in nearby Palauli. The work paid WS $4 per day, and he figured that he could save the WS $50 in three weeks or a month, by which time he would have to return to the other obligations that he had postponed.

BALANCING WAGE EMPLOYMENT WITH SOCIAL RESPONSIBILITIES

Though wage employment necessarily imposes regularity on a person's daily activities, this does not normally rule out missing work sometimes to fulfill important family obligations. One talking chief that I know rarely misses a social ceremony of any kind in his own or nearby villages, even though he holds a full-time wage job. He is an accomplished orator, so the value of gifts (cash, food, and fine mats) that he receives at a ceremony is often large— sometimes even exceeding his weekly pay of WS $39 (US $33).

During the year of my economic survey, this orator received WS $660 (US $560) in cash and purchased goods alone as gifts at ceremonies. This compares to his take-home salary of just under WS $2,000 (US $1,700) per year. If the value of nonmarket gifts, such as pig meat and fine mats (which were not recorded in the survey), were added to the gifts of cash and market goods, his gross receipts from ceremonies would undoubtedly total more than half of his relatively large wage income. His net, of course, was somewhat less than this amount, since at some (but not all) of these ceremonies he must also give gifts of his own. The material gifts he gives, however, often amount to only a stick of kava or a fine mat. The greatest contributions that an orator makes at many ceremonies are the honor of his presence and the words that he speaks. The host rewards him in proportion to the grandeur of each. While this particular *matai*'s income strategy is an extreme example, it illustrates how a bold and clever talking chief tries to manipulate both Western and traditional systems to his advantage.

In a village there are few subsistence or cash-cropping activities that people cannot postpone temporarily, and since the vast majority of rural villagers are involved only in these kinds of tasks, it is possible for them, as a group, to allow special social events, or *fa'alavelave*, to take precedence over every-day work activities. This arrangement causes problems for an increasing number of wage workers, however, who are expected to report to work every day. So far the resolution of this conflict has been largely in favor of the *fa'alavelave*, so that wage workers must either miss the event or miss work.

As in the United States and other industrialized countries, Samoan wage workers often struggle with conflicting social and work responsibilities (and opportunities). In both cases, conflict is more easily resolved because every worker has occasional family obligations to fulfill. Since every wage earner must be absent from work sometimes, it is to everyone's advantage to endorse a work system that allows absences to fulfill those social obligations. Super-visors, for example, find it difficult to prohibit their employees from doing what they themselves do. There is a major difference, however, between the American and Samoan systems. Since Samoans reckon family ties much more broadly than Americans do, a Samoan worker's family obligations are likely to be much more numerous (though individually no more weighty) than a Western worker's. This results in more frequent absences from work, which in turn reduces the efficiency of Western-style businesses and government offices in Samoa.[3]

Samoans frequently leave both their wage jobs and their agricultural duties to attend ceremonies. They do so partly because of their commitment to family and tradition, but also because they are often drawn to the same conclusion by ordinary economic incentives. In a job where the pay is only a few dollars per day, there is little reward for diligence. In contrast, participating in social affairs is not only a moral obligation (and in the case of *matai*, a formal duty), it is also an important source of material (as well as social) rewards. In the short term, the material reward for participation in ceremonies may be a few dollars, a fine mat, a leg of pork, or a few cans of fish. In the long run, the material reward for participation in family and village affairs is nothing less than total economic security.

An unfortunate and unwanted side effect of this choice, however, is that it significantly expands the opportunity that people have for abusing the system. Since supporting one's family is a near-sacred duty among Samoans, employees find it easy to justify unwarranted absences by reference to family obligations (a tactic that is not entirely unknown on American college campuses at exam time). In addition to reducing efficiency, the frequent absence of both managers and their employees makes the supervision of employees (including the managers) more difficult, which sometimes contributes to financial irregularities. And, of course, the reduced efficiency reinforces management's decision to pay employees little, which then lowers their interest in the job.

PAIĒ, OR INDOLENCE

Like many other semi-subsistence farmers, Samoan planters have been characterized in the development literature as having a "high leisure preference." Some expatriates and some Samoans who have returned from long residence overseas are more direct. They often describe Samoans simply as "lazy." An expatriate development agent who had worked closely with Samoan office personnel for three years told me that "Samoans want more money, they just don't want to work for it." American Samoa's nonvoting representative to the U.S. Congress, Fofo Sunia, described the Samoan lifestyle as: "Today you come to work. Tomorrow, why, if you don't feel like it, you stay home" (*Los Angeles Times*, 20 August 1982, p. 5). Urban residents often hold the same opinion about village planters. In a speech to Parliament a few years ago, Western Samoa's Minister of Agriculture joked that perhaps the only way to increase agricultural production in the country

---

[3] I have seen no comparative statistics to support the claim of many Samoan and expatriate managers that absenteeism is higher in Samoa than overseas, but it seems to me to be correct.

was to import Vietnamese "boat people" to work the land. Village planters even say the same thing about each other.

It is readily apparent that Samoan planters are not universally industrious, but to so characterize Samoan society would be more difficult to justify. The relevant question is not whether some Samoans are lazy, but whether Samoans differ much in this regard from people in other societies. And if they do work less, to what extent are the differences due to local economic circumstances, rather than to culturally determined attitudes and values?

When I asked a planter why some neighbor did not produce more copra or taro, or why some neighbor's lands were covered with weeds, he would generally say that the neighbor was *paiē*, "indolent or lazy." But when I asked the same planter why he himself did not produce more, he would reply *E lē sikuea le fa'atau*, "The selling is not square," or *E laitiiti le mea maua*, "There is little to be gained," or *E lē lava le maketi*, "There is not enough market"— all clearly economic reasons. Like many people, village planters tend to judge others by different criteria than they judge themselves. The simple fact is that economic circumstances rarely warrant greater effort or production from village planters.

Some planters are more industrious than others. The range of variation among them is similar, however, to the range of variation among people in other societies. The average level of industry about which that variation occurs may be somewhat lower among Samoans because of the limited economic rewards available to those who do work more. Nevertheless, I doubt that their level of industry differs much from Americans.

In 1982 I talked with Laurence Hansen, the Scandanavian-born manager of the sawmill at Asau, on the northwestern end of Savaii. The government-owned sawmill is enormous by local standards, employing several hundred workers. Laurence had come to Western Samoa on a United Nations contract eleven years before, and he had been manager of the mill for the last ten years. He said that he generally preferred Samoan workers to those back home. "Their strengths and weaknesses are different than European workers," he told me over the roar of the saws, "so you have to organize things a little differently to avoid the weaknesses and take advantage of the strengths. But they are generally willing and hard workers."

Samoans do value personal industry (see Pitt 1970), but they value industry primarily for what it produces, not for its own sake. While Samoans eagerly embraced many of the religious and moral tenets of Protestantism, the work ethic—where work is valued for its own sake—was not one of them. There is no question that Samoans could work harder to improve their plantations and produce more crops. If they could somehow be infused with the Protestant work ethic, they might produce more. But is this a reasonable expectation? The economic analysis shows that, however great or small planters' agricultural labors are now, there is little economic incentive for them to work more.

MONEY, RISK, AND THE SO-CALLED "SUBSISTENCE MENTALITY"

Many development experts believe that another reason Samoan planters (and others like them in other parts of the world) cling to their traditional subsistence farming practices is because they are exceptionally averse to taking risks. Most observers believe, moreover, that this "risk aversion" is the expression of a fundamental personality or cultural trait of semi-subsistence or peasant farmers—part of an all-encompassing, conservative "world view." The evidence from Vaega tells a different story.

The few local families that earn sizable incomes from other sources show little reluctance to give up subsistence production. Of the three families in Vaega that have large and secure incomes from wage labor or business, none grow significant amounts of taro. They buy their taro at the market or from their neighbors instead of growing it themselves. Several other families with high wage and remittance incomes also buy taro regularly. These same families also hire other villagers to plant and weed taro plantations for them.

On the other hand, poorer households that do produce taro have to watch their supplies carefully. They dare not sell much taro, fearing that they might otherwise be caught short and have to purchase their food. This would quickly exhaust their small cash and credit reserves, and ultimately endanger their own food supply. I frequently asked Nu'u why he did not sell a few baskets of taro in the village or at the market when he was short of cash. His reply was always the same: "If our own taro should run out, we would just end up spending the money to buy back the taro that we have sold. And when the money was gone, how would we eat?"

The vagaries of weather, wild pigs, and theft make it very difficult for planters to predict just how much standing taro will be enough to supply their households over the next year. Since Nu'u and the other planters lack the security of sizable cash incomes, they are reluctant to sell taro unless they clearly have more mature taro than their families can eat. They do not want to grow much more than they can eat either. Growing taro is hard work, and since the taro market is small and unstable, they never know if they will be able to sell a surplus.

Taro market conditions changed suddenly in late 1981, and the village planters changed their strategy as well. The recently established YMCA office in Apia offered to buy large amounts of taro for export at prices that were 50–100 percent higher than the government's Produce Marketing Board (PMB) was then paying. The offer was especially attractive because the PMB operated on a quota system and villagers complained that most of the quotas went either to government plantations or to wealthy and influential individuals, many of whom were not even farmers. That left scant opportunity for the common village planter to export taro. The YMCA's plan was to act as a cooperative broker for the common planters.

The people of Vaega had never heard of the YMCA, nor were they familiar with the urbanites who ran it. And the Apia office had not yet exported a single case of taro. But on just the *hope* of a lucrative overseas market for their taro, Nu'u and the other villagers planted 105,000 taro stems (about one-fourth of their normal annual planting) in a single month, with the harvest being earmarked for export through the YMCA.

Vaega planters are indeed averse to risking their cash, but they showed that they are much more willing to risk their labor. Villagers admitted to me that the YMCA had given them no guarantee and that they really did not understand the YMCA's offer. Yet they expended an enormous amount of effort planting taro on just the *chance* that the plan would succeed. Villagers have little money, and they are consequently averse to risking it. They have much surplus labor, however, and they are willing to risk it on the chance of earning more money.

Thus, while village planters sometimes do avoid risk, they do so in response to their conscious appraisal of their circumstances, not because risk aversion is an inherent part of an unconscious "world view." There is no social or attitudinal problem to overcome in getting villagers to produce more crops and to market more of what they produce. Villagers place little or no sentimental value on growing their own food rather than buying it. They gladly do so when these are economically attractive and safe alternatives.

Villagers want to earn as much as they can from their work, but they consider more than just the absolute amount of income when determining their work preferences. Wage labor often has important advantages over family farm labor even when the amounts of income are similar. Once employed, wage income is often more secure than cash crop income. The return is also faster. Wage workers begin to receive their pay within two weeks, while planters have to wait months or even years to realize income from their efforts. Wage workers are also paid more often, usually every two weeks.

Some people prefer some kinds of wage labor over family farm labor for noneconomic reasons. For example, some people are attracted to wage jobs that provide an opportunity for leaving the village. Wage labor may be less strenuous than farm labor. Wage labor may also have higher status than family farm labor. But the current low status of agriculture among Samoans is not a fundamental trait of Samoan culture (traditional or otherwise). Instead, Samoans have gained a low opinion of agriculture primarily because the work is hard and the economic return is low. Those people who have managed to earn greater sums from agriculture—usually with the help of machinery, hired labor, and special treatment from the government—have also gained higher status as a result. The government's frequent public relations campaigns will never significantly raise either the status of farming in the eyes of Samoans, or the size of their harvest. Increased modernization and a steady rise in farm incomes, however, would quickly achieve both goals.

Some villagers do not like plantation work just because their personal interests and abilities lie elsewhere. The observation that many Samoans want to quit farming or want to leave the village, while true, does not distinguish them in any way from people in the rest of the world. Not everyone wants to continue farming when other opportunities appear. Three thousand years of village life have not made every Samoan a planter by choice, nor have they made every Samoan a good planter. Like the peasants of Mexico and the agro-businessmen of the midwestern U.S., Samoan planters realize that as new opportunities appear, fewer and fewer of their sons and daughters will choose the life of the farmer.

But while many Samoans do not want to make their living by farming, there are many others who do. Village farming has many advantages, and outside wage labor has many disadvantages. Though plantation work is often hard and materially unrewarding, when the days are clear the upland plantations are serene, wonderful places to be. People work and rest at their own pace, on their own land, together with their friends and family. I remember sitting with my neighbors—three young brothers, Vila, Seti, and Tevita Autafaga—on an old stone house platform amid one of their upland taro plots. The platform was built hundreds of years earlier, perhaps as early as the Tongan wars of the thirteenth or fourteenth century. Though the family had used the stone platform as the foundation of a plantation shelter a couple of years earlier, the pebble floor was overgrown once again with grass and vines.

We sat cross-legged atop the platform, ringed by *tī* plants with their slender stems and long, reddish-green leaves, while Vila recounted his adventures in American Samoa the year before. He had worked for US $3.50 an hour as a rough welder in the shipyards of Pago Pago. That was grand enough for a youth from "out back," but the pride in his voice was just as evident as he casually exaggerated the nights he spent carousing in the discos around the bay. As we listened to Vila's stories, we looked out across the fields of taro that we had been weeding, past the fallow fields of grass and creeping vines, and over the tops of the coconut palms to the Pacific Ocean three miles away. Vila had brought the family's .22 rifle, and when Seti and Tevita returned to their labors, Vila and I walked through the chest-high taro to the forest edge where we had seen two forest pigeons, or *lupe*, circling among the tree tops 100 feet above. We stalked them quietly, watching them through openings in the canopy, but Vila never got a shot at them and we soon returned to our work.

That was an especially fine day in the upland plantations, but it is important every day to Samoans (as it is to other people) to work in pleasant surroundings, to be their own bosses, and to work in a manner they choose themselves. When they want to hunt forest pigeons on a clear afternoon, they do. When they want to stay three days and nights in the plantation, felling trees and planting taro, they do. When they hunger for fish, they go fishing just inside the curve of the reef where the swells from the southern ocean crash across the coral. In the early evening, they can play cricket with their friends on the village green, and at night they can stroll along the road to Satufia or Pitonu'u where the girls seem a little fairer.

Most villagers want to remain in the village, and many of those want to earn their livings from their plantations. Many more would want to do so if economic conditions were more favorable. Selesele Afele, a middle-aged orator who has sent several of his children to work in New Zealand and has travelled there himself, summed up the sentiments of most village planters:

"There are many of us who want to produce and sell more cases of taro, but the market is bad."

To many Samoans, rural villages like Vaega are ideal places to live, and farming would be an attractive occupation—if only there was more money in it. Samoan planters have shown their willingness to adapt to changing circumstances and to take advantage of new opportunites in cash cropping. Few villagers, however, have the knowledge, experience, or resources to make these opportunites happen on their own. The silver lining in the otherwise dark cloud of village agriculture is that they *are* willing.

A FAREWELL SPEECH

The Department of Agriculture invited me to present these conclusions in a series of public lectures at the end of my field work. When I told my friends in Vaega of the invitation, several talking chiefs hinted that they should go with me to Apia to *tapua'i le lauga*, or "support the speech." I thought it was a splendid idea, but I had to go right away to prepare my maps. They agreed to follow on the day of the first speech.

About thirty-five people from the economic development community gathered in the lecture room at the new Fisheries Office. The group was evenly divided between expatriates and local Samoan officials. The first lecture was on Samoan land tenure and agricultural development, and I was nervous about speaking to a group that included many learned Samoans, most of whom were chiefs. I unrolled a giant map of Vaega's plantation plots and fastened it to the board behind me. When I turned around to begin my lecture, I saw six talking chiefs from Vaega sitting stiffly on the metal chairs at the back of the room. It was just the moral support I needed.

Following local custom, I knew that I should give material expression to my thanks for the men's support. So when the lecture was over and the other people had departed, I took the men from Vaega to lunch at a little Chinese restaurant near the waterfront. After lunch I also gave them each a few dollars *pasese*, bus and boat "passage," and then we returned to the house in Taufusi where groups from Vaega usually stay when they come to Apia. We had with us the final expression of my thanks—a cardboard box full of quart bottles of cold Vailima beer. I was unsuccessful in getting Nu'u to drink any, since he is a church deacon, but I and the other men had no such reservations. After a quiet party, we all fell asleep, stretched out on mats on the wooden floor.

A few days later I said good-bye to my friends in Apia and then returned to Vaega for a final visit. People had been very good to me in Samoa, and the thought of leaving made me sad. When it was finally time to leave, Nu'u and Asiata Iakopo accompanied me on the long bus and ferry rides to the airport on Upolu. There we sat cross-legged on a cement waiting platform, listening for the roar of the jet arriving from New Zealand.

When I first arrived in Samoa, these men had been unintelligible strangers

Photo 43. Return to Paradise Beach.

to me. Now they and many others were familiar friends. I had learned from them and from the other people of Samoa that there is nothing strange or irrational about Samoan planters—whether in their economic endeavors, their social affairs, or their personal lives. At least, I thought, recalling what I would face when the plane touched down in Los Angeles, they are no stranger than other people!

REFERENCES

Asian Development Bank, 1985, *Western Samoa Agriculture Sector Study*. Manila.

Becke, Louis, 1967, *South Sea Supercargo*. A. Grove Day, ed. Honolulu: University of Hawaii Press.

Bellwood, Peter, 1979, *Man's Conquest of the Pacific: The Prehistory of Southeast Asia and Oceania*. New York: Oxford University Press.

Buck, Peter (Te Rangi Hiroa), 1930, *Samoan Material Culture*. Honolulu: Bernice P. Bishop Museum.

Burgess, Richard J., 1981, *The Intercropping of Smallholder Coconuts in Western Samoa: An Analysis Using Multi-Stage Linear Programming*. Canberra: Development Studies Centre, Australian National University.

Davidson, J. W., 1967, *Samoa mo Samoa: The Emergence of the Independent State of Western Samoa*. Melbourne: Oxford University Press.

Fairbairn, Te'o I. J., 1985, *Island Economies: Studies from the South Pacific*. Suva: University of the South Pacific.

Fairbairn, Te'o I. J., and C. A. Tisdell, 1985, "Labor Supply Constraints on Industrialisation and Production Deficiencies in Traditional Sharing Societies." In Te'o I. J. Fairbairn, *Island Economies: Studies from the South Pacific*. Suva: University of the South Pacific, pp. 137–48.

Farrell, Bryan H., and R. Gerard Ward, 1962, "The Village and its Agriculture." In Fox, J. W., and K. B. Cumberland, eds., *Western Samoa: Land, Life, and Agriculture in Tropical Polynesia*. Christchurch: Whitcombe and Tombs, Ltd., pp. 177–238.

Freeman, Derek, 1983, *Margaret Mead and Samoa: The Making and Unmaking of an Anthropological Myth*. Cambridge, Mass.: Harvard University Press.

Gray, J. A. C., 1960, *Amerika Samoa: A History of American Samoa and its United States Naval Administration*. Annapolis: United States Naval Administration.

Government of Western Samoa, 1975, *Third Five-Year Development Plan*. Apia: Department of Economic Development.

———, 1976, *Migration Report*. Apia: Government Printing.

———, 1977, "Recommendations for the Growing of Taro in Western Samoa." Mimeograph, Department of Agriculture, Forests, and Fisheries.

———, 1984a, *1981 Census*. Apia: Department of Statistics.

———, 1984b, *Western Samoa's Fifth Development Plan: 1985–1987*. Apia: Department of Economic Development.

———, 1987, *Western Samoa's Sixth Development Plan: 1988–1990*. Apia: Department of Economic Development.

Hezel, Francis X., 1985, "Trukese Suicide," In Hezel, Francis X., Donald H. Rubinstein, and Goeffry M. White, eds., *Culture, Youth, and Suicide in the Pacific:*

Papers from an East-West Center Conference. Honolulu: Pacific Island Studies Program, University of Hawaii, Manoa, pp. 112–124.

———, 1987, "Truk Suicide Epidemic and Social Change." *Human Organization,* 4:283–291.

Holmes, Lowell D., 1971, "Samoa: Custom Versus Productivity." In R. G. Crocombe, ed., *Land Tenure in the Pacific.* Melbourne: Oxford University Press, pp. 91–105.

———, 1980, "Factors Contributing to the Cultural Stability of Samoa." *Anthropological Quarterly,* 53(3):188–197.

Leung Wai, Sam, 1978, "Food Shortages in Western Samoa: Towards a Solution." In E. K. Fisk, ed., *The Adaptation of Traditional Agriculture: Socioeconomic Problems of Urbanization.* Canberra: Australian National University, pp. 72–92.

Lockwood, Brian, 1971, *Samoan Village Economy.* Melbourne: Oxford University Press.

Marsack, C. C., 1958, "Notes on the Practice of the Court and the Principles Adopted in the Hearing of Cases Affecting 1) Samoan Matai Titles, 2) Land Holding According to the Customs and Usages of Western Samoa." Mimeograph. Apia: Land and Titles Court.

Milner, G. B., 1966, *Samoan Dictionary: Samoan-English, English-Samoan.* Oxford: Oxford University Press.

Moyle, Richard M., ed., 1984, *The Samoan Journals of John Williams, 1830 and 1832.* Canberra: Australian National University.

O'Meara, J. Tim, 1986, *Why Is Village Agriculture Stagnating? A Test of Social and Economic Explanations in Western Samoa.* Ann Arbor: University Microfilms International.

———, 1987, "Samoa: Customary Individualism." In R. G. Crocombe, ed., *Land Tenure in the Pacific,* 3rd edition. Suva: University of the South Pacific, pp. 74–113.

Pirie, Peter and Ward J. Barrett, 1962, "Western Samoa: Population, Production, and Wealth." *Pacific Viewpoint,* 3(1):63–96.

Pitt, David C., 1970, *Tradition and Economic Progress in Samoa.* Oxford: Clarendon Press.

Polloi, Anthony H., 1985, "Suicide in Palau." In Hezel, Francis X., *et al.,* eds., *Culture, Youth and Suicide in the Pacific.* Honolulu: Pacific Island Studies Program, University of Hawaii, pp. 125–138.

Powles, Charles Guy, 1979, *The Persistence of Chiefly Power and Its Implications for Law and Political Organization in Western Polynesia.* Unpublished Ph.D. dissertation, Australian National University, Canberra.

Rubinstein, Donald H., 1985, "Suicide in Micronesia." In Hezel, Francis X., *et al.,* eds., *Culture, Youth and Suicide in the Pacific.* Honolulu: Pacific Island Studies Program, University of Hawaii, pp. 88–111.

Sahlins, Marshall, 1963, "Poor Man, Rich Man, Big Man, Chief: Political Types in Melanesia and Polynesia." *Comparative Studies in Society and History,* 5:285–303.

Shore, Bradd, 1982, *Sala'ilua: A Samoan Mystery.* New York: Columbia University Press.

Thomas, Pamela, 1984, "Society, Land and Law: Land Policy in Western Samoa." *Pacific Islands Law Review,* University of Papua New Guinea, Volume 1 (manuscript).

Turner, G. A., 1884, *Samoa: A Hundred Years Ago and Long Before*. London: Macmillan and Co.

Va'a, Leulu F., 1987, "Early Missionary Work in Samoa." *Samoa Times*. Apia.

Ward, Roger, 1962, "Agriculture Outside the Village and Commercial Systems." In Fox, J. W., and K. B. Cumberland, eds., *Western Samoa: Land, Life and Agriculture in Tropical Polynesia*. Christchurch: Whitcombe and Tombs, Ltd., pp. 266–289.

Ward, G. R., and A. Proctor, eds., 1980, *South Pacific Agriculture: Choices and Constraints. South Pacific Agriculture Survey*. Canberra: Asian Development Bank and The Australian National University.

Weston, Sharon W., 1972, *Samoan Social Organization: Structural Implications of an Ambilineal Descent System*. Unpublished Ph.D. thesis, University of California, Los Angeles.

FILMS ABOUT SAMOA

American Samoa: Paradise Lost? (55 minutes, color) Produced for WNET Television, 1968. Available in the United States from Indiana University Audio Visual Center and several other university film libraries.

An excellent documentary film on culture change in American Samoa. The film shows some of the problems resulting from the introduction of a monetary economy, television, family planning, wage employment for the government and at the fish canneries, tourism, Western-style education, and a colonial government. Filmed in the late 1960s in American Samoa, most of the problems have their exact counterparts in Western Samoa in the mid-1980s—the period discussed in *Samoan Planters*. The film shows many scenes of daily life on Tutuila and in the more remote islands of Manu'a. Individual Samoans speak for themselves about the frustrations and benefits of change.

Teine Samoa: A Girl of Samoa. (22 minutes, color). Produced by Gibson Film Productions, Ltd., 1982. Available in the United States from Journal Films, Inc., 930 Pitner Ave., Evanston, IL 60202.

A sensitive biographical film that shows life in Western Samoa from the point of view of a teenage girl living in Matautu village, Falealili, on the south side of Upolu. This is not entirely an ethnographic film since some of the scenes are reenacted, but the effect is good and the portrayal of the girl's circumscribed life is highly accurate. Unlike most films on Samoa, no attempt has been made to glamorize the scenes of village life.

Chiefs. John Mayer, 1983. (28 minutes, color video) Produced by Pachyderm Films, Honolulu.

Filmed largely at the celebrations of the twentieth anniversary of the independence of Western Samoa in Apia, 1982, but interspersed with many scenes of village life. These scenes include a kava ceremony, fishing, and the tatooing of young men. Scenes at the independence celebrations include traditional dancing and singing, and the impressive *fautasi* boat races. Some interesting historical footage of the early colonial years shows the contrast between old and new. The film presents only the idealized, public face of Samoa from the point of view of its chiefs.

Margaret Mead and Samoa. (51 minutes, color) Frank Heimans, 1988. Produced by Cinetel Productions, Ltd., 15 Fifth Avenue, Cremorne 2090, NSW, Australia. Available in the United States from Brighton Video, 250 West 57th Street, NY, NY 10019.

An award-winning documentary on the debate surrounding Derek Freeman's refutation of Margaret Mead's conclusions in her famous book, *Coming of Age in Samoa.*

The documentary contains archival footage as well as many scenes of contemporary Samoa, including the islands of Manu'a. Many of the principals in that debate, including many Samoans, speak their piece in front of the camera.

Numerous other documentary films on Samoa are available in Australia and New Zealand.

Index